ESPERANZA

Panoramic view showing the settlement patterns of dispersed households so typical of Esperanza. The topography also is typical.

VIKING FUND PUBLICATIONS IN ANTHROPOLOGY
Number Fifty   Colin M. Turnbull, *Editor*

ESPERANZA

An Ethnographic Study of a Peasant Community in Puerto Rico

CARLOS BUITRAGO ORTIZ

Published for The Wenner-Gren Foundation for Anthropological Research Inc.

THE UNIVERSITY OF ARIZONA PRESS   TUCSON, ARIZONA

About the Author . . .

CARLOS BUITRAGO ORTIZ applied his background in anthropology and other social sciences to field investigations among peasants of the intermediate highlands in northwestern Puerto Rico. As a native of the Island, educated in Puerto Rico, Ortiz has encouraged himself and his students to become involved in the problems of Puerto Rican society and a concern with their possible solutions. Author also of a book on the origin and development of agrarian capitalism in Puerto Rico, Ortiz began the 1973–74 academic year in Spain, in pursuit of the relationships between Puerto Rican social history and Mediterranean society and culture.

THE UNIVERSITY OF ARIZONA PRESS

I.S.B.N.-0-8165-0456-3
L.C. No. 73-90915

Table of Contents

List of Maps

List of Photographs

List of Tables

List of Figures

Middle America

Barrio Esperanza in the municipality of Arecibo, Puerto Rico

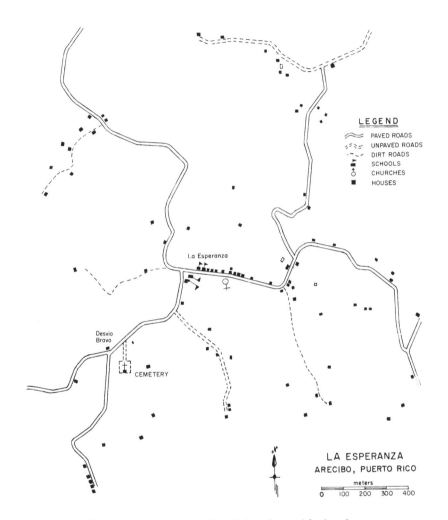

The northern municipality of Arecibo and its barrios

Preface

The fieldwork on which this book is based was done during a period of thirteen months spent in the community of Esperanza in 1962-63. I lived with my wife and daughter in this community, following social anthropology's tradition of direct contact with [the] people. In addition, I have maintained contact with the people of Esperanza through the years by regular visits and, in some cases, formal research. This has enriched my vision of the *barrio*.

Esperanza is still a relatively "traditional" community and my findings still hold. The changes that have begun to appear, mentioned in the relevant sections in the text, have not penetrated deeply enough to alter its fundamental traits.

The materials used in this work are almost exclusively derived from this fieldwork, although some use has been made of written sources. Where such material has been used, acknowledgment is made. As the introduction makes clear, there is a lack of literature dealing with the peasant family in Puerto Rico, and there is none about Esperanza. The works which deal with the family in Puerto Rico, and especially with the rural family, are mentioned and due credit is given.

My debt to many people is eternal and cannot be paid in full. In the first place, the cooperation, hospitality and sociability of my hosts, all the people of Esperanza, made my task easier and more human. They taught me a style of life, a vanishing one, perhaps, but one in which human beings and qualities are recognized as such. The philosophical outlook of Don Paco Concepción, the sense of humor of Don Nicolás Fermaint, the sheer joy of playing the traditional *cuatro* so typical of Basilio Correa and Santiago Rivera, will never be forgotten. Nor can I forget the hospitality and collaboration of Doña Blanca Bravo and Don Diego Bravo, the love for horses of Don Antonio Torres, the hospitality of his wife. I could almost fill a book with the names of persons who gave me their cooperation. To all of them my eternal gratitude.

I received the help of the following government institutions or departments: the district court in Arecibo, the welfare department, and the public works department. The Social Sciences Program, under the direction of Dr. Howard Stanton, provided the financial basis of the fieldwork period.

From Meyer Fortes, anthropologist *par excellence,* I learned the craft of social anthropology. His capacity to teach, while at the same time allowing for the development of my individual capacities, honors the intellectual and anthropological tradition.

Ruby R. Leavitt and Colin Turnbull contributed many valuable comments and suggestions in the final stages. They provided me with a critical background for reacting. To them, my thanks. Last, but not least, my wife and my daughter had to bear the irregularities and inconveniences of the fieldwork period. Their patience (and sometimes impatience) allowed me to become immersed in my task.

The names used in this book are all fictitious to protect the identity, dignity and privacy of all persons mentioned.

C.B.O.

CHAPTER 1

Introduction

Studies of rural family life in Puerto Rico are almost nonexistent. One of the few anthropologists who has devoted some time to this matter has stated: "In Puerto Rico, in spite of a large number of papers and books dealing directly or tangentially with rural family life, there is nothing permitting rigorous comparison with the excellent studies of domestic social structure carried out in Jamaica, Trinidad, British Guiana and elsewhere" (Mintz, in R. T. Smith 1963).

This study starts with the same belief and is an effort to fill part of the gap. In what follows, we will try to demonstrate that Mintz was right by examining briefly some works dealing directly or tangentially with family life in rural Puerto Rico, and later we will describe how this study is an effort to fill the gap. We will aim at demonstrating the need for this kind of study and at justifying its use.

Studies Dealing with Rural Family Life in Puerto Rico

One of the first attempts to study rural life in Puerto Rico was made by J. C. Rosario (1935). This work is a combination of brief historical research with ethnographical observations. His study of the *jíbaro* (country folk) is about rural life in general but Chapters 8 and 9 are devoted to the family. Rosario saw the family structure as a historical "inheritance." The family which he labels patriarchal, is described in the following way: "The father is unquestionably the head of the house. His wife and all the children are expected to obey, and they do obey implicitly" (1935:86). This is the result of the different historical factors:

1

we have traced the Puerto Rican family through over four centuries of its life. We saw how at the beginning it was established upon a very feeble basis due to the unstable elements of the Spanish population, the mixture of races, and concubinage with Indians and Negroes. We observed that the introduction of Spanish families improved the aggregate: which still remained far from being a desirable combination (1935:79).

Rosario's main interest was in the negative attitudes of the country folk towards social change and its causes. As he put it:

The tentative explanation offered by the author as a stimulus for further investigation or perhaps as a working hypothesis, is that the attitudes inherited by the *jíbaro* from his ancestors have been preserved by him with no perceptible change, because his isolation has not allowed for a change in social values (1935:107).

Rosario's work was a pioneer one, and he was well aware of the limitations of his research:

hence the need for a monograph about the *jíbaro* which will be unbiased and objective (if such a thing is possible) and that instead of offering ready-made remedies, will stimulate what is, undoubtedly, the most pressing necessity concerning the subject of this study: namely further research (1935:8).

Steward and associates (1956) contains the results of fieldwork done by several anthropologists in the rural areas of Puerto Rico. This series of studies was not concerned with an analysis of the family, but rather with descriptions of subcultures within the general culture of Puerto Rico. As the director of field research put it: "The concepts have served as a tool in the analysis of Puerto Rico. Contemporary Puerto Rican society is highly diversified and heterogeneous. Our research has shown that there are many subcultures within the larger framework of the national culture and the national institutions" (1956:7).

The studies aimed mainly at a "holistic" description of the components. Out of seventy-seven pages referring to Tabara, one of the communities studied, less than three pages deal with the family. The author does not attempt to go beyond statements like this one: "The family in each household is generally the biological one, consisting of father, mother, and unmarried children—only rarely a dependent father-in-law or mother-in-law" (1956:143).

In the same volume, Wolf's monograph on a coffee subculture follows the same trend. The family is mentioned very briefly as a "labor pool" and a short description of the life cycle is offered, but that is practically all (1956:220–21).

In Padilla's (1956:291–94) study we find a brief section on kinship and the family, which mentions in a general form child rearing, attitudes toward sex, marriage, the family unit and family property and inheritance. The whole of this discussion of the family comprises only four pages.

Mintz's paper in this collection deals with a subculture based on a sugar plantation and in it the same trends are noticed. There is a section dealing with the family, socialization and ritual kinship, but the bulk of the monograph is an attempt to describe the totality of the subculture of Cañamelar. More space is given to economic factors than to a study and description of the family. Statements like this are not followed up:

The predominance of common-law unions and the apparent relative instability of marriage in the community clamours for explanation. Certain other facts are revealed by the simple census above. For instance, Catholic marriage shows general high stability, and only in five individual cases have Catholic marriages been followed by other kinds of unions—in every case by a common-law marriage. Individuals united by Protestant sacraments, on the other hand, and those married by civil procedure, are prevailingly young people (1956:376).

Commenting on the possible relationship between common-law unions and matrilocality:

One cannot but carry away the impression that the women of this sociocultural grouping feel neither suppressed nor misused. Their husbands need them, their contribution to the unity and welfare of the family is of the utmost importance. Women who break off with their common-law husbands, those whose husbands desert them, widows—all may re-marry promptly, and do not become less respectable thereby unless they behave wantonly (1956:379).

This is reminiscent of R. T. Smith's study of Negro families in British Guiana (1956). But Mintz does not pursue the matter further.

Stycos (1958) deals in some detail with family structure. He characterizes the whole of the Puerto Rican family as patriarchal and makes this the basis of his theory on fertility, which is his main interest. The role differentiation between husband and wife is such that there is a "communication gap" with the result that the male, with his almost total authority over his wife, can determine the degree of sexual intercourse and to a great extent the fertility of his wife. Stycos's analysis is subordinated to the fertility problem, and (naturally) to those features of the family that are relevant to the problem. In contrast to the studies found in Steward (1956), he does not discuss economic, historical and other factors that may influence the structure of the family.

Stycos assumes that there is *one type* of family structure in the whole of Puerto Rico despite the fact that several investigators have implied regional differences suggesting that perhaps the coastal regions have some sort of matrifiliation and the highlands family is more "male concentrated." It is plain from this brief survey that there is a lack of adequate data on family structure in particular.

Purpose of This Study and Methods Used

This study is an attempt to throw light on some questions intimately related to the structure of the Puerto Rican family, and in particular, to the rural family. It tries to answer questions as to whether there is one pattern or more than one pattern in the structure of the rural family and what the relation is between this pattern and other factors, such as occupation and religion. At the same time this study aims to provide a background against which social changes in Puerto Rico can be compared and studied. Esperanza is still a relatively clear example of a contemporary traditional community and as such exhibits features which have disappeared, or are in the process of being transformed, in other communities on the island. Thus the comparison of different aspects of the social organization of Esperanza and these communities can be fruitful. It can show the general trend of social change in a society undergoing profound overall changes. For example, the families and people studied by Oscar Lewis (1969) in many cases have a rural background and afford good comparative material.

We also attempt to clarify and conceptualize some key roles in the structure of the family, especially the male role. We try to develop a sociological and structural definition of maleness. Maleness is seen as a complex of social roles, which acquires meaning in relation to other roles within the family, and in some instances in the systems and subsystems outside. In a society which is characterized by a process of rapid social change, this involves the consideration of the way in which the changes in the economic, political and social spheres (including migration to Puerto Rican cities and the mainland) are affecting the male role. On a broader canvas, we explore also the way this same process operates in more urbanized communities and the possible changes in maleness. The hypothesis is that in the traditional contemporary community, like Esperanza, the male role is fundamentally an achieved one, and that it only makes sense when studied within the framework of the whole complex of family roles and from a developmental perspective.

The developmental perspective was pioneered in Caribbean anthropological research by R. T. Smith (1956) in his study of the Negro family in British Guiana. He combined a clear and systematic developmental approach with a structural one, in which the relationships between the family system and external ones were established. In particular, he emphasized the relevance of economic and occupational variables and their influence on family structure and process. This type of approach had been used, among others, by British anthropologists Fortes, Goody, and Leach (1958). In the present study we took this approach as our theoretical point and adapted it to the particular circumstances prevalent in Esperanza, but in many instances, substantial modifications and additions were introduced.

Our first task was to devise a series of hypothetical questions on the pattern of R. T. Smith (1956), expanded with questions based on our own knowledge of Puerto Rican society. This provided an inventory of issues, questions and problems that could arise during the study. We were trying to get a panoramic perspective. With this series of hypothetical questions we installed ourselves in Esperanza.

For a period of about two months we contented ourselves with simply making contact with the people of the area, to get some insight, and to become accepted. Normal interaction increased our initial understanding of the social organization, and we began to get "the feeling." As the situations were not structured, it provided a basis for the more formalized interviewing that came later. As an excuse for moving around, a very simple census was started; this provided an opportunity for speaking with the people and explaining what we were doing.

After this initial period, we took the hypothetical questions and our daily notes and started to structure a questionnaire, the general organization of which followed R. T. Smith (1956).

We realized that it would be impossible, in the time and with the facilities at our disposal, to use statistical procedures with the goal of having precise statistical indexes. The aim was simply to gather enough numerical information to give reasonable support to our descriptive statements. Our interviewing program had to vary with the availability of respondents, the difficulty of the problems, and the time available for the study. This explains the fact that the size of the sample quoted varies in different sections of the study. We did, however, endeavor to be representative in that we tried not to concentrate our inquiries on just one area of the community but to distribute them evenly. In some sections of the study, data based on special surveys made outside the questionnaire are included, for instance, the 204 households in the tobacco section in Chapter 3.

The following number of interviews were carried out for each section of the questionnaire:

The Present System—153 (Section A)
Household: Organizational Features—50 (Section B)
Census of Household Composition—167 (Section C)
The Time Factor in Relation to the Structure of the Household—30
   (Section D)
The Kinship System and Marriage—50 (Section E)

The variation in the size of the sample and interviews is an indication of both the time required and the intricacy of the problems. The census, for instance, was a relatively straightforward task compared to ascertaining the facts concerning the time factor in household structure.

It should be emphasized that the questionnaire was used primarily as a framework for free interviews, discussions and observations of the kind usually followed in ethnographic fieldwork. We were able to record two complete interviews (covering every point listed in the questionnaire) with two informants selected for their expert knowledge of their community, one male and the other female. Thus any question or problem that arose spontaneously was fully followed up.

The use of interviews proved to be a very fruitful technique for gathering certain types of data. It was useful as a general survey of the community, but the more formalized and standardized the aspects we studied, the better. As a technique for gathering descriptive situations, it was less fruitful. In many cases, the writing up of long descriptions and answers created a relatively stiff and formalized type of interaction that could become a negative factor in our relations with the people. In some cases, when this situation began to emerge, we abandoned the formal interviewing and started some kind of informal interaction. Later, we returned and continued the interview.

The reaction also varied with the personality of the subject. Some people reacted with suspicion to a visitor asking questions and writing down the answers. For others, the interview was a recognition of their importance, and they enjoyed giving every answer. Happily there were enough people of this kind to make our research relatively easy and representative. People who did not respond in a positive way were approached with other techniques available in the arsenal of the social anthropologist, but the formal interview, divided into several short ones, yielded a great quantity and quality of information.

We also interacted with the social system and culture we were studying, seeing it from the inside, not merely noting and observing from the outside. The combination of many different techniques leads to a heavy agenda, but it pays in full.

The "center" of Esperanza. A store is at the left, the school at the right, and the Catholic Church at the far right.

CHAPTER 2

Ecology and Economy

Barrio Esperanza, the subject of our study, is located in the northern part of the island of Puerto Rico. It is a section of the municipality of Arecibo, a coastal town which constitutes the political and economic center of the region.

Esperanza is a wholly rural agricultural region about 5 to 6 miles from the town. Topographically, it is a transitional area between the coastal plains of the north and the more rugged mountains of the island's interior regions.

Ecology

The topography is a combination of semilevel and rugged surfaces with a series of rounded hills, mostly of limestone, which tend to be dominant. The maximum altitude of these hills is around 300 to 400 meters. This is not high, but the abundance of these hills contributes a great deal to the ruggedness of the region.

Esperanza receives a large amount of rainfall, although there is a relatively dry season that extends from the end of December to March. According to government records of the last forty-eight years, the average rainfall has been 57.83 inches. May is the month with the highest amount (10 inches) and then from August to the beginning of December it is nearly 8 inches. There is a broad correlation between the seasonal level of rainfall and the agricultural cycle, with the period of harvest tending to fall roughly in the "dry" season and the planting and waiting periods in the "wet" months. But it is not a very clear and exact pattern, for there is frequently some overlap.

The temperature range varies little during the year, although the months around January tend to be a little cooler than the rest. The lowest temperature we recorded was around 58°F at night and the highest around 95°F during the day, but the average daily variation is from 15° to 20°.

The original tropical vegetation has virtually disappeared, and what was originally dense, subhumid, tropical forest can be found only in some isolated spots. This is due to the intensive destruction of the forest for farming purposes and for charcoal manufacture. At the present time, the only surviving remnants of forest are on the hilltops, which cannot be cultivated because of their limestone composition. Deforestation has also accelerated the process of erosion, and the Puerto Rican government (1953) has calculated the erosion is well advanced in almost the whole region.

The area covered by the study comprises approximately 9 to 11 square miles. It does not correspond to a political division, but there is a good deal of overlap between the social criteria we used and the political divisions. What impressed us as we came to know Esperanza was the great sense of solidarity shown by its inhabitants. It is emphasized that, in contrast to neighboring units or regions, people say, "We are from Esperanza," and distinguish themselves from other regions like Bayaney and Santa Rosa. Even people who live outside the official limits (as printed on official maps) on the periphery acknowledge the fact of "being from Esperanza." This was also demonstrated in the range of kinship connections and *compadrazgo* ties, a theme discussed in more detail in a later chapter.

Esperanza, as a political unit, covers more than the area we selected for detailed investigation, approximately 16 to 17 square miles. Within the limits of that area there is a population of about 2,105, according to the latest government census figures. The sample we used includes about half the population of the whole region. Of the 370 households named in the census, we dealt with 225, all of them located within the 9-to-11-square-mile area of the study.

These population figures give the whole area a relatively low density per square mile in comparison with the figures for the whole of Puerto Rico, which has a density of 650 persons per square mile according to the census, as compared to 100 to 500 for Esperanza.

The population of the area is composed mainly of "white" literate people, descendants of Spaniards who settled in the area. Some informants state that the original settlers came from the Canary Islands. This claim is very difficult to confirm for the whole sample, as our general synchronic approach did not admit much historical data, but a substantial group of families have this belief, as we were able to verify many times.

In the last century the economy of the region seems to have revolved around the cultivation of coffee, changing in the latter years to the cultivation of tobacco. Old people with whom we talked could remember and describe the big farms, and one can still see in different parts of the region the remains of the places where they used to process the coffee. The coffee was exported to Europe, mainly to Spain.

It appears that coffee suffered an economic setback at the end of the century because of hurricanes, and also because the island passed from Spain to the United States in 1898 as the result of the Spanish American War.

According to informants, the coffee industry gradually declined thereafter and was replaced by tobacco, but coffee did not disappear entirely. Tobacco was also exported to Europe and another cash product, sugarcane, was beginning to make headway. It appears, from the scanty information we could gather, that sugarcane began to develop in the region in the last century, but that it really advanced in importance as a cash crop in the period 1900–10. Thus it is significant for the region that it has a relatively long history of operating within the limits of a cash economy and in that sense wage labor has been an important feature of the economy for at least 150 years.

Side by side with this cash economy there has always existed a mixed sector. The peasant with his small plot of land, rented or owned, has invariably produced for his own household as well as for the city market. In that sense, then, the whole region may be said to have always had a mixed economy, subsistence and cash.

Economy

The region as a whole is a purely agricultural one, with no industry whatsoever within its limits. Out of 154 households we included in a survey, 124, or about 80 percent, were headed by people who earned their living from the soil as farmers, as wage laborers on the land, or both.

Three great clusters of farming activities dominate the economy: sugarcane, tobacco and minor food crops (yams, plantains, sweet potatoes, corn and similar crops).

SUGARCANE

The cultivation of sugarcane in Esperanza is basically a commercial and large-scale enterprise. Out of approximately 579 *cuerdas* under cane (since a *cuerda* is 97 percent of an acre, this study will treat them as equivalents), 165 belong to twenty-one farmers, and the rest (414) belong to only two absentee owners. Thus the bulk of the land (80 percent) under sugarcane is farmed as two large-scale units, while the rest is worked in units averaging about 8 acres. Of the total farmland, approximately 50 percent is under cane.

The big farms rely to a great degree on mechanization, especially during the harvest. But mechanization is permitted only up to a certain level, due to the pressure of the labor unions and to the nature of the work (as cane cutting cannot be done by machine), with the result that it has remained a source of work for many household heads in Esperanza.

The small and middle-sized farms employ almost no machinery throughout the whole process of cultivation and harvesting due to the lack of capital, the small size of the farm, and the topography, which is quite steep in some farms. Most of the work is done by hand, and the only type of machinery is the truck that carries the cane to the mill. The cutting and loading is done by wage laborers, many of them farmers who also own their small or middle-sized piece of land.

By direct observation during the sugarcane harvest it could be verified that at least 100 households of our sample were engaged in some way in sugar production. Either they owned sugarcane farms, or some members of the households were employed as wage laborers, or both. The big farms employ from thirty to fifty men during the harvest, and the small and middle-sized farms employ between three to fifteen men only on a seasonal basis.

An important feature of the sugarcane industry is that it operates in accordance with a definite seasonal pattern of planting and harvesting. Workers are very conscious of this, and they call the growing season the "dead season" because economic activities in the area are "dead." The harvest season begins around January and continues for five or six months, up to May or June.

TOBACCO

Tobacco is the other cash crop that is economically relevant in the economy of Esperanza. In contrast to sugarcane, this does not employ much wage labor, as most of the work is done by the household head with the aid of his family. In a group of 204 households, about 97 were engaged in the production and cultivation of tobacco. The farms are not large, and they range in size from half an acre to 12 acres at the most.

The crop is sold to a cooperative in the nearby town of Utuado, located to the southeast of Esperanza. This institution operates through the whole island of Puerto Rico. It provides the initial resources to the farmers by making loans, providing fertilizer and other things needed in tobacco cultivation. The cooperative buys the crop at the end of the harvest, and if there is any favorable balance the farmer can either take the cash or use it as a basis for future loans and other financial operations (Table 2.1). Some large farmers in other parts of the island fulfill the same function as the cooperative.

Tobacco has greatly contributed to filling the gap produced by the dead season in the sugarcane industry, alleviating the financial burden

Table 2.1—Production, Value of Production and Profit of a Group of 20 Tobacco Farmers (1961–62)*

Quintales (100 lbs.)	Total Value (Dollars)	Profit (Dollars)
16.59	677.25	47.15
20.68	834.44	399.87
8.18	319.38	54.61
10.52	403.70	159.85
26.28	993.02	517.68
45.64	1852.26	837.80
19.73	774.70	337.55
23.29	918.57	367.16
52.76	2167.89	1068.13
13.15	515.68	188.70
11.71	470.57	314.95
13.50	527.12	183.89
23.70	929.09	336.46
14.05	583.18	246.53
6.75	288.62	155.28
13.52	518.18	63.57
11.14	410.00	102.95
19.58	778.63	156.25
6.31	259.83	88.39
2.22	82.83	23.31

*Figures from the Utuado cooperative; include farms of different sizes and levels.

many households otherwise suffer due to lack of work. The tobacco harvest falls roughly in the dead season of the sugarcane cycle, so that when the harvest period of sugarcane comes, many farmers are free to earn some money working in the cane fields. Farmers whose tobacco is late complain that they cannot take work in the sugarcane industry.

Favorable market conditions have made the tobacco farmers relatively well off. Most of them manage to make a small, and sometimes fair, profit after deducting costs.

MINOR CROPS

This sector of the economy of Esperanza produces both for home consumption and for the urban market, mainly for Arecibo, the economic center of the whole region.

Almost every household manages to have the use of land on which to cultivate food crops. In a survey made in a sample of 152 households, 138 had control over such a piece of land under different forms of tenure (Table 2.2).

Table 2.2—Households Having Control of
a Piece of Land

Type of Tenure	Number of Households
Owners	67
Squatters	48
Rented	18
Sharecropper	5
Do not have or control land	1
Not known	13
Total	152

Both the size of these plots, which vary from a quarter of an acre to 80 acres, and their forms of tenure are highly varied. In the larger farms not all the land is under food crops of the kind we are discussing here, but at least 5 to 25 percent is.

The main products cultivated in this way are: sweet potatoes, bananas, yams, corn and plantains. These are regularly planted and cared for by the household head, his sons (if present) and perhaps a *compadre* or nearby kin.

There is a very close relation between this type of agricultural activity and tobacco cultivation. For the land on which tobacco is grown is also used to grow other products. The tobacco is planted first, and allowed to grow to 3 or 4 feet high. Food plants are then added, beginning with sweet potatoes. These grow very slowly, and in the meantime the tobacco harvest is begun. This process takes some weeks. The tobacco leaves are stripped off by stages, beginning with the lower part of the plant (the older leaves) and ending with the higher parts (the younger leaves). The leaves are cut and then dried in the farm's warehouse or barn. In this way Esperanza's farmers maximize the use of the same piece of land, and can take advantage of the fertilizers that have been deposited in the soil for the tobacco plants. All this is done during a one-year period.

Other products are grown on almost any available piece of land, sometimes near the tobacco. Corn (maize) is grown immediately after the tobacco and sweet potatoes. It can be cultivated and harvested in less than three months in the period (March-April) when the tobacco harvest has been finished and the farmers have not yet started to prepare for planting again (June-July).

As stated before, most of the production in this sector of Esperanza's economy is used either for domestic consumption or for the market. In a sample of 122 farmers engaged in this type of farming, 84 kept 40 percent or more of their output for domestic consumption. This confirms the mixed character of food production in Esperanza.

Although we were not able to obtain statistical information on this point, our knowledge of Esperanza suggests a very general but direct relationship between the size of the farm and the percentage allocated for home consumption. Small farmers (or peasants—the terms are equivalent in Esperanza and are so used here) can produce less of cash crops like tobacco and sugarcane. People who grant credit to farmers for cultivating any of these crops always give it in an amount proportionate to the size of the farm. These factors tend to increase the cash available to the large farmers (those who own more than about 60 acres) and to decrease the cash for small farmers. Cash is also needed to purchase food outside the home, and so the peasant-farmer (cf. Redfield 1956) is led or forced to increase his production for home consumption.

The goal of farmers in Esperanza is to be able to plant either tobacco or sugarcane or both, but no financial or other return can be expected for at least six months from the time of planting. The farmer adapts himself to the situation, and minor crops become an insurance policy against hunger. The result has been that the larger farms tend to increase the production of cash crops like tobacco and sugarcane and decrease the production of minor crops, compared to the smaller farms. Farms where more than 90 percent of the agricultural production (excluding tobacco and sugarcane) is allocated to domestic consumption are probably some of the smallest in the whole *barrio*.

At first, there is not much deliberate effort to produce these minor crops for the market. People plant them to have food at times when cash is scarce. But if there is a small surplus (or if prices of a certain market are high), they might travel to town and market their product there, or they might sell it to middlemen who are operating locally. Transportation for these products is provided by small trucks that fix their charges according to the bulk and weight of the product.

The part of the crop that is intended for home consumption is either used immediately when ripe, or it is stored until needed as usually happens with sweet potatoes. The diet of the peasant varies according to the crop which is being harvested.

DOMESTIC ANIMALS

Domestic animals comprise a very important sector of Esperanza's domestic economy. The principal animals are the hen, cow, cat, dog, horse and pig. The cow is mostly used to produce milk for the household; no milk is sent to the market. Yields are relatively low, and the reason the peasants give for this is that they do not have the money to feed or care for the cattle adequately. Herding cows is the province of children (especially boys) and women. Most households have at least one cow and perhaps one or two calves.

When the cow's milk yield falls below a certain average, it is sold for meat either in the town market or to a middleman. This can also happen if the family needs cash for an emergency.

The cat is brought into the household to chase and kill rats and the dog to protect against unwelcome visitors (especially when women are alone in the house). The dog also helps to kill pest animals such as rats and a species of wild squirrel that eats crops like corn, sweet potatoes and even sugarcane. Dogs are also used in rounding up livestock at the end of the day.

The economic importance of the horse has greatly diminished with the introduction of the motor car, but it is still frequently used, especially in places where there are no roads. Horses are also useful for transporting crops to centers for truck loading, and peasants use them when they go to local stores to buy foodstuffs and other household items.

The pig is raised primarily to be slaughtered and eaten at ceremonial occasions like baptisms, weddings and similar events. But if the family needs some cash for an emergency, a pig may be sold to a neighbor or taken to the town marketplace and sold there.

Chickens are commonly kept. Hens are kept both for the pot and for the egg production. Cocks are bred for cockfighting, the favorite pastime of the males in Esperanza, and great care is taken to prepare them for the cockfighting season.

Many other kinds of poultry such as turkeys and pigeons are also kept, and are left free to wander around the household. Peasants state that this is a cheaper way to rear them, as they cannot afford to buy enough special food to feed them adequately. Usually they are fed special food only once a day, either in the evening or late afternoon. The manufactured feed sold in town contains maize, wheat and fish among other things.

Emigration to the United States is another factor that must be taken into consideration if one is to understand the economic system of the region. Of the two types of emigration, permanent and temporary, we shall deal here only with the latter. Permanent emigration is excluded because it was impossible to follow up such cases. Here we are interested in household heads who belong, and continue to belong, to Esperanza and maintain a household there, and who emigrate only for a relatively short period of time, such as one month or one year.

Emigration takes place during the months of April, May and June, when work in the sugarcane fields is ending and the tobacco harvest is finished. This is the period of the year when people are most likely to have some cash in hand with which to buy the things needed for a stay in the United States.

Kept with the help of informants, a record of people who emigrated to the United States during the period of our fieldwork shows that the great majority were going only for a short time as temporary migrants.

Most of the people who emigrate for short spells are married and heads of at least elementary families. The pattern in this case is to go to the United States to work and save with the intention of buying a piece of land in Esperanza, or paying some installments on the farm's mortgage, or of making basic repairs to the house. Such household heads may emigrate regularly, establishing cyclical patterns.

Of the twenty-six emigrants during April, May and June, twenty-four were cyclical. The two remaining were family units that migrated permanently. In terms of status, sixteen of the twenty-six migrants were heads of households and families, three were heads of families but not of households, four were not family heads, and the status of three was unknown. Of the twenty-one cyclical migrants whose status was known, seventeen were married and four were single.

In a larger but less detailed survey made in 150 households, a total of 308 persons were found to be in the United States. Of those, 221 were males and 87 females, which suggests that the male tendency to emigrate is stronger than the female. We were able to gather information on the type of emigration for 285 of the 308 absentees, and of those 129 were said to be in the United States on a temporary basis and 156 were there permanently. These data indicate that about half of the people of Esperanza who are abroad in the United States at any given time are expected to return to the island.

Out of the 308 emigrants, 119 were between the ages of seventeen and twenty-eight, and in the age range of seventeen to thirty-five, there were 160. This means that people who emigrate tend to be in their most productive period of life, and also in the age range when most people in Esperanza marry, between twenty and thirty.

If age and sex are considered, the same trends appear. In the age range seventeen to twenty-eight years, 144 are males and 58 females. This confirms the statement made before that more males emigrate than females, which implies that there is more pressure on males to emigrate.

Emigration is thus a significant feature of the economy of Esperanza, which is affected both by the drain of a great number of people who have emigrated permanently to the United States, and by the fact that a sizable number of migrants return home regularly, mostly male household heads, whose wives and children live permanently in Esperanza.

MIGRATION AND FAMILY STRUCTURE

It is crucial at this point to understand certain causal patterns that influence the development of the family. One such framework is the economic or, to put it another way, the occupational. In communities like Esperanza the economic pattern is particularly closely related to other areas of family life. There is a definition of "being a man" that begins in a sense with some sort of economic autonomy and leadership. "Being a man" is not an abstract definition; it is a social role deeply embedded in the context of family life. A man must head a family to be a man; he must be married. Being married means achieving adulthood, but to be an adult there must be economic autonomy. As in many other societies of Hispanic and Mediterranean origin, some spheres of social life seem to be defined as masculine ones. The process of becoming a man is embedded in the family structure, but the position of the man in its structure is closely related to the economic world and also to the political one. Men engage in economic activities as leaders of their families, and it is men who take part in political activities. The classical study of an Andalusian community in the south of Spain by J. Pitt Rivers (1961) illustrates the cause pattern: men operate as economic leaders of the household, and being a man is being able to operate successfully in this capacity.

The man is the link between the domestic realm of family life and the outside world. Like the Greek shepherds described by Campbell (1964), masculine roles operating within the family connect with other levels in society. The shepherd goes to town to engage in patron-client relations and in so doing enters into a somewhat competitive relationship with the patron. Like his counterpart in Esperanza, he tries to establish some kind of permanent link with these people. In Esperanza, *com-*

padrazgo relations established with many persons provide the male with a pool of resources which he can manipulate, in the same way as the Greek shepherd seeks to manipulate his patron. Family roles are integrated with patronage roles. The domestic and communal levels of these communities come into contact with higher levels, provincial and national. Different networks are integrated in these ways.

Other factors are also closely related to the role of the man in this community. The description of the *barrio* emphasizes the static aspects, but migration enters as one of the factors. The migration factor is not exclusive to Puerto Rico. The Caribbean, as a classical colonial area, has tended always to look to a faraway metropolis (Williams 1966). In the case of Puerto Rico, it was Spain until 1898, when the United States took over the island colony. England, France and Holland have played, and in some cases are still playing, a similar role. The migration process emerges as a constant factor in the Caribbean (M. G. Smith 1962b), closely related to development processes in the social structure, and in this case at least, in the structure of the family.

Migration in the Caribbean has many facets and many trends, only some of which are relevant for our purposes. The direction of the movement and the motivation and status of those who migrate are of special relevance. People tend to move from the colony or former ex-colony towards the metropolis for mainly economic reasons (Hernández Alvarez 1967; Philpott 1968) and if they return it is either through economic necessity, or perhaps due to a recession in the metropolis, or because of a desire to get established back home, or simply to visit. Migrants tend to be mainly young males, at least in the Puerto Rican case. Migration provides a means for transcending the unenviable single status and getting married. In the face of negative economic conditions at home that would not permit them to achieve the adult role required of the community, migration provides the solution. The traditional way of starting a family is modified accordingly. With land so scarce and with lack of financial resources, people, especially males in the process of becoming "men," move outside local and national boundaries to be able to achieve social maturity. In this way a compromise is achieved between the traditional pattern and the new one in the male-headed family. People can assume their social roles, but the economic basis is not provided within the community's territorial boundaries.

This does not always provide for a male-centered family structure in the Caribbean. The constant movement that migration imposes tends in many cases to alter this aspect of local family structure or organization. In Esperanza, for example, the stability that can be expected from a male-headed family is frequently altered by the need for migration. We say "need" because the economic situation is sometimes so negative that males are forced to migrate. Unemployment or a poor harvest can critically diminish the family's resources. People live in a cash economy where transactions are made in cash, at least partially. Credit (*fiao*) can be obtained in local stores in the *barrio* and in the town of Arecibo. But credit operates within certain limits, and people know them well and can expect little help in time of real need. All these contingencies, then, force the male to migrate. Some never return, and others develop the pattern of cyclical movement referred to previously.

Similar patterns hold for many areas in the Caribbean: people, especially males, trying to find some sort of effective solution. In many cases the male is not able to stabilize the situation and the female-headed domestic group tends to emerge. This aspect of family organization has been long commented upon and disputed among students of Caribbean society, and all kinds of causal explanations have been advanced. Authors like M. G. Smith, although not negating the relevance of economic interpretations, try to reduce the analysis to certain minimum but required principles of family organization. Writing about some of these aspects, Smith remarks:

Apart from such socioeconomic conditions as migration, the interhousehold movement of adults tends to exhibit the influence of conjugal and consanguineous ties, and these are also important in governing the residential distribution of children. The simple fact that mating relations may take alternative forms, and that all these alternatives influence the constitution of linked household groups, will show that family and domestic relations are by no means conterminous, and that the former cannot be reduced to the latter (1962b:8-9).

Our contention is that the economic variable, among others, is one of the most relevant for understanding the structure of the family, and also for explaining the process of change of roles within it. In this case, we see the intimate relation between economic opportunities for adult males in metropolitan or relatively industrialized areas, relative impoverishment in the local community, migration and change in family leadership patterns. There is a whole range of variations, but the central theme is economic.

If we take a look at the Caribbean in general, certain clear trends can be seen. Puerto Ricans (including the inhabitants of Esperanza) migrate to New York and other areas in the United States. Jamaicans and other societies of British origin migrate to Great Britain. In the Lesser Antilles, as discussed by M. G. Smith (1962b), we find migration toward Trinidad, Curaçao and Venezuela. These latter are areas of relative economic growth. Even little St. Thomas, in the United States Virgin Islands, with its flourishing tourist economy, receives a full-sized migration from poorer islands nearby.

What G. K. Lewis states in relation to the United States Virgin Islands constitutes a condensation of our thesis:

Perhaps the single most remarkable fact of the Virgin Islands way of life is that its economic base, in the form of the majority of the labor task force, is alien, constituted of non-American immigrants settled, legally or illegally, in the various island communities. Initially coming from the neighboring British Virgin Islands and then from the more distant Leeward Islands group, they have been refugees from the desperate poverty of their Caribbean background, responding to economic opportunities in the more affluent American possessions (1970:3-5).

OCCUPATIONAL STRUCTURE

A good idea of the occupational picture of Esperanza can be arrived at by looking at Table 2.3. Most of the occupations are directly related to agriculture. Most people fall into one of the first two categories, farmer

Table 2.3—Occupational Structure

Occupation	Number
Farmer	93
Wage laborer	43
Merchant	4
Public car driver	2
Carpenter	8
Prison guard	1
Watchman in school	1
Mason	2
Barber	3
Clerical worker (government)	2
Shoe repairer	1
Janitor	1
Industrial worker	1
Car driver (government)	1
Watchman (industrial)	1
Foreman (agricultural)	3
Priest (Protestant)	1
Artisan (musical instrument)	1
Total	169

Note: Subjects stated their occupations in their own words, and in some cases more than one occupation was given. A total of 154 household heads were interviewed.

or wage laborer, and many fall into both. Many people have more than one occupation, as for example small farmers who often also work as part-time wage laborers, a feature frequently found in many agricultural communities in Latin America (O. Lewis 1960).

The merchants are people who usually work full time at their occupation, as no hired labor is employed in the stores. The public car drivers also work full time, plying to and from Esperanza in this area.

It can be readily seen that there is little occupational differentiation in Esperanza. The fact that many people follow more than one occupation makes differentiation on the basis of occupation almost impossible. This is a man's occupational world, and few women participate in it. Some women work in the school's dining room as cooks, and some work in the tobacco harvest (not in the field, but in the warehouse or barn), but these possibilities exhaust their occupational opportunities, and this is directly relevant to the internal organization of the household.

There is a group of about fifteen teachers who come every day from the town to work in the school, but in the evening or in the late afternoon they return to their homes. There is also a nurse who is on duty during working hours in a small dispensary. Esperanza depends heavily on the outside world for the satisfaction of many of its public health, economic, religious, educational and political needs. A "floating population" engaged in providing these services is always to be found there. There is, therefore, no core of professional or technically trained people in Esperanza who could form a middle stratum between the big landowners and the small farmers and wage laborers.

CHAPTER 3

Household: Organizational Features

The household in Esperanza is both a kinship unit and a residential group. It usually includes a male head, his wife and their children. The pattern is quite different from the one described by M. G. Smith (1962b) for the British Caribbean where the elementary family and the household do not coincide to the same extent.

On the average, the number of people found in a household is approximately five. In a sample of fifty households, we found an average of 5.48. This emphasis on the individual household should not obscure the fact that there are enduring and frequent relations between households, especially between those united by kinship and *compadrazgo* ties. These come out in the visiting patterns. Asked when they had last seen or visited their kin, most of them said that they had seen them within the last few days, or that they see them frequently.

The terms most commonly used for describing the household are family (*familia*), home (*hogar*) and house (*casa*). They are almost used as synonyms and people are quite conscious that they refer to the individual household.

The household is perceived by its members as an economic, moral and solidarity unit. It has the function of rearing children, providing food, clothing and shelter, affording companionship, and enabling authority to be exercised over subordinate members.

People talk eagerly about their families in a way which indicates the importance they attach to them. Answers like, "One can exercise authority in it," "Because one needs a home to live," "It is good for the rearing of children," "To have a wife, that is the principal thing," demonstrate this domestic focus.

The Household Dwelling

Whenever possible each family is sheltered under its own roof. Houses vary in size and number of amenities in relation to the means available to the family, but there is a common pattern in their general design, use and furnishings.

PHYSICAL CHARACTERISTICS

Most of the houses in Esperanza are constructed of wood, cement and sheet metal. These materials are brought from outside the area, except for some wood that is available locally. All of the houses are single-story constructions; they usually have about five rooms, but poor people's houses tend to have fewer. Of these five rooms, probably two will be bedrooms. There is sometimes one room reserved for meals, the way a dining room is set aside for this purpose. Out of fifty houses visited, only eighteen had a dining room specially reserved for meals.

Most of the houses have a verandah in front, in addition to having a living room. Only thirteen houses in a sample of fifty were found to have a bathroom. This applies also to toilets: only three in fifty had one inside the house; latrines are detached. The kitchen is usually located in the rear of the house.

DIFFERENT USES OF ROOMS

The different rooms of the house are not used exclusively for their manifest purposes, but have many extra uses, and a description of the house is incomplete without some description of this diversity.

Sleeping rooms of the house are also used as bathrooms by many families. As there is no piped water supply, water is brought from the well or river, and the person takes his bath in the room. Bedrooms are also work rooms in which the women do their ironing, especially when there are visitors in the house or the household head is sitting in the living room.

The verandah is a sort of lobby in between the outside of the house and the living room. Visitors wait there until someone answers their knock, and they are invited to come in. In a formal way it is a place to sit in the evening after the work of the day. Not all the houses have a verandah and poorer ones generally lack it.

The living room is in a sense the center of the house. It is the place where visitors are received, where the family gathers in the evening to rest, converse, hear the radio or watch television (a very rare amenity up to now). If somebody is on the verandah and a friend comes walking near the house, he or she is invited to "come up" (*subir arriba*) into the house. Here the visitor chats and sips his cup of coffee, the traditional beverage that must be offered to any guest.

In the night, the function of the living room can change, and it might be used as a sleeping room for a visiting relative or for one or more members of the family, if the house is not big enough. It is not unusual to see a collapsible bed tied to the wall, for "emergencies" as they say.

Even the kitchen can have more than one function. In addition to its normal use for cooking, many people use the kitchen as a place to bathe. Most of the baths are taken in the latrines, however, where a person can have more privacy than in a room, as the latrine is detached from the rest of the house. In this way most of the latrines really become a combination of bath and latrine.

The area round the house is called the "patio," and a great many of the household activities take place in it. Flowers are planted in the patio, domestic animals are fed in it, the cow is milked there, children play there, women do their washing there. It is not uncommon to see a group of males sitting in the patio talking and watching a cockfight or drinking.

Most of the houses are 600 square feet or less. A larger house is very rare indeed, and it must be remembered that economic considerations influence the size of a house. Most of the people try to reduce building costs by calling on kin to help with the labor, using local woods, buying second hand (used) boards, but even in this way it requires some cash to build a house in Esperanza, and for the peasant $200 or $300 is a large expense.

The usual practice is to build the minimum facilities and then expand and improve when circumstances allow. Cheaper materials may later be replaced by better ones. This regularly happens around Christmas when they get some money from last year's tobacco harvest or the bonus from the labor union agreement with the sugarcane farmers.

The lifetime of a house varies with the quality of the materials used in its construction. In the past most houses were built of local woods, which are very hard indeed, and they could last up to 150 years. But with the disappearance of the forests, materials came to be imported, and the wood imported from the United States and other countries is soft wood that is not so resistant to tropical conditions. The framework is commonly made of local woods, and the rest (floor, walls, doors, windows) is made of imported materials.

There is great variation in the length of time taken to construct a house, but inquiries in thirty-six households gave figures varying from five days to one year. On the average (using this census as a source) it takes fifty-three days to build a house.

Renting houses is almost nonexistent in Esperanza, and it is normal for the head of the household to own his house. Out of fifty houses surveyed, thirty-nine were the property of the household head, four the property of relatives, three the property of others, and in four cases no information was available. The situation is rather different with regard to the ownership of sites although the tendency for the household heads to be the owner is maintained. Of fifty households, thirteen sites belonged to squatters (not paying for use of land), five homes were located in land which was the property of relatives, twenty-four sites were the property of the household head, four houses stood on rented land and one site had been bought and was being paid for by installments.

Land is more expensive than a house. Anyone proposing to build a house, and who desires to buy a piece of land for this purpose, must bear in mind the increase in his costs. The solution in Esperanza is to beg for a piece of land on which to build a house. Recourse may be had to one's own relatives, the wife's relatives, *compadres,* neighbors: in fact anybody one feels might help. A house site so begged is usually a piece of land that does not have any economic value, such as a hilly place or an eroded plot. In this way, if one does not have a piece of land of one's own, one can still put all one's economic resources into the cost of the house. A person who has a piece of land available but denies it to one who requests it to build a house is severely criticized and is called an *esmayao* (miser), a derogatory term.

FURNISHINGS

The living room, being the social center of the house, is generally well provided with facilities. It will have a pair of rocking chairs and one or two other chairs in the better off families, and in poorer families at least a big wooden bench. Almost every house has a radio, and the peasant is proud of it and announces that he hears the news every day.

The walls of the living room (and also of the sleeping rooms) are a reflection of the realm of family life. Family photographs of weddings, religious pictures and images and statues, calendars, farmer's almanacs and decorative figurines adorn the walls of the peasant's house. Virtually everything of some emotional, pictorial or religious value is kept by the family and hung on the wall, where it remains for years.

If the living room is used as a dining room, a small table with two chairs serves as the place to have the meals. If there is a special room being used as the dining place, a bigger table with four chairs will be used. If the family can afford it, a cabinet with cups, cutlery, and all the implements used for eating and drinking will be found in the dining room, where it serves decorative purposes.

Each sleeping room is usually occupied by a big luxurious bed, and perhaps a smaller and less luxurious one. The big one will be used by the married couple to sleep in, and the small one by smaller children. If children are quite small, probably a cot or hammock (*coy*) is used.

The kitchen is the most neglected place in the whole house. In spite of being the place where women spend most of their time, less care is taken to keep it in good condition. Perhaps this is because the bulk of the people previously used charcoal as a fuel for cooking, and the great amount of smoke that comes out of charcoal blackens the walls and roof of the kitchen, in spite of a hole in the wall or roof that serves as a sort of chimney. Although the kitchen is neglected, great care is taken to improve the appearance of the living room and the sleeping rooms. The front of the house is well taken care of, and the back is fully forgotten.

Husband-Wife Roles and Physical Space Distribution

In a very general way the roles of husband and wife are reflected in the distribution of space inside the house and its surroundings. The concepts of *arriba* (up) and *abajo* (down) define the area of operation of wife and husband. Up (*arriba*) means basically the kitchen, the backyard and the sleeping rooms, which are the "feminine" areas of the house. This is where a woman is expected to be found, doing the chores of the house. Here she is busy cooking the food for her husband and children, ironing the family's clothes, and cleaning the house. A good wife is not a show off (*presentá*). This means that she keeps herself busy in her area and is not seen in the front part of the house or going around in the neighborhood, as summarized in the saying: *"Una mujer debe estar en su casa atendiendo a su marío (marido) y hijos y no caminando por el vecindario"* (A woman should always be at her house caring for her husband and children and not going around the neighborhood).

The man is expected to be down (*abajo*) and this means (in terms of physical distribution) that he is expected to be outside the house, either in the farmland or in the tobacco barn. There are also some places around the house, such as the verandah, where the man keeps certain things like the *machete,* saddle, hoe and other tools that are considered "masculine" (*del hombre de la casa*). Houses are built a few feet from the ground and the storage space beneath the floor is also male territory. The barn is another place where the man keeps his things.

Thus spacial distribution reflects the social differentiation of the roles of husband and wife. This is a consistent pattern all through Esperanza which we were able to verify by direct observation.

This physical separation was noticeable in replies to questions about the kitchen. Most men stated that they never went into the kitchen as that was not the place of a man, but of a woman. Most of them said that they just sat down at the dining table and ate what the woman had prepared. In many cases they would not even sit at the dining table as they were out working on the farm (the wife carried the food to them), or they would sit in the living-dining room, but not at the table.

The women never touch men's belongings (or tools), and in all the time we spent in Esperanza we never saw even one woman take anything from the "masculine space" (cf. Arensberg 1937).

Patterns of Eating and Sleeping

The way the family eats and sleeps reveals much about the intimate functioning of the household. In Esperanza there is no clear-cut pattern in eating arrangements, although there are certain recognizable norms. Most of the time, age is a criterion. There is the value that adults deserve more respect than children, and so they are served first and occupy the best places at the table. This is embodied in the frequently heard injunction: "elders come first" (*los mayores alante*). Among adults, men are served by women, who eat in the kitchen, or after men have finished. This gives one a glimpse of some of the distinctions that are observed in Esperanza's households. The same differentiation operates in the kitchen. When questioned, most men said that it was a good idea for men to know how to cook, but when asked if they knew how and if they actually cooked, the numbers in the affirmative were almost none.

Sex and age modify and influence the sleeping arrangements. Except for the married couple, the norm is to separate persons of opposite sex. This segregation cannot always take place, and sometimes they are forced by crowded conditions and lack of space to sleep in the same room.

If this happens, age is taken into consideration. Small children are placed in the same room, as they "do not yet have a wicked mind" (*niños no tienen malicia todavía*) and are not conscious of sex.

They are deemed to lack the necessary sophistication to be aware of sex and sexual relations. The term *malicia* (wickedness) implies that a person has *malicia* when he understands that sex is a pleasure and must be searching for it. The child, because of his lack of understanding, does not search for it.

Young children can either be placed all in the same room, or they can sleep with adults in the room. But as they start to grow up they are segregated. In crowded conditions the living room is used as a sleeping room at night.

Ownership of the House and Lot

Not all houses are constructed on plots that are the property of the household head, nor are all the houses owned by the household head. Household heads (mostly males) try to own the house and the lot, but they do not always succeed in doing so.

The ideal pattern is to have the ownership both of the house and of the lot, but the most difficult thing to own is always the land. The result of one survey we made shows that about one household head in every two succeeds in doing so, as twenty-five out of fifty household heads were the owners both of the house and the lot where it stood.

Most of the people who own the houses are male household heads, but there is no legal or customary prohibition against a woman owning a house or lot. It is very difficult indeed for women to become household heads, however, widowhood being perhaps the main reason or condition that permits them to assume this role. Women are also practically excluded from the outside sphere of the family, where they could enter the occupational system and accumulate the economic resources that are necessary to construct a house and/or to buy the lot. The cultural expectation is that the woman, when married, should concentrate on the job of looking after "her" household and her husband.

Headship of Household

There is a basic dichotomy that permeates all segments of Esperanza's family organization. The differentiation between household head and housewife (*jefe de casa y ama de casa*) delineates two clearly defined segments of family structure.

On one occasion we interviewed a woman who was living alone with two children, having separated from her husband. The husband was living in the United States, but when we tried to interview her, she resisted and stated that he was household head although he was absent in the United States. They were separated, but as the man was sending her money, she still thought of him as the head. Only after prolonged visits and exhortations was she able to answer our questions, and even then we could notice the reticence in her answers, many times adding, "If my husband were here he could answer that better." They have been separated for more than two years, and from the information I could gather, there was no hope or possibility of their reuniting. She was using the phrase, "If my husband were here," to cover her uneasiness at the performance of a role that was new for her and that was clearly the prerogative of the male. This shows the degree to which women accept implicitly that the role of household head is a male one.

In another house, when asked in what areas he had authority, the household head summarized his functions by saying, "I have authority in the *machete* (bush knife), *azada* (hoe), *caballo* (horse) and *sombrero* (hat)." The *machete* and *azada* symbolized his role within the occupational world and as provider, while the *caballo* and *sombrero* symbolized his status as an adult male. Only adult males wear their hats while riding and then only if they are married and a head of household. In short, it is taken for granted in Esperanza that household head means male household head. A woman thrown momentarily into that position feels uncomfortable and vacillates in reaching decisions. Many times in that context we heard the phrase, "If . . . X were here . . . ."

All persons interviewed had a very clear idea of what the household head is supposed to do, of what his obligations and rights are. In the economic sphere the expectation is that the household head will fulfill his basic role of provider for all the material needs of all the members of the household. The most explicit symbol of this is when the peasant sets out on Saturdays and other days to buy the supplies needed for the household, both foodstuffs and other provisions. People notice and say, "There goes X to buy the *compra* (literally, supplies bought) of *his* house."

On the moral level he must be "an example" (*un ejemplo*) to his children, and must see that they are "well behaved" (*porten bien*) persons. The peasant scheme of values emphasizes the harmony that must be maintained in social intercourse, and no father likes his children to have bad reputations. This is well summarized by the term *respeto* (respect), and every father is watchful and tries to see that his children behave with *respeto*. The father is responsible for the conduct of his children, and although the mother has more frequent contact with some children, for example, the daughters, it is the father who is morally responsible for the behavior of the household as a unit.

On the jural side the authority and responsibility of the father is even more pronounced. He is legally responsible for his wife and his children, and this holds even in cases of separation or divorce (a very rare thing in Esperanza). On practically all matters dealing with the external relations of the household, he takes the leading part. This does not mean, for example, that the wife cannot inherit in her own right, but that if she inherits anything, she will have to tell her husband and ask permission to fulfill the due processes of the law, and in all this he is expected to exercise his authority.

This clear dichotomy is matched on the other side by the role the woman plays in the internal structure of the household. She has practically no role in providing the economic resources, but is responsible for seeing that everything operates well in the household. The house must be kept clean, domestic animals taken care of, the meals cooked. This is taken for granted, and no woman who is a good housewife would ask her husband what her duties are, or neglect them.

The connection between the different roles can be clearly seen in the economic context. Again the man belongs "down" (*abajo*) while the woman's place is "up" (*arriba*). This means that the husband is expected to go out of the house to earn his living, while the woman must remain "up" in the house. Most husbands say, "I bring the *compra* (supplies) to the door (front door) and leave it there, where my wife will take it into the kitchen." An old saying in the area is: "A man *arriba* does not bring any beans into his house" (*El hombre arriba no sube habichuelas*). Beans symbolize the total food supply the man is expected to bring into his house, being a permanent item in the food of the peasants. If the man fulfills his role of provider, then the woman can fulfill her role of housewife. These are the ideal patterns, and they are practiced most of the time by the majority of the people concerned.

In a sample of fifty households, only three were headed by females, and of these, two were headed by widows and the other was headed by a woman who had separated from her husband. But even this woman showed great uncertainty in her behavior. She told the people that her husband was going to come back to live with her and their children, and to the writer's inquiries about who was the head of the household, she replied that her husband was the head.

In contrast to this, male household heads are established by marriage. This means that men marry and live in a house of their own with their families (wife, and later, children). Men usually marry between the ages of twenty and thirty (see Tables 10 and 11 on marital status and sex in Chap. 6). Thus they come to be household heads relatively early in their lives, while the majority of women (few as they are) who become household heads do so as a result of widowhood, a condition that is normally reached only in the later stages of the individual's life cycle.

To illustrate the roles and how the differentiations operate, we describe briefly the cases of three household heads of different socio-economic levels.

Xavier is a squatter who lives on the land of one of the old families of Esperanza. He is an easygoing person, and has the ability to make friends with anybody. He does not cultivate the soil in a regular way, although he plants some minor crops as a sort of hobby. Xavier is well acquainted with politics and politicians, and he is the informal representative in the area of the party in power in Puerto Rico. As he suffers from a chronic illness, he receives a pension from the government. His wife is one of the few women who work outside the home in Esperanza. She works as a cook in the dining room of the government school, and her salary plus Xavier's pension are the sole sources of cash income of the family.

Xavier is without any doubt the head of this household. His authority over the household's members is acknowledged by all of them. He is always engaged in the "outside" things, like taking care of his horses or his cocks and doing his chores as informal representative of the party. This last work involves a lot of visiting and talking with people, something Xavier likes very much.

Xavier's wife spends much of her time (about six hours daily) working outside the home, and her regular complaint is that she does not have enough time to take proper care of her home and husband and children. She is always saying that her daughter and mother (who take care of the house while she is away) do not do an efficient job, and that she is the only one that really "understands" the whole thing. When she comes back from her work in the late afternoon, she is busy around the house cleaning and doing other chores. She is the one who prepares the dinner, while her husband goes for a walk or sits in the living room, perhaps chatting with a visitor.

Xavier's wife is in charge of the internal issues of the household in spite of the fact that she works outside the home. Her complaints about the house care and the inefficiency of her mother and daughter reveal this clearly. Xavier, on the other hand, is the *de facto* and jural leader of the household, and is busy in outside and masculine affairs. He inquires of his wife to see how things are going inside the household, and comments if he finds anything at fault.

He makes the decisions about house purchases, for even though his wife is a wage earner, he is the one who controls the finances of the household. When we inquired who was the "boss," he would start laughing and look amazed at the question and make the comment, "Decide that for yourself."

MANUEL

Manuel is one of the property-owning farmers and owns something like 40 acres of land. He cultivates tobacco and sugarcane as cash crops, but he produces also some products for domestic consumption. His income is relatively high by Esperanza's standards: around $3,000 a year. Manuel's economic resources allow him to employ some wage labor, at least in the sugarcane harvest. He works all the time on his farm and does not go outside to work as a wage laborer.

This is a household where the roles of husband and wife are clearly differentiated. Manuel occupies himself fully in the "outside" functions, while his wife is busy performing her duties in the kitchen and in other "feminine" areas. Manuel performs among other things the following tasks: farming, buying supplies (*compra*) and clothing, and keeping watch over the way things are going inside the household (wife's work, children's behavior).

His wife is a fulltime housewife, as she does not work outside the home. She is in charge of the kitchen, washing, ironing, and house cleaning. When her husband is out farming, she has to carry his food to him and also the coffee that is drunk at ten in the morning and at three in the afternoon.

Manuel is quite an authoritarian personality, but it would be unfair to qualify him as a despot. He keeps a watchful eye on everything around the house, but does it with a combination of the "stick and the carrot," and only in extreme cases or situations does he lay down the law in a decisive way.

CARLOS

Carlos is a farmer who owns (with his father) a farm of 20 acres. He cultivates tobacco and sugarcane and also some minor crops, both for the market and home consumption. In general, he belongs to an intermediate socioeconomic level, being neither of the lower nor of the higher level in Esperanza. He also works as a wage laborer during the sugarcane harvest, and in turn he employs some wage laborers in the harvesting of his own sugarcane.

Carlos is always working either on his farm or on somebody else's. Following the pattern in Esperanza, he is in charge of outside matters in relation to his household. He is the sole wage (and cash) earner in his house and controls the financial transactions. His wife is a fulltime housewife, and never leaves the house; she cooks, cleans, and does the washing. We noticed that she was a shy personality and that she hid in the kitchen when any visitor approached the house. Only after we greeted Carlos were we able to exchange a few words with her, and this only with a great effort.

Carlos is not an authoritarian personality, but neither is he an easy-going man. He is a very resolute person who never raises his voice, but assumes that everybody in his house knows his own responsibilities. He, like Xavier and Manuel, is in full charge of his household.

The Social Context of Male Roles and Conflict

There are certain contexts that constitute the areas where the male roles are played, with all the stresses and tensions that are involved. We suggest in this section that communities like Esperanza and, in broader terms, the Puerto Rican society and societies and communities of Hispanic, North African and Mediterranean origin can be compared, and show similar patterns in the ways and places where males play out their roles (Buitrago Ortiz 1970). There seems to exist in these societies the requirement that the male role has basic public aspects, that these aspects must be fulfilled in the open. The concept of the public area appears to be a constant factor in the male situation. The process of being a male is a public one. Another relevant factor is that the male role is not an ascribed one. The male role is achieved, and there exists a functional requirement that it must be validated constantly. One must demonstrate that one is a man; at one moment you may be a man, but it is assumed that you could change the next. The role must be played properly and constantly in front of the community, in the open.

In many Mediterranean societies the cafe seems to be an arena where males meet to prove their masculinity. Verbalization of the aggressive kind, bragging, heavy drinking and sometimes open aggression tend to structure a sequence of expected behavior. In the playing out of the role, everybody must be alert, because the other is also always on the alert. It is a dynamic situation that generates a state of constant tension. No one has characterized this attitude better than the British anthropologist Campbell (1964). Speaking of the young man who is becoming a "real man" and referring to some specific aspects of this process, he states, in terms very much reminiscent of Esperanza:

The community will gradually form an opinion of his prowess as a shep-herd, his fearlessness on the high ridges, his devotion to a sick or injured sheep, and his skill in grazing. It is difficult to say how this opinion is formed, since unrelated shepherds seldom work together. Possibly the estimate is sometimes inaccurate. But the critical moment in the development of the young shepherd's reputation is his first quarrel. Quarrels are necessarily public. They may occur in the coffee shop, the village square, or most frequently on a grazing boundary where a curse or stone aimed at one of his straying sheep by another shepherd is an insult which inevitably requires a violent response. In any case some account of the event becomes public property. If the quarrel occurs before unrelated bystanders, the community may obtain a reasonably factual account of the fight. If it is not witnessed by an impartial audience, the contestant with the fewer marks of injury and the greater number of persuasive kinsmen wins the day. It is the critical nature of these first important tests of his manliness that makes the self-regard . . . of the young shepherd so extremely sensitive (1964:280–281).

It seems to us that the requirements of the male role impose heavy strains and stresses in these types of communities, which rely heavily on the male-centered family structure. In a traditional and somewhat static situation like the one described by Campbell, the role playing assumes an almost ritualized form. In Esperanza (and elsewhere in Puerto Rico) we have a somewhat different situation, with the intense process of social change that influences the functioning of the family and its related roles. One Puerto Rican anthropologist, Seda Bonilla (1969a), has for many years studied the relation between the process of social change and the personality of the man who undergoes the migration experience and returns to the small town, and has postulated the emergence of a disorganization of anomic character in these people. They want to reject the traditional patterns of behavior in favor of what they perceive as the "right" American ones.

Seda Bonilla draws up a model in terms of a conflict of generations. He mentions the old generation which operates within the framework of traditional values. Even though he criticizes a certain inability to operate successfully in that framework, he goes on to state that the patterns and values had some sense, that the old generation had a clear picture of their social world, and tended to act accordingly. The rules of the game were clear and structured and the individual had some sense of security and achievement.

In contrast, the new generation is composed of young people, many of whom have undergone the experience of migration to the United States. Seda Bonilla portrays them, mainly young males, as confused, disorganized, with no clear picture of what they want to be. They have a vague idea of certain value orientations that they define as "American," such as being a "cool cat." The main thesis is that of marginality, where the traditional values and orientations are rejected and something "new" is aimed at. But this attempt fails; the result is anomic behavior. For Seda Bonilla, these males are alienated and confused; they cannot function as articulate, autonomous human beings. They are caught in a conflict from which they escape, or try to escape, by open undirected aggression and similar means. His book constantly mentions verbal and physical aggression as a regular mode of behavior, in trying to cope with the tensions and stresses of this marginal condition.

In our opinion, however, Seda Bonilla loses sight of the continuity that exists between the old and new generation. For instance, he mentions the fact that these young men have informal meetings in which they resort to verbal and physical aggression, to a kind of behavior where they make fun of one another. The main characteristic is a predisposition to fight for anything, to externalize, in spite of trying to be a "cool cat." The aggression is undirected, anything can serve as an object, even inanimate things.

We would modify Seda Bonilla's model a little in terms of an interpretation. The continuity, slight as it may be, is there. The interaction pattern is very similar to the *relajo* pattern as described by students of Puerto Rican society, but only in its structural aspects (cf. Lauria 1953–67). The content of the relationship, its basic motivation, has been transformed. In the past, in the traditional society or community, the *relajo* pattern constituted one of the main avenues for playing out the male role. As stated before, this role, with its varied implications, is closely related to the structure of the family and is one of the connecting links between the domestic levels in the Puerto Rican society and the outer or "higher" levels. It is an achieved role that must be validated constantly. The *relajo* model, then, appears to have a "function" in the traditional society. What has been maintained is the predisposition to deal with the other in some kind of antagonistic way, but without the relatively clear conviction typical of the past. The young males seem to reject values that in the past were part of the male role, but at the same time their attempts to incorporate new "American" values have not been completely successful. The reactions then, are not structured and directed. Their manifest behavior reflects their psychological confusion.

There is another dimension of the problem that Seda Bonilla seems to have missed. He is more interested in the process of social change and tends to forget one factor that in a sense is inherent to the situation. We refer to the generational factor. He is comparing and contrasting two different generations, two groups of people in different stages of their life cycle. This forgotten aspect tends to result in his analysis being made purely in terms of a process of social change. But the generational aspect locates individuals in different sectors of the social system, and to some extent this implies some degree of difference in terms of values, world views and social norms. The generational factor is implicit in his analysis, not explicit. His thesis is not refuted by our comments, but complemented; an implicit factor is made explicit. His interest in dynamic aspects of the social system tends to neglect the structural aspects inherent in the situation.

But in general this model, with modifications, can be applied to Esperanza. In a broad way, there appears to be more continuity and fewer problems. Esperanza seems to be a more isolated community, not only geographically, but in terms of social interaction with the outside world. This statement should be qualified, as migration is part and parcel of Esperanza and not an abnormal happening. Seda Bonilla's community appears to be a more urbanized area, and Esperanza is more rural and traditional. The conflict between generations is less violent. Our contention is that there is probably less discontinuity and psychological disorganization than Seda Bonilla supposes. The two generations of males can be seen interacting in places like the cafes, the horse market and the vigils. The tone of the interaction is always antagonistic, there is the constant bragging and verbal aggression, the heavy drinking, and the playing of musical records in the jukebox. But it is more ritualized, more structured, more "traditional."

For example, we have seen friends engaged in a process of playing billiards, which has become a popular game in cafes everywhere in Puerto Rico. The males in Esperanza flock to the *barrio's* cafes in the late afternoon, after the working day. They invite each other for a bottle of beer and for a game. They play all through the late afternoon, and the spectators closely watch the game, make comments, drink beer, and pass from the role of spectator to that of player. We took part in these games for more than a year, and our experience confirms that aggression of all sorts seems to be relatively controlled and restrained. We watched people who sometimes were on the point of overt aggression, but the participants were always able, sometimes by subtle use of ridicule, to divert or dissolve it. A male on the point of fighting would not be taken seriously (*no tomarlo en serio*) by anybody. A joke could be made, everybody would laugh, and solidarity would be restored again, to be challenged a few minutes later. The system reflects greater flexibility and can handle (or so it seems) tension and stresses better than Seda Bonilla's community.

But this does not mean that the situation is a completely stable one in Esperanza. Migration influences the youngest males, many of whom have been educated in the schools of the nearby town of Arecibo.

As they finish their high school courses, they are confronted with a dilemma. They can stay in the *barrio* and work the land when it is available and if they are willing. But opportunities for owning land are few, and agricultural tasks rank very low in the scale of values of young males. They have been educated in a public school system that emphasizes the values of industrialization and urbanization and that relegates agriculture to a secondary place. They tend to hear from people who have just returned from the United States that, *"ahí si hay pesos"* (literally: there you have the dollars). Even some "traditional" farmers who have worked in the past in the United States sometimes compare the quality and quantity of farm land available there with that of Esperanza. The comparison is almost always in favor of the United States's farm land. The overall result is that males in their most productive years tend to migrate to the United States to get a start in life. When they return, temporarily or in a permanent way, the change is noticeable although with less violence than in Seda Bonilla's community. They speak constantly about the *Estados Unidos, El Norte* (The North), or *Niuyor* (New York), *el boj* (the boss). Their scale of values tends to look to an urban setting and towards industrial occupations.

The general process of social change seems to lead in the same direction in both types of community, that described by Seda Bonilla and Esperanza. The whole society is being urbanized and industrialized, and this is altering the norms of the roles. Both communities were predominantly rural in the past and migration to the United States was totally unknown. The opening of these communities has placed these roles in a state of stress. To the "natural" conflict of generations, we can then add the process of disruption of the content of the roles, and the result is some kind of anomic behavior. People seem to abandon one way of behaving for another, but the process is not complete. The traditional definition of "becoming a man" is then under great pressure. The general process of economic and social change alters the normative content of the roles in the domestic realm of the social structure. In this case we have economic and social forces coming from the outside and "opening up" these communities. This process has been studied in communities where the traditional male role is similar to the community studied by Seda Bonilla and by us and the impact is similar. The research done by Lopreato (1967) in the south of Italy could summarize our contention, though his work and conclusions are nearer Seda Bonilla's than ours.

In the preface of his book, he states:

Among the many transformations shaping human society today, one stands out both for its intensity and for its generality. Everywhere agricultural people are being seduced from all directions, with products, ideas, and values manufactured in the great urban centers of the industrial world. Human society seems to have every intention of transforming itself into one colossal city of teeming bureaucracies and industrial complexes. Peasants want to be peasants no more. At least, they are no longer willing to suffer the privations—economic, social, and political—that have been the secular characteristics of their status. At the first opportunity they leave their fields to seek the economic and social opportunities of the city. Some take their families, never to return to the old village. Others shuttle back and forth between village and city, playing a direct role in the "urbanization" of the agricultural world (1967:13).

The Social Conflict of "Traditional" Male Roles

Every Sunday in Esperanza an event takes place that reflects in a very clear way some of the most important aspects of the man's role in this social system. For lack of a better term, we will call it the horse market. The event is mainly a meeting of horse riders of Esperanza and nearby *barrios*. Visitors from other barrios come, but the majority of those present are from Esperanza. One of the horse owners and riders, Pablo, owns a country store, where he sells beer, rum and foodstuffs. The place also has a jukebox and a billiard table. Near this store there is a big back and side yard, which can accommodate more than twenty horses and from forty to perhaps seventy persons. This is the setting where the event takes place.

Every Sunday from about ten in the morning, Pablo opens his store, and perhaps an advance party of one or two riders come in. They talk with the owner, have a beer, play a couple of records from the jukebox and perhaps sit for an hour or two on the outside, squatting (*ñangotados*) and conversing, or simply loafing. The process continues in the same vein until about 1:00 p.m. At this time horses and their riders start arriving. By 3:00 p.m. there are more than twenty-five horses and also some fifteen to twenty people, who are no longer riders or never were.

The number of people present at any time varies, as they do not remain at the market all day. They come and go, but there is always a substantial group there. The event continues until the early evening hours, and by six or seven o'clock at the latest, it has normally finished and all the horses and riders are gone.

The occasion is a male one and women are fully excluded. We never saw a woman there, not even Pablo's wife, who remained inside her home. The men who come to the event are adults, and the age range varies between eighteen and fifty years. We estimated that at least

70 percent of them are married, and the rest, who are single, would be those in the youngest age range. Most of them are horse riders and go there with their horses, but some go on foot: the latter are usually riders and horse traders who no longer practice the trade, but are so devoted that they cannot stay away from it. Xavier, one of our informants, was one of them. He seldom rides a horse any more (he is more than fifty years old now). But when Sunday comes, Xavier cannot resist the temptation. He puts on his best clothes, his hat and states, *"Voy a dar una vuelta por casa de Pablo"* (I am going to see what is happening at Pablo's place). Some of those who go are not or have never been riders, but they are only a minority, as most males in Esperanza like horseback riding and have at least a superficial acquaintance with it.

The event, to the outside observer, presents a colorful picture. The jukebox operates at full volume; some men play billiards and shout. Others chat with their friends and drink either beer or rum. Outside in the yard, ten or fifteen horses patiently wait for their owners who have them tied to a post. Somebody is doing business and is discussing horse prices with another, while onlookers watch.

Out in the road in front of Pablo's store, three or four riders are engaged in a race, each one trying to prove that his horse is the fastest. The picture is one of movement and of constant and never-ending conversation.

Pablo's place is located in front of the road that cuts through Esperanza's "center," where the church, the stores, the school, the medical dispensary and a cluster of houses are located. It is strategically situated. During the market on Sundays, groups of horsemen continually come and go from Pablo's store; it is the center of male activities in the *barrio* during that day.

The market fulfills more than one function. From the economic viewpoint, it is the place to buy a horse if one needs it. There are also some people who practice the trade of selling horses with a view to making a profit. Zacarías and his father Rubén both have quite a reputation as dealers. People say that they can sell anything, meaning that they can sell a horse in poor condition for a relatively good price. They sometimes buy old and sick horses, and after taking good care of them for a few weeks, they can manage to disguise and sell them. People in Esperanza state that Zacarías and Rubén think only about horses (*no piensan mas que en caballos*).

The market also performs the social function of bringing the men together. It is here that our main interest lies, for the market is the place where man's role in the social system can be studied with particular profit. We have seen how the man belongs to *abajo* (down) and how his role as provider is emphasized in the internal organization of the household. The attendance at the market and his behavior there is also part of being a man and being by implication a household head.

After a man provides for the members of his household, he can engage in other behavior that is expected of a man in the full sense of the term. This means that he can go into the market alone and can remain there for the whole day and later does not have to give account of his whereabouts to anybody, as children and women are supposed to do. When Sunday comes, everybody in the family knows that the head is going to the market when they see him putting on his best clothes and taking his hat, spurs and whip. Nobody questions him, and before going he tells his wife in a matter-of-fact way. On the road he probably meets others who are also going, and they ride together and talk about their expectations for the day; who is going to sell his horse and who is going to buy.

One of the relevant features here is the horse-man-fertility configuration, as we will call it. We noticed in our visits to the market that men said that they did not like to ride mares or castrated horses, as a stallion would feel attracted by it and would try to mount the mare or gelding. The argument they put first was that it was dangerous, as the stallion would come up from behind and could kick them. But it gradually became evident that this was not the only reason. Some stated that they did not ride mares or geldings because that is "for women" (*eso es para las mujeres*). They felt that it was an insult to their masculinity to be seen so mounted. The preference for a full man is supposed to be a vigorous stallion, to own this type of horse, and to demonstrate that he can control it. One of the things that men most admired was when Zacarías, who is the best rider in Esperanza, took a wild horse and rode it until he dominated the animal. Tomás, who was present, made the following comment: "To a rider like him I am willing to give my horse, even if he kills it."

When men behave in this way in Esperanza, they are reinforcing their roles as men. Men are supposed to be courageous and sexually aggressive. Fertility (*fecundidad*) is a means of demonstrating masculinity. Women are expected to be submissive and passive. A castrated horse is supposed to be like a mare (*como una yegua*). So when a man refuses to ride a castrated horse or a mare he is refusing to be associated with feminine qualities. Only women usually ride mares or castrated horses. Further, if a horse tried to copulate with his mount, it would try to do so from the back, and the rider would feel ashamed. The shame is in part related to the fact that he would find himself in the position of being attacked from the rear, similar to the way in which homosexuals (*maricones*) have sexual relations. People would liken his position *vis à vis* the stallion to that of a homosexual (feminine behavior) having sexual intercourse with another homosexual. It would involve a reversal of roles.

Another fact to be noticed in this connection is the association between marriage and fertility. The socially approved way of being fertile is within marriage, and fertility is associated with masculinity. The result is that men avoid any situation in which they could be associated with nonfertility ("a man is a fertile horse").

The spurs and the whip that the man uses when riding a horse could be placed in context here. They are the tools by which a man can control and fully dominate a horse. The man who can do this is *cojonudo* (has guts) and is considered a full man. He can impose his will on the horse, and the horse obeys him. When a man goes to the market, he never (if he rides a horse) goes without spurs and whip. We were not able to follow the matter deeply, but we have the impression that when they carry the spurs and whip they feel more masculine. It is as if they were symbols of the virility that men must show.

The type of behavior at the market is also perfectly consonant with the active role expected from men in Esperanza. There is constant bragging and discussing and a disregard for money. A rider boasts that he can ride better than anyone else and is willing to bet on that. Another states that his horse is the best one and shouts his desire to be bet a bottle of rum on a race. A third invites some friends for a drink, stating that he will pay for everything as he has plenty of money to spend. Sometimes this behavior leads to conflict, as when a man shouts at another that his horse is the worst in the market. If both are drunk this can lead to insults and to a fight to "prove that I am a man and not a coward" (*para probar que soy un hombre y no un cobarde*). But friends usually intervene, and it all ends with an invitation to share another drink.

The horse market is then primarily the place where the men of Esperanza can act out their masculinity. During the week all of them have been working hard; but on Sunday they can, aided by their horses (those who own and bring them), demonstrate that they are *machos completos* (full men). They drink, they shout, they spend relatively large amounts of money. By being generous with the money they demonstrate that they are not *esmayaos* (stingy), and that they, not their wives, have the money and can spend it. Both are qualities that are prized in the head of the household. The association with the horse, with the implication in terms of masculinity, is strictly along the same lines.

It should also be noticed that during the week no similar event is celebrated. It is only held on Sundays, which is the day when one is not supposed to work. All week the men have worked hard, demonstrating their responsibility as providers of their households. Only one day of the week do they "throw the big party." It is a definite segregation between work and leisure, but both are equally involved in the same theme—masculinity.

Some Public and Private Aspects of Female and Male Roles

Conflict and stress at the local level is an expression of structural principles. When conflict takes place between people of the same community, we find social roles expressed. For example, gossip, which is activated basically and almost exclusively by women in Esperanza, can be viewed as a way of "being a woman," equivalent to men's behavior in public places, as described earlier. Gossip (*chisme*) is intimately related with the female role. It is practiced constantly in this community and follows a regular pattern. It is practiced only by the female sex; no men should even be present. People assume that *"chisme es cosa de mujeres"* (gossip is a woman's thing). Women chat in some corner and the behavior is the opposite of that of men. Conversation is carried on in a hushed tone, almost in a defensive way, taking care that nobody else can hear. They exchange secrets and information about others. Any misbehavior by the *barrio's* inhabitants is commented upon. If somebody's son stole something and was arrested by the police, it is immediately passed around through gossip (*chismeando*). If Pepe or Pablo got drunk last night at the *barrio's* cafe and were thrown out by the owner, even that is commented upon by the gossiping women (*las chismosas*). Thus, while men shout and brag and play their social roles in the public places, women practice theirs in a covert and almost imperceptible way. The ways of being a man or a woman imply a different, almost opposite behavior. But it is interesting that in both cases conflict is more or less institutionalized and can thus be dispelled within certain limits.

Talcott Parsons's concept of instrumental and expressive roles becomes relevant for an analysis of these roles in Esperanza (Parsons and Bales 1955), but his dualistic model must be modified. He assumes that within the structure of the family there exists a basic dichotomy between the husband-father and wife-mother, the former carrying out the fundamental instrumental roles and the latter the expressive ones. Our assumption and modification state that both husband-father and wife-mother have both instrumental and expressive roles, within the family structure and outside of it, but intimately related. The roles we have been studying are not segmented or partial ones like husband or wife, but what we would call "general roles" that involve the whole of the person. Being a man or a woman implies a total conception of a human being and not just a sector of his social personality. In a community like Esperanza the instrumental role of the husband-father is played in the farm or in an occupation outside of the house. His expressive role is fundamentally acted in the cafes, in the horse market, at the vigils. Women play their instrumental role within the domestic realm as housewives (*amas de casa*). Their expressive role can be played inside the house, but it implies a lot of visiting as well, going to the store, going to church: she has to go out. We think that Parsons's distinction is helpful, but tends to neglect the concept of person. That is, when a woman is playing out her expressive role, she is also being a total human being. One special aspect of her personality is being emphasized but her womanhood does not dissolve; it is fully present. The same situation holds for the man when he goes to the cafes, the vigils and other public places. The strains and stresses of fulfilling roles are isolated and localized in specific situations and places.

Gossip is also part of the process of social control. People, especially women, fear *"el que dirán"* (literally: what would people say) as the means of having secret negative and unknown comments made about them. It acts as a sort of moral pressure. People even assume *a priori* that when somebody is gossiping (*hablando de ellos*) about them they are evaluating them in a hostile way. If anybody gets a piece of information about you, it can be used against you; it is a sort of moral deficit; ego is at the mercy (potentially) of alter. This can explain, at least partially, why gossiping is a secret act between two persons of the same sex and roughly of equal social status, who can interact in a relatively intimate way, or at least pretend to. Women in Esperanza always talk about the absent alter and in this way they avoid a direct confrontation between themselves. Gossip appears to provide a release for hostility by expressing hostile and negative feelings about those absent. For example, it would never occur to two women to start evaluating each other in a negative way when both are present or talking between themselves. A direct confrontation is always avoided. Thus gossip becomes a private and secret way of solving and channeling conflict. In this sense it is quite different from the way that males play out their roles in public places; the expressive aspect of maleness is public while the corresponding aspect of being female is a private affair.

It is rewarding to compare gossip in Esperanza with the data gathered about the same subject by Oscar Lewis (1969) in La Esmeralda. In a general way, there is some similarity; women are the ones who gossip; men are not expected to behave in that fashion. But women in La Esmeralda, located in an urban setting, behave in a somewhat different manner. They can enter and stay in public places like cafes. The impression one gets is of an overlapping of masculine and feminine areas of social behavior, instead of the neat divisions operating in Esperanza. Compared to Esperanza, La Esmeralda exhibits a series of deviations from the traditional pattern. Women are more extroverted, even in public. They are extremely aggressive, while men, at least from the data gathered by Lewis, appear to be less aggressive than men in Esperanza. The traditional model we have discussed for Esperanza has thus been deeply altered in La Esmeralda.

This supports the contention which has been discussed by other students of the Caribbean and seen in the work done by R. T. Smith in British Guiana (1956), that the process of social change has brought about structural transformations in the urban and increasingly in the rural family, which have tended to destroy or drastically alter the instrumental-expressive aspects of both men and women in their so-called traditional form. The basic changes appear to be less aggressive behavior on the part of men, more stress and strain in the process of being a man; in the woman, more extroversion and aggressive behavior. This has transformed the character of gossip; it is less secret, with more direct confrontation and even resort to direct violence. Lewis's (1969) pages are full of data that point in this direction.

The interior of a tobacco shed. Little tobacco can be seen, as the harvest season had almost finished.

CHAPTER 4

Economic Aspects of the Household

The household in Esperanza is closely associated with the cash economy in which its members take part, both as producers and as consumers, as we have indicated. Household heads work as wage laborers and many of them also as farmers producing at least partially for a market. The money they earn is spent on household necessities and other articles in the nearby town of Arecibo or in the stores of Esperanza.

From an inquiry made in fifty households it was found, on the basis of information given by household heads, that forty-seven of the fifty units satisfied at least 50 percent of their essential needs (clothing, food) through cash transactions. The emphasis here is on manufactured items like clothing, shoes, canned food, pasteurized milk and similar articles. The stores in the *barrio* carry some of these items, but their supplies are often limited and lack variety. Hence people often go to town for their provisions.

On the other hand, we also find that there is a whole segment of the household's economic activities that is confined to the home. The main items produced at home are: milk, eggs, meat, and products like sweet potatoes, yams, and on some farms, coffee. Of the fifty households previously referred to, forty-one stated through their heads that they produced these items for household consumption. This condition is quite consistent with the mixed character of Esperanza's economic system.

Household members state that the purpose of rearing animals is for an "emergency." Either the animal must be sold for urgently needed cash, or slaughtered to provide food on a special occasion, or to nourish a sick person. The animals are bought by the household head, and then the wife and the children take care of them. They cannot do anything with the animals without his consent.

Man and His Economic Role

The man's productive role is essential for the welfare of the household as he alone can earn the cash which is necessary for satisfying its needs. Out of sixty-six persons working outside the household, only ten were women and several of the latter were only working part time. No household was financially dependent on a woman's earnings.

The great pressure placed upon men to enter the external occupational system is reflected in the early age at which they go to work as wage laborers. Of sixty-six persons surveyed, fifty-six had entered the labor force before twenty-one years of age. From the data available and our observations, it seems that men start work between the ages of fifteen and twenty. They have therefore worked for a few years by the time they marry, usually in their early twenties. This experience helps to equip them for the role of household head and provider for their families.

Men enter the labor force for the first time in two ways. They either enter on their own initiative by searching for work on their own or through the help of their parents (particularly the father) who may take the active part. The father expects that his son will be a hard worker, and if the son is slow in demonstrating his aptitudes, the father will start pushing the boy. In many cases the son has worked many times with his father on the land, and the values of hard and honest work have been gradually acquired in that process.

Since Esperanza is an agricultural region, it can offer the entrant only that type of wage work. For any man who wishes to stay in the area and work and get married there, this is the only possibility.

It is usual for young single males who work to contribute towards the expenses of the parental household, although it is not demanded of them that they give all they earn. It is part of the parent-child relation to be a good son; contributing towards the household costs is considered a filial duty, at least while the person is single. Not to do so would be to show ingratitude, as one should help those "who gave you your life and have reared you" (*los que criaron a uno*). This is especially relevant in relation to the mother, because she has no opportunity to earn cash, unlike the father who may continue to work for gain until his sixties, or even seventies.

In one group of fifty households, there were only eleven unmarried adult males who were working. They ranged in age from seventeen to forty years, but out of the eleven, seven were twenty-five or less in age. We were able to get information about the extent of their contribution to the household income in nine cases; six helped the household and three did not give anything. This pattern is general, and it can be safely said that most single males who work contribute towards the household's income.

As has been noted, being head of a household requires that the man be a good provider. The concept of a good provider includes, among other things, that he should have, if at all possible, a small piece of land to cultivate. He should also have the reputation of being a hard worker, which means that he works regularly for wages in Esperanza as well as on his plot and at any other work that turns up. People say that lazy men do not make good husbands.

This requirement of economic self-reliance makes it almost impossible for a man to marry and establish a household before he is employed. In only two situations does this happen: when the couple has engaged in premarital intercourse; or when the couple gets married voluntarily, and the wife stays in the house of her husband's or her own parents. In the latter case, it is considered a temporary phase while the husband goes to work in the United States to earn enough money to set up a household of his own, either in Esperanza or abroad. The former is a situation where the marriage is hurried on, and the girl's family, especially her father, does not rest until the couple gets married. Both are rare situations. The normal and expected pattern is for a man to be working if he wants to be able to get married, so that he can establish his own household immediately.

In a situation where the husband is not working, and the couple lives either with his or her parents, the patterns of household headship are clear. The husband is considered a complete failure. We could not find an actual case of this kind, but from what people said, it would be a sorry state for a man. He would not have authority in the place where he lives, and even the authority over his wife and children would be lost to some extent. The obverse of this situation is the great importance placed upon neolocal residence, and the intimate relation between the role of provider, male headship and, to a lesser extent, common residence. Two elementary units under the same roof invite trouble, as the role of man as a provider is a key one for the existence of the household. The presence of a married couple with either parents is thus always just a temporary phase.

Residence in the house of his or her parents is temporary. The main reason given for delaying the establishment of the household is the lack of economic resources. Sometimes a man has the income but it is not sufficient to construct a house, so the couple has to wait. If things are bad in Esperanza, men anxious to get married may wait a few months, but then they get restless and fly to the United States to search for work (*buscárselas*). As soon as the husband has some sort of accommodation in the United States or the money to return to Esperanza and build a house, he will set up his own household.

In the case of one young couple who married while we were in Esperanza, the man went to the United States. He was able to get a job there while his wife stayed at her parents' and his parents' house alternately. In less than five months he sent his wife the money for her fare and now they live in the United States.

Table 4.1 shows the patterns of residence immediately after marriage. The heads of these 50 households were asked, first, about the normal patterns of residence in Esperanza when there were no obstacles to establishing a household. Second, they were asked to say what would be done if the couple could not set up a household. The answers show the preference for a neolocal residence after marriage, and the virtual absence of preference for joint households.

Table 4.1—Type of Residence Preferred Immediately
After Marriage

First Choice		
Independent	49	
Wife's Parents	1	
	—	
	50	Total
Second Choice		
Wife's Parents	13	
Husband's Parents	8	
No Preference	24	
Others	5	
	—	
	50	Total

FOOD PURCHASES AND HOUSEHOLD

On the average the household spends about $90 a month on food; the amount varies, of course, with family income and other economic resources available. This food is supplemented by domestic production. The peasant diet shows a definite pattern and starchy foods predominate. Typical meals would be:

Breakfast (5 a.m.-9 a.m.)	Oats, eggs, fruit juice, coffee or Biscuits, bread, eggs, coffee.
Lunch (10 a.m.-12 noon)	Rice, beans or Sweet potatoes, rice and codfish.
Dinner (4 p.m.-6 p.m.)	Rice, beans, fried potato chips or Rice, beans, fried meat.

Rice and beans are regular features of the peasant's table, and coffee with milk is drunk at frequent intervals during the working day. Sometimes illegal rum is drunk as an aperitif before dinner.

Food purchases are made by the household head either in Esperanza's stores or in town. It would never occur to the man to let his wife or any other woman of the house do the buying of the foodstuffs. He earns the money and he is the one who can go out to perform that duty. It is part of his duty as a head of household, it belongs to the *abajo* (down) sphere that is strictly a man's world. To let a woman make the purchases would be to change her role as housewife and to place her in the *abajo* sphere. The act of bringing home the supplies symbolizes the role of the man as the provider and demonstrates that he can feed his family. It is also complementary to the activity of the wife in cooking the food. Peasants see these duties as interdependent. When Alfonso told us: "I bring the supplies into the verandah and from there my wife takes charge of them, because it is her duty and I do not have anything more to do with it," he was referring both to this interdependence and to the short division of labor and role.

The custom is to buy weekly, and most purchases are made on credit. When times are good you pay, and when they are bad you rely on your good credit established in better times. People buy in the same place for years, so the owner knows and trusts them. The credit system is similar in its structural features to the one found in the Irish countryside, as described by Arensberg (1937). For instance, there is the shopkeeper-client relationship, based on confidence, called *confianza* (trust). If this element of trust disappears, the whole relationship is wrecked.

There is a relative difference, however, if we take into account the amount of cash at hand in each case. It appears that the peasant in Esperanza has more cash available more frequently than the Irish peasant as described by Arensberg. Many of the peasants in Esperanza work as wage laborers part of the time and are paid weekly. Also, agricultural produce is sold more frequently in the town market in Esperanza than in Ireland. The market is only twenty minutes away by truck and is accessible daily if desired. At the market, payment is made in cash immediately. The cooperative in Utuado can offer loans to the peasants, who will later sell their tobacco crop to the cooperative. All these factors, it seems to us, make the peasant in Esperanza less dependent on the credit system and at the same time increase his capacity for paying cash.

As in Ireland, the credit relationship is more than just a purely economic transaction. The statement "to pay off a debt entirely is perforce to dissolve the relationship" is also true in Esperanza. To stop buying in a store means a complete break with the store owner and his family. As Arensberg states, "one loses, not only a customer, but a friend, quite literally" (1937:173).

The result is that, as in Ireland, the relationship is maintained through the years and people value its lasting duration. From time to time (weekly, monthly or yearly) they pay something (*abonan*), but never the whole amount as that would imply they were going to buy in another place.

The store owner in Esperanza, as in Ireland, has to behave in a very subtle way when he wants some payment. Never, during our entire stay, did we hear a storekeeper ask a regular client in any way if he was going to pay the whole debt. When he has finished with the customer and is adding the figures and entering the total in a notebook in which he keeps the records, he usually asks in a matter of fact way: "Are you going to pay (*abonar*) anything?" This is asked only once and the question is not repeated.

The storekeeper knows that he depends on a whole complex of relationships to keep his business going, and the clients know that they depend on the storekeeper; so a balance is struck and, as in Ireland, a *modus vivendi* is agreed upon and institutionalized.

There is another way by which payment can be made for goods bought on credit. Some store owners are also farmers and have squatters living on their land. The latter may be employed as wage laborers on the storekeeper's farms. They regularly buy on credit at their employer's store and a deduction is then made from their wages to cover the cost of the items they have bought. This system still plays an important part in the economy of Esperanza.

Household Routine (Housewife)

The domestic sphere is truly the province of women, and more in Esperanza than in many other places, as the whole system of values encourages the woman to remain at home, busy with her family and household chores. An outline of the daily routine of a woman is given, taking three cases from different classes as examples (class stratification is described in Chap. 13).

SCHEDULE A—LOWER UPPER CLASS

Dolores is the wife of Miguel. She is a woman in her early forties, and her husband states that she is in full charge of the house. Her working days begin very early in the morning. She is the first person in the house to awake, and by six-thirty in the morning, she is in the kitchen preparing and serving the breakfast for all the members of the household. During this same period she manages to find time to feed the domestic animals in the backyard. By seven all members of the household have had their breakfast. The household includes three boys who attend the local school and a girl, the eldest of the children, who attends school in the town of Arecibo. The boys are gone by seven-thirty as they have to walk to school, which is about two miles from Miguel's house. The girl is taken to town by a *público* (cars that offer commercial transportation from Esperanza to Arecibo) and she is also on her way by seven-thirty. Miguel goes to the farmland to begin his tasks for the day at about the same time.

Around eight o'clock, Dolores takes a short trip to the place where her husband is working to give him some coffee. It is not far from the house, so she is able to return in a very short time to continue her routine. From eight-thirty, after she returns, she is alone in the house, busy with her household chores. At this time she usually washes the family's clothes and also may iron clothes already washed and dried. If she has any spare time, she does some house cleaning and tidying. By eleven-thirty she goes into the kitchen and starts preparing the midday lunch. When it is ready, if Miguel has not returned, she takes his lunch to him as she knows he cannot come to the house. As the children are away at school (they eat in the school's dining hall), Miguel and his wife have lunch together, either at home or on the farm. After lunch she returns to her house, or he goes back to the farm.

By one o'clock, Dolores is alone again in the house and continues her tasks. After washing the dishes she usually finishes cleaning the house. At two in the afternoon, she prepares coffee and carries it to Miguel. She drinks coffee with him and returns to the house immediately, as she still has more work to do.

Around four-thirty, the children return from school, and she has to see that the boys start helping, especially outside, with the cows and the horse. The girl helps her mother in the kitchen and with other household chores. At this time, also, Dolores starts cooking dinner, as she knows that Miguel will be hungry when he returns, usually around five. When he returns he dines immediately, alone at the table, while Dolores and her daughter serve him. After he finishes eating he goes into the living room to rest. At this time dinner is served for the rest of the family, who sit at the table, excluding Dolores, who eats in the kitchen at the same time that she is serving her husband. When they finish, mother and daughter wash the dishes together and clean the kitchen.

By seven Dolores has finished and is free to rest in the living room or in one of the bedrooms, where she chats with her daughter or the others. If there is anything else to do, like sewing and mending, she does it a little later. By nine o'clock, Dolores and the rest of the family have gone to sleep.

SCHEDULE B—MIDDLE CLASS

Elena, the wife of Lázaro, also rises relatively early. By six o'clock she is already in the kitchen, preparing breakfast for the whole family. These include Lázaro and the children, who must walk to school some three miles away. Lázaro and his wife are in their early fifties. After breakfast is finished, the children leave the house for school, Lázaro goes to the farm, and Elena is alone in the house. The first task is to wash the dishes. After that she starts her household cleaning by sweeping the floor of the whole house. She then moves on to other tasks, among these sewing and washing clothes. She is busy with these tasks until about eleven-thirty, when she must leave everything and start cooking lunch, as Lázaro returns around twelve to the house to eat. Until one o'clock Elena is busy attending her husband. The children are at school and eat at the school dining room, so Elena and Lázaro eat together without them.

After lunch, Lázaro retires to take a nap before returning to the fields, while his wife clears the table and washes the dishes. This is also the time when she does some minor chores like preparing or selecting some food that she will cook the next day. Around three o'clock she serves coffee to her husband, who comes from the fields. When he returns they have coffee together.

After three, Elena begins preparing dinner and checks on the children, who have already returned from school. They do not help much in the house as they are too young. If they want any refreshment, she will take care of that. In the meantime, she continues her work in the kitchen. By five or five-thirty, the dinner is ready and everybody in the family is home; Lázaro and the children are sitting in the living room or chatting outside in the front patio. She calls them to the table. Lázaro eats before anybody else; after he finishes, Elena takes care of the children. Serving the dinner to the family and then washing the dishes occupies Elena until seven.

She then takes a short rest. But the working day has not finished, and between eight and nine in the evening, she washes any dirty laundry and does some ironing. With this she has ended another working day and shortly afterward goes to bed.

SCHEDULE C—LOWER CLASS

Felicia is the wife of Timoteo, a squatter who lives on the land of one of the biggest landowners in Esperanza. Timoteo is a part-time carpenter, who also works as a sharecropper on the land of his mother, a widow, who does not cultivate the plot she inherited from her husband. Felicia rises at about six o'clock in the morning and immediately starts to prepare breakfast. Her husband and the rest of the family rise a little later, but by seven everybody is up and all have had their breakfast. A little before eight o'clock, the daughters (they do not have any sons) leave for the local school, which is relatively near, less than a quarter of a mile away. After Timoteo and the children have left, Felicia washes the dishes, as she likes to keep her kitchen in a clean and organized manner. After this she starts cleaning the house sweeping the floor and making the beds. She also takes some time from house cleaning to feed the domestic animals, which include hens, chickens, some roosters, and a pig.

At ten in the morning, her husband, if he is working nearby, comes home to drink his mid-morning coffee. This she always has ready so that whenever he comes he will not have to wait. After her husband goes out again, she starts the preparations for lunch. At eleven-thirty, she serves lunch to her husband and eats with him. After washing the dishes, she goes again into the backyard, where she gives the domestic animals their second feeding. This takes place at about one in the afternoon. Felicia then continues her house cleaning. After she finishes, she does the laundry and ironing. By the time she finishes at about four, it is time to start preparing dinner. She goes into the kitchen, cooks, sets the table, calls the family to dine. By six-thirty she has finished washing the dishes and spends a few more minutes putting the kitchen in order. After she has finished with the kitchen, she has a last chore to perform: she goes into the backyard for the last time to check if all the domestic animals are locked up for the night. After that, at seven, she is free and sits down with the family on the verandah or in the living room to chat with her husband and the children.

Situation Where Male Fails in Role of Provider

Households where the male is absent or incapable of fulfilling his economic duties as provider are virtually nonexistent in Esperanza. If the male is absent it is only for short periods of two or three months in the United States. When questioned, people state that if a man is unable to support his family he would either emigrate to look for a job in the United States, or the government would assist him.

There is a series of factors that effectively exclude the possibility of the man's being absent or incapable of supporting his household. Naturally, death of the male household head places the household in a special position in this respect, but apart from this factor, the others now to be discussed prolong and reinforce the position of the male in the household as provider.

In the first place, the introduction in recent years of a system of social security has provided a man with a regular income even when he has retired. This tends to maintain his position as the economic leader. To this can be added the fact that the family can appeal to the government's welfare department for financial help and usually receive it. This income is usually controlled by the man in spite of its being assigned to his wife. Men also tend to work well into their sixties or seventies, in spite of having a pension from the government. To do this is to violate the law, but informal arrangements are made between employers and employees to circumvent it. The credit pattern also tends to help the male retain his predominance. Even if he is unemployed, he can continue to make purchases in a store, sometimes for as long as a year, on the promise of payment when he gets work.

As a last resort, a man can migrate to the United States for a time, work and save money, and come back again. And there is also the close relation of parents and children, which in this context means that single children and, to a lesser extent, married ones who are working should help their parents. In a situation like this the children who give money or goods do so to the father, who then determines how it shall be used.

In Esperanza, female heads are usually widows. Such a woman rarely looks for a job. She is usually in her fifties, an age when it is extremely difficult to find work either in Esperanza or in the town. But various solutions are available to her. In many cases she inherits her dead husband's social security pension, and she is entitled to one-third of any property he leaves, such as land or houses. Again the sons and daughters can help their mother in two ways. She may go to live with one of them, or she may be regularly visited and looked after by her children. This is what people in Esperanza mean when they say, "There are no people living alone in this area."

General Picture of Household Economy (Cases)

Two specific examples may serve to illustrate more clearly the general view of household economy.

CASE 1—MATIAS

Matías, the head of the household, is a man of forty-six years, and his wife is a little younger. There are seven persons in the house:

Matías, his wife, four sons and one daughter. The daughter Julia is the oldest child, being eighteen years old. The boys are eleven, twelve, fourteen and sixteen, respectively. No other persons live in the house.

The house was built thirteen years ago, but Matías could not tell what it cost. He owns the house and lot, and he also owns a farm of about 28 acres. Another 13 acres are the property of his brothers who have migrated from Esperanza, but he cultivates these and is their *de facto* owner. He has rented something like 10 acres from a nearby farm, which makes a total of 51 acres that he controls. This places Matías well above the average landowner in Esperanza.

A great part of his farmland is used for cash crops. Last year he produced 2,500 lbs. of tobacco, and on 15 acres of the best land planted in sugarcane, he produced 28,000 lbs. of sugar. All of these products were sold. As can be expected, Matías employs wage labor during the sugarcane harvest. In addition to those two cash crops, he uses part of his land for crops like sweet potatoes and yams, and part of these are consumed within the household.

Matías has ten cows, one horse, some chickens, a dog and a cat. The boys take care of the animals, and his wife has somehow managed to cultivate and sell tobacco, a thing that he states with a mixture of pride and bewilderment.

The relative self-reliance of his household means that Matías is not forced to look for wage work. He owes around $1,600 on the 28 acres which he bought in installments, and also states that he buys the family clothes on credit at a cost of about $150 yearly.

He denied having any cash savings, but he was once in need of some money (a relative had died), and he told the writer that he was going to the bank to take some money out of his account. He was not able to estimate his annual expenditure or household budget, but his income can be reckoned at around $2,000 to $2,500 a year, which places him above the average in the area.

CASE 2—GILBERTO

Gilberto, a man in his fifties, is the head of the household; at present four persons live in the house, all related. There are Gilberto, his wife Eva and two sons. One of the sons, Isidro, is separated from his wife. José, the other son, is an invalid who remains all day in his wheelchair. Isidro does not help his father regularly, and this has brought complaints from his father and mother that Isidro is worthless (*no sirve pa ná*).

They live in an average-sized house, about 640 square feet in area. Gilberto states that the house cost him around $2,200 to build. It has three sleeping rooms, living room, dining room, kitchen and balcony.

The materials used in the construction were sheet metal, wood and cement. It was built about ten years ago.

Gilberto owns both the house and the lot and also about 8 acres around the house that constitute his farm. This is the only property he owns, and he has been paying installments on his farm, on which he still owes some money.

He works his land in a very intensive way, and the farm is in full production. Last year, according to Gilberto, it produced 1,000 lbs. of tobacco, 1,200 lbs. of maize, 1,200 lbs. of sweet potatoes, 400 lbs. of pumpkins and about 400 lbs. of yams. All the tobacco and maize were sold. Of the sweet potatoes, 800 lbs. were sold. The yams were used for domestic consumption. The 200 lbs. of coffee produced were used for the household's consumption. Gilberto also works in the sugarcane fields for wages as soon as one tobacco crop is gathered.

The domestic animals on his farm are a horse, two cows, some pigs, chickens, a dog and a cat. Except for the horse, the animals are looked after by his wife. Sometimes they sell one or two animals, especially when they are in need of cash.

Gilberto calculates that he owes about $300 to the food store and to a furniture shop where he bought some goods on the installment plan. He claims that he has no savings; his stock is his capital. He says that he spends about $40-$50 a month in food purchases and clothing, out of a total annual income in the region of $1,200.

Consumption Patterns

As usually happens with low cash income units, the people of Esperanza spend most of their cash on items such as food, clothing and medicines. But even within this relatively low level of cash income, certain special patterns of consumption stand out. There are certain preferred items the peasant will buy, often on credit.

Among these preferred articles are radios, television sets, beds, dining room suites and many similar items. Sometimes it is surprising to find a radio worth $150 or more in a household whose income is quite low. The contrast with the rest of the furniture is quite marked. The same thing happens with beds and living room furniture.

The two items which are most frequently bought on installments by poor people are radios and beds. Other items are not found so frequently. The upper classes naturally buy other things besides these. Most of the houses in Esperanza have a radio, and even in sectors where there is no electricity, they have battery-operated radios. Television sets are scarcer, and out of more than 370 households in Esperanza less than 20 houses had them. The things people buy are in general related to their income. In the upper levels one finds more and higher-priced television sets, more high-priced beds. It is rare to find someone buying beyond his capacity.

The peasants' system of values does not encourage thrift, however. They spend a relatively large amount of money on rum, cigarettes, cigars, and in betting. Although this money is spent by men, wives do not speak harshly about their husbands' extravagance as this is accepted as associated with the role of the man in the household. When entertaining guests, the host seems to be trying to impress them with his ability to fulfill that role, a male prerogative. This is part of his role as household head, and being a good host means he is a good household head.

Certain foods, such as meat, canned food, fish and many imported items are considered to be luxuries; that is to say, they are bought only for special occasions such as Christmas, weddings and baptisms.

The habit of buying on credit is firmly established, and the peasant has responded to the appearance of installment buying by purchasing certain items that he could not have bought before. A relatively large part of their income is spent on the essentials, but people also manage to buy things elsewhere considered luxuries. Inquiries made in fifty households revealed that forty-two households spent 50 percent or more of their total income on essentials such as food, clothing and medicines. Of these same fifty households, thirty-three stated that they spent part of their income on parties, rum, cigarettes, billiards and cigars. The same inquiry also revealed that manufactured goods like furniture, radios and refrigerators were bought. The scale in these fifty households ranged from a $50 table radio to a $500 television set.

Cattle grazing and resting from the sun's heat on a farm.

CHAPTER 5

Composition of the Household

As already indicated, the majority of households in Esperanza have male heads. Out of a sample of 167 households surveyed, 156 were headed by males. This is consistent with the fundamental distinction operating in this society between the man as husband-provider-household head and his wife as housewife. The role of the woman as significant mainly in the domestic sphere is shown or reflected in the tables on household composition and headship. As will be seen, the household in Esperanza operates in accordance with clear basic principles.

Composition of Households with Male Heads

Each of the 156 units occupies an independent house integrated on the basis of kinship ties. The majority are domestic units composed of husband, wife and children (Table 5.1). The rest of them can be derived from previous domestic units. Of the 156 households headed by males, 132 are composed of husband, wife and at least one child of both spouses. Households composed of husband, wife and no children number 14. These are mostly units which have reared their children and now live either alone or have some close relatives living with them. Another 6 households are composed of the husband-fathers and the children, the men being either separated from their wives or widowers. The result is that of 156 units, 152 can be traced to an original elementary unit of husband and wife and, later, children. In a total of 819 persons living in male-headed households, only 7 are not related by ties of kinship to the head or his spouse.

Table 5.2 further substantiates the fact that the basic unit of the male-directed household is the elementary family of husband, wife and

Table 5.1—Structure of Domestic Groups Headed by Males

Type of Unit	Number
Husband, wife and children	132
Husband, wife, alone or with relatives	14
Husband, children	6
Others:	
Husband and mother-in-law	1
Two brothers	1
Brother and sister	1
Domestic unit whose head is not a household head (another is the household head)	1
	156 Total

children. In 146 households, the wife and her mate (legal, religious or consensual) are found together, and the great majority of male heads have been properly married, either by the judge or by the priest. Out of the 146 wives present, 140 are legally married and 6 are living in consensual units.

Table 5.2—Composition of Households with Male Heads
(Sample: 156 Households)

Category	Number
Head	156
Head's spouse	146
Children of head and spouse	384
Children of daughter of head and spouse	38
Kin of head's spouse	25
Children of son of head and spouse	17
Kin of head	18
Adopted children	12
Children-in-law of head and spouse	11
Not related	7
Son of brother-in-law of head	1
Aunt of previous wife of head (dead)	1
	816 Total

The largest single category is that of children of *both* parents. Children from previous unions are not usually brought into a later union. Two factors tend to minimize the number of these children: first, the stability of marriages and, second, the fact that when people remarry they are usually in middle age or at a later stage in their life cycle, so the possibility of having children is minimized, and their previous children are already married. In any case, the number in the sample is almost negligible.

As can be seen, these households are child-rearing and conjugal units. The average number of persons per household is around 5.2. It can be seen from Table 5.3 that most of them are two-generation units, but there is a clear trend towards increasing the number of generations from two to three around the age range forty-one to fifty and onwards.

Table 5.3—Number of Generations in Households
(Sample: 167 Households)

	Male-Headed Households							Female-Headed Households						
Number of Generations	1	2	3	4	5	6		1	2	3	4	5	6	
Age Range	Number of Households						Total	Number of Households						Total
0-30	0	17	0	0	0	0	17	0	0	0	0	0	0	0
31-40	1	27	3	0	0	0	31	1	1	1	0	0	0	3
41-50	0	22	11	0	0	0	33	0	2	1	0	0	0	3
51-60	1	23	9	2	0	0	35	0	2	0	0	1	0	3
61 or more	8	15	16	1	0	0	40	1	1	0	0	0	0	2
Total	10	104	39	3	0	0	156	2	6	2	0	1	0	11

This seems to be related to certain features of the composition of the household group (Table 5.2). After the husband and wife and their children, the category of children of daughter of the head and wife is the largest one. If we add the children of the couple's son, the number increases considerably. This marked incidence of children of offspring of the head and his wife (see below) may be partly responsible for the average number of people per household and for the trend towards becoming a three-generation unit in the head's later years.

The ideal and the practice of postmarital residence in Esperanza is the independent household, but not all people who marry achieve this immediately or at all. There is the practice of living with parents as a temporary measure until full independence can be achieved. It also seems that this is quite consistent with other features of Esperanza's family structure. More daughters marry and live in this temporary fashion in their father's household than do sons who marry.

An emphasis on the man as head of the household and his clear role as provider, with his wife limited to the domestic sphere, is quite consistent with these temporary solutions. The son is more reluctant to stay with his father after being married, as this in some measure means that he is still under his authority. Living in the house of his father-in-law is at least a symbol that he has gone away from his father, and has achieved at least that small degree of independence. On the other side, the daughter, living in her father's house and still under the father's authority and having the expectation that her role will be in the domestic sphere, will continue with less resistance to play the temporary role of daughter. She is less pushed toward the independent household than her husband.

When a young couple stay in a parent's household for some time and have children there, they contribute toward converting the household into a three-generation unit. In this way all the principles involved can be seen to form part of a consistent pattern (Table 5.2).

Table 5.4—Married Persons Living in Their Father's Household
(Sample: 167 Households)

Sex	Number	Number of Children	Husband or Wife Resident	Age Range	
				19-28	29-38
M	5	10	5	5	0
F	11	24	6	8	3
Total	16	34	11	13	3

Tables 5.4 and 6.1 demonstrate the significance of these arrangements for tranforming two-generation units into three-generation ones. Out of thirty-eight children of daughter of head and his wife in Table 5.2, twenty-four are the issue of married daughters living in their father's household. Ten children out of the seventeen children of sons of head and wife belong to married sons living with their fathers. In both cases the result is the same, to extend the number of generations living in the household.

A look at the ages of males and females in Table 5.4 indicates that these couples, taken as a group, are just starting their family cycles or have not been long in this process. Most of them are in their twenties.

In this society, children rely to some extent on their parents to get a start in their married life. This is more so in the case of the daughter than in the case of the son, and it is logical for it to be that way. Males are the ones who must start the households, and they are the ones that go out into the occupational world in that process. The fact that a daughter stays with her parents means that her husband has not achieved full personality as the leader (moral, economic and jural) of his family, and so the girl's parents (especially her father) to a great extent retain control of her and sometimes of her children. It is highly significant that out of eleven husbands in the households where the daughters lived with their fathers, five were in the United States working. It is a sort of compromise; a man is allowed to get married, but he must prove his ability as a household head. In the meantime, the wife's father retains control of his daughter.

This does not mean that all couples in this situation will establish themselves in an independent way. Some may remain permanently with the wife's parents, or the husband's. But this is rare in Esperanza. Even the single mothers are kept under control, in many cases with the hope that a suitor for them will appear.

The rest of the children of the daughter or son of the household head and spouse are children whose parents either have died, have gone to the United States, or are absent from Esperanza. In some cases these children "have been asked for" (*pedidos*) by their grandparents. In Esperanza, grandparents sometimes formally request one of their children to give them a child to be reared. Although they will be reared by their grandparents, such children do not lose their rights or personal status in their parents' household.

The next category of relatives in the composition of the household, those of kin of head or kin of head's wife (Table 5.1), demonstrate that in this aspect the system is to a great extent bilateral. Kin of the head's wife are twenty-five, while kin of the head are eighteen. The emphasis is on the direction of the head's wife's kin, but is not clear-cut enough to warrant any definite statement. The main categories within them are the mothers, brothers and sisters of either the head or his spouse.

Adopted children number twelve and the husbands and wives of daughters and sons form the next category. Unrelated people comprise only seven out of 816 persons included in the sample, which shows the force of kinship ties at this level.

Composition of Households with Female Heads

There are only eleven households with female heads (Table 5.5), and out of those, at least seven are derived from former elementary units of husband, wife and children. These units are now composed of the wife and children, and in six of these seven cases, the head is a widow and the other a former widow who remarried but separated from her husband. The three units remaining consist of three units each with a widow living alone (but very near to her kin) and a unit of two sisters, single and with no intentions of getting married. Only widowhood or separation or being single can elevate a woman to the position of household headship.

There are some children of children of the head present in two households, and so only these have three generations. One additional household has five generations.

Table 5.5—Composition of Households with Female Heads
(Sample: 11 Households)

Category	Number
Head	11
Daughter of head	13
Children of daughter of head	7
Son of head	5
Kin of head	2
Children of son of head	2
Daughter of daughter of head's dead spouse (alone)	2
Great granddaughter of head	1
Adopted daughter of head	1
Daughter-in-law of head	1
Daughter of adopted daughter of head	1
Sister of the wife of head's son	1
	47 Total

CHAPTER 6

Developmental Sequence of the Household

The concept of the developmental cycle is so well known as to permit us to waive a detailed discussion of it. Fortes, Goody, and Leach (1958) and R. T. Smith (1956) can be consulted as good examples of previous uses of the concept in fieldwork and theoretical analysis.

Establishment of the Household

In Esperanza, the mere fact of having married and set up a separate residence is not enough in itself to establish a household. These factors, marriage and common residence, give a man a start towards establishing a family of his own, but other things must follow. Among these the most important is the birth of the first child. Only after this event do people really consider that particular couple a family in the full sense of the word. After five or six months people start inquiring "*¿ Cuándo llega?*" (When will it arrive?) and when the first child is born, people say: "*Ahora si están unidos, sin hijos no hay unión*" (Now they are more united, without children there is no union). Husbands told us that "*Después del primer hijo uno quiere más a la mujer*" (After the first child one loves his wife more). In a broad sense everything done to establish a new household is a preparation for, and culminates in, the birth of the first child.

The existence of the family is validated in other ways but these are secondary; only a child of the union can complete a family. *Esperanzeños* could not conceive a situation of a couple being childless for a long time, and we could not find a single case in our inquiries. Their typical reaction was one of astonishment and they stated: "*Uno se casa para tener hijos*" (One gets married to have children).

This conclusion was verified in interviews. Of thirty-two household heads interviewed, twenty-two stated that the real starting point of the household is the birth of the first child. This opinion was consistent with the conclusions drawn from direct ethnographic observations and from expressions of views in ordinary conversation. It is an expectation of people of both sexes and almost all ages. The birth of a child to a newly married couple, at the proper time, is looked forward to. If it does not happen, something has gone wrong and gossip starts.

In a very basic sense then, a household is not considered normal until it fulfills certain conditions in a regular way. The man must be working; if possible he must also have a piece of land. The couple should have their own house in an independent place. The man must be a good provider and the woman a good housewife and mother. The people say that: "When a man is working hard, has no vices, his wife is at home all the time taking care of the children, everything goes well in the household."

To be a drunkard (all drunkards are males) is to violate these values, and it is signficant that some of the worst drunkards in Esperanza were people with "no obligations," that is, single or its equivalent. If he drinks in excess, he is drinking "the children's money" and is considered a bad husband and an irresponsible person.

The basic dichotomy permeating the whole of Esperanza's family structure is quite explicit here. In answers to questions about the organization thought to be characteristic of a household, informants always emphasized this differentiation of husband-provider and woman-housewife. As one informant said: "The work of all men here is to labor on the land, the woman in this place performs the tasks of the house. Small children are in school, and when they reach maturity they emigrate."

The process of establishing the household is one in which the male plays the leading role. The man must be able to buy or build a house and to obtain a site. He must also buy at least some pieces of furniture for the house. Among these the most important is the bed where the couple is going to sleep. If there are enough resources, they might be able also to buy a radio, a mirror, and perhaps some rocking chairs and furniture for the living room. But all these things depend on the man's economic resources. The introduction of installment buying in the stores in town has allowed many people to purchase household goods by payments, and people recognize the changes in this situation by commenting, "If you do not get married now, it is not due to lack of money. Anybody can get married these days."

Out of thirty household heads consulted, twenty-eight stated that it was necessary to save money to get married. The arrangements for getting a house are more varied and most of the respondents stated that men usually built the house, and if they did not build it, they would buy it. Houses are rarely rented, as most people who have a house live in it. As was seen in the previous chapter, the people who cannot establish an independent household live with their parents when they get married while they continue to struggle to establish their own households.

Significantly, it appears that the temporary phase of staying at a parent's house until a couple can become independent is not a new arrangement in Esperanza. Among the thirty household heads, seven lived either with their parents or their wife's parents until they got their own house. The duration of the stay depends upon many factors, but mainly on the time it takes the husband to get together the necessary resources to set up an independent household. Some couples have remained only a few months, and others have been forced to stay longer, sometimes one or two years; there are also those exceptional couples who make their stay a permanent one.

It is certainly easier to own a house than a plot of land. The usual practice is for people to rent land, buy it on installments, or obtain a free plot and then to concentrate all their resources on building or buying the house. In this way they maximize the resources available. Their difficulty in obtaining land of their own is indicated by the figures. Of the thirty household heads, only five had a plot of their own when they established their household immediately after getting married. The rest did not own a plot, and were forced to rent or find a free plot as squatters.

It seems that a young couple receives help in obtaining a plot from all sides. Only ten of the thirty household heads stated that they established themselves fully on their own without any help, either from relatives, *compadres,* neighbors or friends. The rest received help from relatives (of both sides), friends and *compadres,* in that order. People resort to every available source of help. Our knowledge of Esperanza and our experience there confirms this fact, which in the field of kinship means that neither side is emphasized above the other. What matters is who can provide the help, and not the kinship relationship.

The type of help is varied. It can range from financial assistance to buy the plot to cooperation in helping a man build his house.

In Esperanza, the marriage ceremony and the reception, as it is called, are the normal process of establishing an independent household. The lack of any other ceremonial procedure is very evident. The other form of mating practiced in the area is consensual marriage. This form involves cohabitation and role differentiation between male and female, with an implicit acceptance of mutual rights and duties and behavior that follows more or less the same pattern as legal or religious marriage. The difference between them is that consensual union is not binding in terms of law or religion, and does not confer the same high status of legal or religious marriage. People try to avoid this type of union, although the condemnation of public opinion is not necessarily harsh, and can even be lenient as long as the couple behaves in a respectable way. In legal and religious marriage, the rights of the parties are explicitly specified, which is not the case in consensual unions. A mother and children of a consensual union may have to resort to the court in extreme cases, which are rare, to validate their rights, for example to economic support (see Chap. 11 for a more detailed discussion). There is no special ceremonial and ritual procedure with respect to a couple who moves to an independent household to live in consensual union, and consensual unions are less likely to continue as a form of mating, as Esperanza is increasingly enmeshed in a system that defines and codifies everything.

HOUSEHOLD DEVELOPMENT

In the initial stage the composition of the household is relatively simple. It includes the husband and wife and perhaps another person. It is a two-generation unit in less than a year after marriage, as the first child normally comes within that period. People of both sexes marry between the ages of twenty and thirty.

Both husbands and wives state that the early stages of establishing a household involve the hardest work. The wife has to care for young children and is tied to the house. The husband has to work all day outside the house either locally or, if he is a migrant, in the United States. But this does not mean that the husband is marginal to the internal functioning of the household. Husbands are most of the time in daily contact with the happenings of the household and in some cases they ask for a daily report from their wives. There is a well-defined concept of household headship, and this is one expression of it. A man who does not keep watch over his household is termed a *descuidado* (irresponsible) and heavily criticized by the community.

Even at this early stage of the developmental cycle, we find some extra familiar persons being incorporated into the household. In our small sample of thirty households, it was found that in at least fourteen cases, relatives were living with them. Most of these were kin either of the wife or the husband, and only three were unrelated to either spouse.

There is one factor that must be taken into consideration at this stage, when men are struggling to establish their households. If Tables 6.1 and 6.2 on age and marital status are examined in some detail, it can be observed that in the age range of zero to eighteen there are more

Table 6.1—Age and Marital Status: Males

Age	Single	Married Legal and Religious	Consensual Union	Consensual Widower	Separated Legal and Religious	Separated Consensual	Divorced Legal and Religious	Widower Legal and Religious	Single Father	Total
0-18	214	0	0	0	0	0	0	0	0	214
19-25	21	8	4	0	1	0	1	0	0	35
26-35	11	23	2	0	3	2	0	0	0	41
36-45	8	38	1	0	0	1	0	0	0	48
46-55	5	29	1	0	0	1	0	1	0	37
56-65	3	22	1	0	3	0	0	0	0	29
66-75	2	19	1	0	0	0	1	0	0	23
76-85	2	8	0	0	0	0	0	2	0	12
86-95	0	0	0	0	0	0	0	1	0	1
96-105	0	0	0	0	0	0	0	0	0	0
Totals	266	147	10	0	7	4	2	4	0	440

Table 6.2—Age and Marital Status: Females

Age	Single	Married Legal and Religious	Con-sensual Union	Con-sensual Widow	Separated Legal and Religious	Separated Con-sensual	Divorced Legal and Religious	Widow Legal and Religious	Single Mother	Total
0-18	194	0	1	0	0	0	0	0	0	195
19-25	23	27	3	0	0	0	1	0	2	56
26-35	6	40	3	0	0	0	0	1	1	51
36-45	1	40	0	0	0	0	0	2	1	44
46-55	2	18	0	1	0	0	0	2	0	23
56-65	0	23	0	0	0	1	0	7	0	31
66-75	0	8	1	1	0	0	0	4	0	14
76-85	1	0	0	0	0	0	0	6	0	7
86-95	0	0	0	0	0	0	0	1	0	1
96-105	0	0	0	0	0	0	0	1	0	1
Totals	227	156	8	2	0	1	1	24	4	423

males (214-195) than females, outnumbering them by nineteen persons. But an examination of the age range of nineteen to thirty-five yields the opposite result, with 107 females and 76 males. Many men are in the United States, working to save money to get married, or if married, working there to improve their economic position and that of their households. Some of these migrants never return, but many have households in Esperanza, or prospective wives, and these are the ones who do return. If the man's stay in the United States is prolonged, this can have several results. Either the man sends for his family, or the family sends for the man. If neither action is taken, trouble starts and the relatives of either spouse may involve themselves. Gossip brews, the man is characterized as irresponsible, and in extreme cases, the wife can return with her children to her parents. But events like this rarely happen.

As the cycle evolves, the household takes on a more complex composition. In Table 5.3 it can be seen that in the age range of forty-one to fifty, households with three generations appear fairly frequently and the trend is maintained. It is at this stage that children begin to get married, and some of them settle for a time in their parents' house.

Kin of the head's spouse, and kin of the head also may be incorporated at this time (there are certain people who can be incorporated at any time, as grown children, unrelated people and others). People in Esperanza pride themselves on the fact that nobody lives *alone,* reflecting one of their basic values: that everybody must have a home. In this way everybody is ideally incorporated into a household, and it is a fact that there are practically no persons living alone in Esperanza.

There is another factor that influences household composition. Table 6.1 shows a group of thirty-one single males who are over twenty-six years of age. The corresponding figure for females is only ten. These single males comprise different categories in the composition of the household, but the great bulk of them are sons of the head and his wife. The rest are kin either of the head's wife or of the head. These people are, so to speak, casualties in a battle. They are adult males but still dependents. They have failed to fulfill the complete role of household head that is expected of them. Yet they do not establish themselves to live alone, but instead incorporate themselves into existing units. This is testimony to the extent to which Esperanza's inhabitants regard household headship and marriage as interrelated. It seems that not all men can achieve the degree of economic self-sufficiency that is needed in order to be able to establish a household.

All through the cycle (Fig. 1), the male is in complete control of the household, and his wife is limited to the domestic sphere. There is no point at which women begin to increase their authority, and when

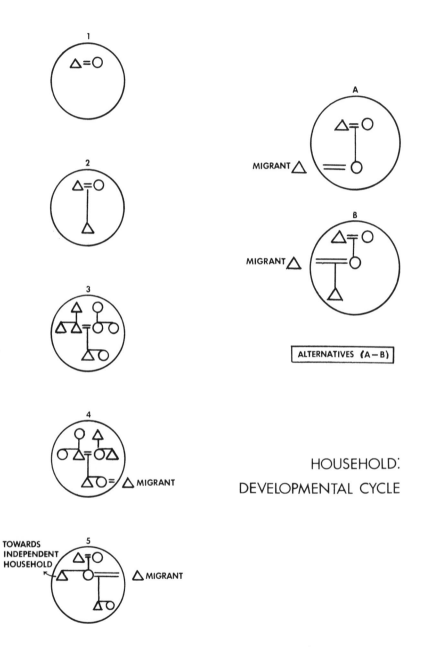

Figure 1

questioned on that matter they only stated that they *understood* their husbands better after being married for some time. This factor tends to level the relation between husband and wife, but with the implicit and never discussed assumption that the man is the head. A man can be absent from the household at any time and nobody dares ask him where he has been when he returns, but a woman or child has to ask for permission and let it be known when she or he is back. There are some speech usages which show neatly the division of areas of behavior and authority recognized in Esperanza. When people say "women's affairs" (*cosas de mujeres*), they mean the domestic sphere; when they say "men's affairs" (*asuntos de machos*), they mean outside the domestic sphere. Going out alone, especially on holidays and at night, drinking, going to cock fights, going into the town of Arecibo alone are *asuntos de machos*.

In the sexual sphere this can be translated in the following way: a man who has an affair outside the house is very smart, very *macho* (male), but a woman who does it is simply a *puta* (prostitute). A wife tends to ignore and tolerate a husband who has an affair, unless he becomes irresponsible toward her and the children. The man never tells his wife about these adventures; to confess anything would be an unmanly thing to do.

CHAPTER 7

The Individual's Life Cycle

Certain aspects of the life span of the individual in Esperanza throw a great deal of light on family structure when studied from a sociological viewpoint, especially when looked at in terms of the total social structure.

Birth

In every human society the life cycle of the individual begins with birth, and some of the most important rituals and relationships arise then and are intimately related to it, in Esperanza, as elsewhere.

Children in the past (twenty years ago) were born predominantly at home in the *barrio,* but things have changed; today most of them are born in the government hospital in the town of Arecibo. As soon as a woman thinks she is pregnant, she goes to a doctor in town, either a private practitioner or a government doctor, who examines her and, if he finds her pregnant, prescribes treatment for her. Most of the expectant mothers of Esperanza today go to a government prenatal center.

These changes have brought about the virtual disappearance of the midwife. In the past there were many midwives in the *barrio,* related to the practice of giving birth at home. There was practically no need to seek help from the town, and the midwife was responsible for prenatal care and follow-up in the postnatal period. Although there are still some midwives, not one is practicing in Esperanza.

The majority of births now follow a standard procedure with regard to medical care. When the time comes and the woman feels labor pains, a car is called and she is taken to the hospital. If the husband is present, he will do this, but if he is away working, a relative or neighbor will perform this service, and someone will be sent to inform the husband. In cases like this, *compadres,* neighbors and kin of either side come into the picture, an aspect that will be treated in detail later.

At this stage there is a virtual separation of husband and wife, as the woman is taken into the hospital and the husband is not allowed to assist or participate in childbirth. But even here the male-female dichotomy so fundamental in Esperanza can be seen at work. Women assume the initiative in a situation like this and say that "men do not understand these things." The male role now is a passive one, while the women dress the expectant mother, comfort her, and wait for the car that will take her to the town's hospital.

The man helps, but only at the request of the woman, and if he tried to help directly and on his own initiative, he would be told to keep quiet and not to interfere.

There are no rituals or kinship preferences at this stage, except perhaps that the wife's mother may come to stay before the birth to care for her daughter and relieve her of some of the heaviest household tasks. This is an expression of the close relationship between mothers and daughters.

After the birth, the father is allowed to see his child, and usually close kin and others are also allowed this privilege. They, especially the father, are anxious to see who the child will look like, and jokes will be made about it. In Esperanza, fertility is greatly admired, and the father and mother will be happy to have a new member in the family. There is a great fuss about dressing the child in a proper manner, and as hospital clothes are considered too drab, the child is changed into brighter clothes brought from the outside as soon as possible.

In about five days the woman returns home, and many an old mother complains that in these modern days mothers do not get the care and rest they deserve, and state that in the past they used to rest forty days (*la cuarentena*) in the house and could not go out.

Today the seclusion period has practically disappeared and no woman keeps the forty days. But the majority spend at least some days resting in the house. That can vary between two and fifteen days, depending on the duties she has as a housewife, the amount of help relatives and others can give her, and her physical condition after the birth.

Customary practices with regard to the umbilical cord once again emphasize the male-female dichotomy. The cord is placed in a different place according to the sex of the child. That of a boy is placed in a hole in the farmland so that he will become a good farmer, and that of a girl placed in the kitchen under the kitchen fire so that she will become a good cook. Sometimes a girl's cord is placed in the sewing chest in the hope that she will become a good housewife. This two-fold practice clearly symbolizes the expected roles that each child performs when members of a household as adults.

Naming practices vary in Esperanza. In the past it seems that there was more uniformity, judging by the names the old people have. Most of them were taken from the Catholic calendar, and the name of the child was automatically chosen. Each saint had his or her day, and the date the child was born was looked up on the calendar, and the name of the saint appearing that day was given to the child. That is why today most of the old people in the *barrio* have typical Christian names like José, María, Jesús, Pedro. A look in the farmer's almanac hanging from the wall solved the problem.

Some names are still chosen in this way, but today the wife takes an active part: husband and wife look for a "beautiful name" and choose one they like. The name is usually a Christian one, but it is not the one of the saint appearing on the calendar on the day the child is born. Sometimes the wife chooses it alone; sometimes the husband. Relatives may also influence the selection. There is no rigid pattern in this process.

Baptism

In Esperanza, people recognize and practice what they call three types of baptism: water baptism, church baptism, and bishop baptism (confirmation). Here we deal with the first two types.

Baptism needs for its full performance at least two godparents, one of each sex, and preferably husband and wife. They should be on good terms with the child's parents, and the father of the child chooses the godparents. He may consult his wife, but he makes the final decision.

After that, he and the prospective godparents arrange for the date of the ceremony and the party that follows. It may have to be postponed for months if the father or godparents do not have sufficient money to hold it immediately. The day of the ceremony, the child is taken to church by his or her godparents, where a priest officiates. During the ceremony the child is held around the body by his godfather, while the godmother holds the feet. The meaning of this arrangement could not be explained by anybody in Esperanza, but the fact that it is the man who holds the child is of significance. After this is finished, the godparents take their godchild to the house of the parents.

There the child's parents are waiting, and until the godparents arrive with the child the party cannot begin. After the arrival and some final arrangements, the party begins. Drinks are served by the father and the godfather, who acts as a cohost. At the same time the child, in his or her best attire, is fondled by the people present. No gifts are given to the child by anybody, except perhaps by the godparents, and these are not worth much in money value. After some hours, a meal is served but does not appear to have any ritual significance. When the meal is finished, songs are improvised in honor of the child, and the dancing begins. This continues for hours, until at last the people begin to drift away to their homes, and the party ends. This is the general pattern, although some details may be changed. In some cases a cake is made for the child and the guests, most of them children. In instances like this, it looks more like a birthday party than a baptismal party.

The other type of baptism, water baptism, is closely related to church baptism, and usually comes before the church baptism. It does not involve any party or ceremony. The godparents come into the child's house and perform the act in a few minutes. The godfather pours water over the head of the child, says some prayers and makes the sign of the cross and that ends the water baptism. Peasants explain that the water baptism is a provisional measure to insure that if the child dies he will not die a *moro* (Moor, i.e., non-Christian) and will be able to go to heaven.

Baptism then, marks an important stage in the life of the people in Esperanza. By means of it a person becomes a Christian and his salvation is assured, at least while he is a child and does not "have the use of reason." Later he will have *capacidad* (capacity for responsibility as an individual) when an adult.

The basic importance of this ritual at this stage in the individual life cycle is to introduce the child to the world of Christians, under the tutelage of his godfather who acts formally as a sort of spiritual guardian for the godchild. Baptism has many other implications, but they will be analyzed later in connection with *compadrazgo*.

Breast Feeding and Weaning

In spite of many changes brought about by the introduction of modern medical practices, the feeding of children in their first years of life continues to be carried out along traditional lines. Most of the children are at first breast fed by their mothers, and shortly afterwards they are bottle fed. The pattern is a very irregular one, children being fed when they start crying. In our sample of thirty households, twenty-five mothers had breast fed their children, and twenty-one stated that they did so whenever the children cried. But the period of breast feeding is not long, and on the average it lasts only a month. Manners (1956) reports a nonfixed schedule for one year in Tabara. In Esperanza, children are changed to the bottle after the first month. The main reason given by mothers is the lack of milk from the breasts.

In general, even older children are fed whenever they want to eat, but gradually they are trained to the three-meal-a-day schedule of the peasant. Very early in their lives they start eating solid foods, as the peasants do not hesitate to feed children any type of food they think they will like. They start this in their first year of life, probably after the sixth month. In most cases weaning seems to be a gradual process, and parents (mothers especially) do not place much emphasis on it. The child is started on solid foods and for a time he feeds both on them and on the bottle, but gradually the bottle is abandoned. If children still use the bottle by the time they go to school, they are ridiculed; going to school means that you are getting "big" and big children do not feed on the bottle. But this happens only in very exceptional cases.

As to the way they wean the children from the breast, this may be a more abrupt process. In some cases children are made to sleep separately from the mother, and if they cry nobody takes any notice. But the majority of the mothers told us that as children got used to the bottle they forgot the breast, and so the transition was made.

The children eat the same starchy foods as the adult, and no special cooking is done for them.

Paternity and Maternity

The roles of father and mother are clearly defined in Esperanza. Paternity is a very strong sentiment, and few fathers would deny that this or that child is theirs. It is formally acknowledged by giving the father's surname to his child. A child who does not know who his father is or who bears the surname of his mother feels out of place and tries to evade the problem if put to him in a conversation. Bearing the surname of your father means that you are the product of a legal union, and that you can state who your parents are.

When questioned in this matter, people emphasize certain aspects that make it crucial that you should know who your father is: respect (*respeto*), inheritance rights, and the duty of the father to rear his children. The first means that there is in the father-child relationship an element of authority and behavior control, something approaching an attitude of reverence. The second aspect means that the relationship must be clear-cut, so that there is no ambiguity over the inheritance of land or property or, in these days, insurance policies. The third defines as a strict duty that a father must rear his children, who are defined as such by the transmission of his surname. In the last case, the role of provider is being emphasized in an implicit way.

That the concept of paternity is well defined is illustrated by the following example. A man, who lived with a group of his siblings on their farm, had a reputation in the community for being an irresponsible person. He was lazy, dirty and hostile. But this man so negatively characterized by the people put up a big battle for the possession of a daughter when his consensual wife abandoned him. The matter was brought to the attention of the government social worker who deals with these cases in a special family court, and the man went to court to fight for the possession of his daughter. Only reluctantly did he give way when the case was decided against him.

The corresponding conception of maternity is somewhat different from that of paternity. People state that the mother is the one who "rears you" (*la que cría a uno*), but here they refer not to any function as provider but to the fact that the mother is the one person in the household who takes care of you, who is more frequently in direct contact with you. The image of the mother is that of a person who sacrifices herself for her children, and who is all love and care. The father is respected, while the mother is loved.

The two different roles as perceived and practiced by both participants reflect the division of male and female and its implications in the family structure of Esperanza. The father, head of the household, must be respected because he has the authority and the power to punish. The mother, by contrast, is more tolerant and knows how to deal with the children and to intercede with the father in favor of the children. The two images complement each other in the actual structure of the household as a functioning unit.

In Esperanza, then, we find a clear and interdependent conception of paternity and maternity, and this shows a striking degree of consistency with the role structure of the household as a unit.

Childhood

The child is constantly supervised, even though he is allowed a certain freedom of movement. Children are kept within sight of the mother, and most of the time in the company and supervision of their brothers and sisters. After they can walk, they are allowed to play in the yard, while the mother works in the kitchen and other parts of the house. She makes frequent checks as to where they are and what they are doing. Older children, perhaps six, seven and eight years old, are put in charge of the younger ones, and they are punished if they do not take proper care of them and something happens.

There is no apparent sense of urgency in the matter of toilet training. If the child defecates or urinates on the floor of the house or in a similar place no fuss is made. This does not happen frequently, and evidently some sort of education is achieved in this particular. Toilet training starts around three years of age, and parents said that it could not be started at an earlier age because the child is not ready yet and cannot learn.

Corporal punishment is seldom used, and when it is used, it takes the form of a few strokes with the father's belt or with a wooden stick. Children are usually warned by shouting at them in advance, and the punishment is not always carried out. Also an occasional slap can be given to a child who is misbehaving. Babies are not punished, and it is only to children of three years and over that punishment is applied. The mother, as the person in most frequent contact with the children, is the one who actually applies the punishment, but if the offense is a big one she will report it to the father on his return home, and he will then punish the child. But this is rare and during our stay in Esperanza, only once did we witness corporal punishment.

Children have plenty of contact with their father, who sometimes takes them to the plot of land he is working on, and there they try to help in whatever way they can. But most of the time they remain near the home, where they play under the supervision of the mother and elder siblings. When the father returns from work in the late afternoon, he sits down on the balcony, in the living room, or in the open air, where he plays with his children. He does not see as much of the children as the mother is able to do, but nevertheless a considerable degree of contact is maintained in the father-child relationship.

Around the age of six, children are sent to school for the first time. The school itself is situated in the *barrio,* so children are not forced to go far for their primary education. Peasants are well aware of the utilitarian value of formal education, and they send their children to school in order that they may be able to "defend" (*defenderse*) themselves better in a world in which education has become increasingly necessary as a qualification for rewarding employment. If they have a diploma, the peasants say, then they would be able to get a better job than just doing agricultural work, which requires a lot of physical effort. As they say in Esperanza: "That (education) is the only capital that the poor can leave to their children."

Even before they go to school, children are being educated in the roles that a man and a woman are expected to perform in Esperanza, Boys go with their fathers and help them in simple agricultural tasks, and also take care of animals. The girls remain in the house and help their mothers in washing, carrying water, house cleaning and so on. In this sense the male-female dichotomy is being emphasized in the pre-school age (for a similar pattern, see Wolf 1956). Boys are not allowed to perform female tasks, or girls, male tasks. For the boy to do that would be to behave in a girl's way and for the girl to do it would be to behave in a masculine way, a reversal both sexes equally wish to avoid.

Sexual Patterns

Esperanza, like every social system, has institutionalized ways of dealing with sex. Children learn the appropriate ways of behaving not directly from their parents, but by being punished or scolded when they violate the norms. Sexual discussions between children of the opposite sex are strictly forbidden, and any form of sexual play is taboo. The main mechanism used to inculcate ideas on the appropriate sexual behavior is physical segregation. This is practiced in sleeping arrangements, and in other areas of family life such as bathing and excretory habits. The child, up to the age of around three, is considered not conscious of sexual behavior. But the older children get, the more conscious they become, and it is said that they have "malice" (*malicia*), and this could lead to wicked sexual behavior.

If we examine the educational process of the child within the family, it can be seen that certain attitudes are emphasized constantly, and the child must learn these by heart. In Esperanza, the attitudes that are given importance are those of being well brought-up (*educado*) and being able to respect others. These are instilled both in males and females. It is difficult to describe what they mean by being educated and being able to show respect. The aim seems to be to produce a well-behaved person, who emphasizes harmony in his social behavior, who does not offend anybody. Obedience is an important element, as one should obey one's father, one's teacher, the priest (cf. Manners 1956). Respect implies a sort of social distance, of social segregation, of not "touching" the other person, and at the same time being able to be on friendly terms with him or her. These are the items that are emphasized. Sex is scarcely ever mentioned by adults in the presence of children or of persons of the opposite sex. It can be mentioned only when all present are adults of the same sex. If children are present and a sexual joke is made, they listen but they must not join in the laughter.

The position can be better understood if we see how the incest rule operates. This is the fundamental sexual prohibition in Esperanza. A male who commits incest is expected to commit suicide and not wait for the law to punish him. We have good reasons to believe that this is what happens. Out of five cases that came to our knowledge (from the last thirty years), four ended with the suicide of one party. The figure of the incestuous person is even stereotyped as that of a person who has hanged himself from a tree.

To prevent father-daughter incest, father and daughter minimize the amount of physical contact between them. N, a man of about fifty-five, told us that he never kissed his daughters because of the sexual danger involved. Coupled with this physical segregation comes the respect that the daughter should have for her father (cf. O. Lewis 1951). He is seen as a revered, somewhat authoritarian figure. And, *vice versa,* he should protect his daughter from other men (as all men are seen as sexually aggressive). Thus physical segregation is reinforced by the element of respect.

In the mother-son relationship, the elements assume a somewhat different connotation. The element of physical segregation is present, but it seems to us that this segregation is not so extreme as that between daughter and father. The mother is "desexualized" in relation to her son. This is done by making her something of a quasi-religious personality, a person who can even be willing to die for a child (a son in this case). Patricio told us that his dead mother was a saint, that the mother is the person one loves most in the world. While he said this, tears rolled from his eyes. He also said that he was always with his mother. Informants stated that "one does not see one's mother as a woman." Mauricio made the sign of the cross every time he mentioned the name of his dead mother, whom he also considered a saint. Love for a mother is thus not incompatible with respect.

In the brother-sister relationship, physical segregation is severely enforced. They sleep in different rooms and avoid nakedness and any bodily contact. They should not engage in any type of game involving physical contact, because these provide a temptation for sexual intimacies, which must be avoided at all cost (cf. O. Lewis 1951). With regard to respect, the situation is rather similar to the father-daughter relationship. The brother must naturally respect his sister. In addition, he assumes the role of her protector and operates as a sort of father figure, protecting his sister from other men. It is not by accident that this happens. Both the father and the brother are males, and male values emphasize sexual aggression. That is why it is said in Esperanza that the brother should act toward his sister as a second father. These values are instilled in the boy from childhood, and it is a common sight to see young boys protecting their sisters from the other boys at school.

Transition Towards Adulthood

The transition towards adulthood is a gradual process, in which the person gradually acquires those patterns of behavior that define him or her as an adult. In Esperanza, there is a clear conception of this process. For the female, the change from a girl to a woman is intimately related with marriage. The process of becoming a woman is more than just one of having grown up physically. Everybody sees that the girl has become taller, her hips have broadened and so on. When she menstruates for the first time her parents consider her a woman. But she has to have what people call *capacidad* if she is going to be considered an adult. This is a combination of mature behavior and some basic experience that would allow her to perform her role as a housewife efficiently. She should know how to cook, sew, and care for the children and for her husband. She is considered an adult when people think that she can fulfill this role adequately. There is also an age criterion around which the female must begin to act as an adult, and this is from eighteen to twenty.

For the male also, although age and physical growth are necessary, they are not sufficient. The elements that define his adulthood are a little different. If in the woman they emphasize her future role as housewife, in the man they are the elements that will define him as a household head. He is defined as an adult when he is an independent person. This means he has a job, perhaps a piece of land, some resources, and a house. Again the intimate relationship between marriage and adulthood becomes relevant. If the man has these, or the capacity to have these, he is in the process of becoming a full-fledged adult. Of course, he must behave in a mature way, but if he has the qualifications described above, he is considered to have behaved in that way.

In courtship, the relationship between the prospective son-in-law and father-in-law is vital. The whole courtship period could be summarized as one in which the future husband tries to gain the favor of his future father-in-law. Of course, he must also have gained the assent of the girl, who has relative freedom of choice.

There are several formal occasions when the sexes come into contact in a regulated way, which permit a man to declare his intention to a girl. At vigils, parties and even in church this can be done. If the girl answers in the affirmative, the male—if he is "serious" and plans to marry her—must visit her house to speak with her parents, especially with her father. It is he who has the key role in deciding if the courtship can continue.

During and before the courtship, there are patterns of behavior that must be followed in relations between young people of opposite sexes. The youth is supposed to behave with respect towards the girl but, at the same time and within that framework, he must take the initiative in all matters. If the couple is formally engaged, he must visit the girl at her parents' house on certain days of the week, which are appointed by the girl's father. Ideally, an adult must be near the couple during visiting time to prevent any excesses. Throughout the whole process of courtship and marriage, it is the father who must protect the girl, and only at the end of the wedding ceremony does the father feel able to relax his vigilance. Stycos (1958) describes a similar pattern.

The crucial relevance of this role can be seen in the rare cases of premarital pregnancy or elopement. It is the general expectation that the most aggrieved person in such a case is the girl's father. He angrily pursues the man who performed the deed until reparation is made, which usually consists in getting the couple to a judge and marrying them. In this way his responsibilities as a father are transferred to a great extent to the husband. Somebody must always take care of a woman. Elopement or premarital pregnancy endangers this normal transfer and it is up to the father to see that it is completed in the usual way. If the man escapes, the girl has to stay at her parents' house and acquires a reputation as a "light" girl, which means, in the *barrio's* terms: "If she has done it with one, she can do it with more (men)." This makes it difficult for her to secure a husband, and only by demonstrating "chastity" for a few years can she hope eventually to marry.

Young people, both men and women, do not have very clear ideas about marriage, but the expectations they have show clearly their recognition of role differentiation within the household. Men say that they want a wife who would care for them and give them children, and women complement this picture by stating that they want children and a house and a good husband. The general attitude towards getting married seems a positive one, and the concern of many old people in Esperanza is that in their opinion young people today marry too readily, without having any *capacidad,* and later they have problems.

Marriage marks the individual as a fully fledged adult. In a sense it is closely related to the first important ritual in the individual's life cycle: baptism. Baptism signified his initial entrance into the community as a Christian, and in this later stage the individual makes a second entrance, this time into the adult world. Both form part of the physical and social development of the person.

Old Age

It is expected that when people are old in Esperanza they will be respected and obeyed. This is the ideal pattern and it is one in which young people are expected to obey almost automatically. Even today the old people retort to the young ones that "they may know much that is in books, but we know the real things that come only with experience."

As a part of the life cycle of the person, age has somewhat different implications for a man and a woman. A man has almost always headed a household and exercised the role of provider, and it is not easy for him to abdicate those functions when the time comes. That is one reason why men work almost until they die, and that means well into their sixties and seventies. Even "retired" men with no need to work are always on the move doing something. Octavio, whose sons are all married and who does not need to work, is always doing odd jobs around his farm, and people comment that if these old men sit down and stop doing anything they will die.

Today they would not lose authority in most cases if they ceased to work, because the system of social security could enable them to maintain the role of provider. There is also the moral content of the role of household head, and even in the few cases where the household head is old and does not work, and another man (e.g., his son) is the one who earns the money, the household head has a great share in deciding how the money shall be spent. There is a moral obligation *not* to deprive old men of their authority, at least not completely.

Most men whose wives die before they do or who get divorced, remarry very soon. In the case of old men, they state that it is very hard for them to take care of themselves and of the house, and that they need a woman in the place, as women are the ones who understand how to perform household tasks. If they cannot remarry, since there is no tradition of people living alone in Esperanza, they tend to live with their children.

The position of the woman left a widow or divorced is different. She has never had to provide for the household, as her role has always been in the domestic sphere. In this context, it is easier for her to go to live with some of her children, and she will not remarry. In some cases she may inherit some property and land and remain in her home, living there with some close kin and children or grandchildren.

Esperanza is consistent in the way it looks after its old men and women. The man avoids becoming dependent on others and so maintains the masculine values of independence and self-reliance; the woman, who has always been dependent, can make an easier transition, usually shifting her dependence from one household to another.

Peasant's house, with the peasant in working clothes. Part of the family can be seen. The small shed at the right is a pig pen.

CHAPTER 8

The Kinship System

The kinship (*parentesco*) system of Esperanza is a relatively narrow one, both horizontally (intragenerationally) and vertically (intergenerationally). We avoid using the term "descent" when dealing with the kinship system of Esperanza as social anthropologists use it to describe societies with corporate lineal groups (see Campbell 1964), and this could lead to confusion. People in Esperanza acknowledge kinship relationships from ancestors of both sexes, but there are no corporate groups.

Our informants could go back only to the level of their grandparents, and almost nobody had any knowledge or memory of their great-grandparents. Only one or two people could remember anything about them and then only in a very vague form. On the horizontal level recognition extends to cousins, especially first cousins, after which the relationship tends to fade, people of fourth cousin range or more being called *parientes lejanos* (distant relatives). One of our informants phrased this as follows: "But even when they have died ... people ... pay homage to their memory. In the people that are alive ... in the first place, the parents, in the second place, brothers and sisters, in the third place, the grandparents, after that first cousins, then third cousins and distant relatives (*parientes lejanos*). That is the order."

Within these limits, kinship is recognized in Esperanza. It seems that many people have at least one distant relative in the area. It is usual to see people on Saturday and Sunday exchange greetings in the stores and inquire about family events. These are the two days that people come to the center of the area, where they shop, go to church or just stroll nearby. They meet, in this way, their brothers and cousins, those kin who live within the limits of Esperanza. But they say that in the past they had more kin in the area, that many people have gone to the town of Arecibo and to the United States. People very commonly go to town to visit kin who live there, and when we inquired, the regular answer was that they used to live in Esperanza. Our informants also used to say that once there were lots of people in Esperanza, but now the area was "empty." They were exaggerating, but reflecting a clear trend. It is probable that local kinship connections were more varied as well as more numerous in the past.

Inheritance is formally bilateral, as women can inherit property in their own right, either as wives, daughters, sisters or mothers. But what gives the system a male bias *de facto* in this area is the fact that women are excluded from the extradomestic occupational world. If they inherit land, they cannot cultivate it and have to rely on their husband, a son or brother, or some other male relative to do it.

Expected Behavior Between Kin

In the matter of actual social contacts the system is fully bilateral, as a glance at the composition of the household shows. Contacts are maintained with relatives on either side, and no discrimination is made in terms of address or behavior, as many degrees of relationship are recognized on the father's as on the mother's side. The actual number of relatives and the degree of contact with them is determined by the amount of actual intercourse, and not by formal principles. This does not mean that there are no principles, but only that the principles do not emphasize one side at the expense of the other.

These are the general features of the kinship system, and we now turn to a more detailed discussion, taking Ego as our point of departure.

EGO'S OWN GENERATION

The emphasis is on harmony and cooperation between full siblings. The element of respect also enters, especially in relation to age and sex differences. Brothers should protect their sisters, and certain types of contact between them should be avoided. They should not come into any physical contact, nor should the brother be present when his sister is in a naked or seminaked state. People verbalize this special treatment of the sister by stating: "You have relations of trust (*confianza*) with your brothers and sisters, but the trust is different when you are dealing with your sister."

Relations between brothers are very close and enduring and do not end with the marriage of the brothers. Brothers are expected to help each other, and the elder must watch and take care of the younger. The rule is that an older brother must be called *usted*[1] by the younger ones, a term of address that implies respect.

Emphasis is placed on the fact of being "children of (both) father and mother" (*hijos de padre y madre*), meaning by this full siblingship. Although it is asserted that half-siblings are treated in the same way as full siblings, there seems in practice to be a slight difference in behavior and in the degree of contact and cooperation.

Relations with cousins reflect the bilateral character of the kinship system. People stated very clearly that cousins on either side were treated and addressed in the same way, and added that between a sibling and a cousin there is a big difference in terms of trust, cooperation and degree of intimacy, though some cousins could become like brothers if the circumstances permitted. With a brother and sister you have more confidence than with a cousin.

Beyond the first cousin relationship, the degree of contact and social intercourse with more distant kin is minimal or nonexistent. The fact that second cousin marriage is permitted in Esperanza demonstrates the narrow character of the system. First cousins should not marry, and there is additional reluctance to do so, as some people state that marriage between close relatives can cause the offspring to be mentally defective.

FIRST ASCENDING GENERATION FROM EGO

Relations with the father are permeated by reverence (*reverencia*), obedience (*obediencia*) and authority (*autoridad*). A child must recognize that his father is the head of the house, that he commands authority and respect. This is the basic tone of the relationship. The mother, by contrast, can be more lenient (*más alcahueta*).

The term *alcahueta* refers to a kind of mediator, a go-between, a procuress. The term is sometimes applied to people, especially women, who carry messages between lovers and who tend to use their verbal abilities to praise the people they serve. It is used here to explain the role that the mother plays between the children and the father. When people say that a mother is *alcahueta* with her children they refer to the fact that she tends to be lenient with the children, and is offering them too much affection (*le está dando demasiado cariño*). She sees this as a compensation for the lack of love from the father, who is expected to be authoritarian. When she thinks the father is too strict, she

---

[1]*Usted* is a term which implies either respect, distance, or formality. *Tú* is the more intimate form of address. It implies either closeness or equality when used by two or more persons in addressing each other. Both terms are important indicators of status differences. Thus, a person of higher status can use *tú* in addressing one of lower status, and the latter will respond with *usted*.

acts as the mediator, offering love. She manipulates the situation in such a way that everybody is satisfied at the end. Children should also respect the mother, but it is not the same type of respect as for the father. With father it is fear and obedience; with mother it is love and trust.

Relations with aunts and uncles are again equally balanced on both sides. They are seen as secondary fathers and mothers and as such are treated with similar respect. But there is less restraint in the relation, and a restricted joking relationship can sometimes be maintained. Jokes can be made between aunt-niece or uncle-nephew, but they are not as personal or frank as they would be, for example, between friends. It is always emphasized that the aunt and uncle are the siblings of the parents.

SECOND ASCENDING GENERATION FROM EGO

Many of the informants did not know their grandparents on either side or had only a very vague memory of them. Those who knew and came into contact with them described their relationship with them as a mixture of respect and affection (*cariño*), with the affective element tending to predominate. Grandparents are characterized as good-natured, indulgent personalities. This corresponds with our experience and with the data on the composition of the household. If you have a married child in your house, there will probably also be at least one grand-child, and this is the one that is going to be spoiled (*malcriado*) by the grandparents.

Terms of Address

The terms of address are definite and vary in relation to the marital status, age, generation and sex of the person. Brothers and sisters are called by their first names, which implies equality. But sometimes age alters this and the respectful term of *usted* is used to address older siblings. When siblings become *compadres* they address each other by *usted,* but the implications of this will be discussed in a later chapter.

Cousins are called "cousin" (*primo*) or by their first name. If older than Ego they are addressed as *usted*. If of a different sex, the use of *usted* implies respect for that sex.

The father is addressed as "father" (*papá*) and if his name is not used, as *usted* (see Fig. 2 for consanguineal kinship terminology). The mother (*mamá*) is addressed in a similar way. Sometimes a diminutive like *papito* or *mamita* (little father and little mother) can be used, but

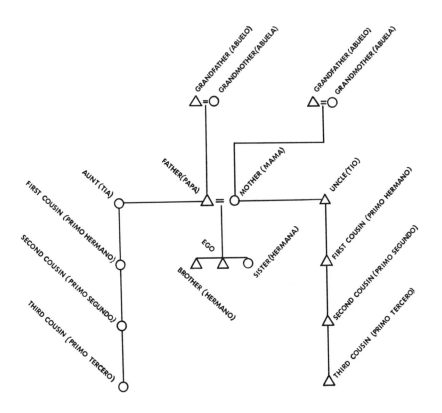

KINSHIP TERMINOLOGY
(CONSANGUINEAL)

Figure 2

that depends on the particular character of the persons involved. Even with the diminutive, *usted* is also used, so that the element of respect is always maintained in this configuration.

The same terms of address are used for uncles and aunts on both sides, and the relationship (uncle-*tío,* aunt-*tía*) is stated. If age and sex differences exist, *usted* would be used to denote respect. If equality tends to prevail, the first name is used, but even here (as with the father and mother) *usted* is used.

Grandparents (*abuelos*) tend to be addressed by the relationship term but in a diminutive use, such as *"abuelita"* (meaning little grandmother), and *usted* is added. The diminutive conveys the good-natured personality of grandparents, while the *usted* implies the respect due them.

People with no kinship or other ties in the community are placed in a special position and called *particulares* (individuals). They are addressed initially as *usted* if adult and *tú* if minors. If they have more formal education, they are called *usted,* even if the person addressed is younger than the speaker. In this way the system is able to handle the problem of how to address strangers.

The Meaning of Kinship in Esperanza

It is very difficult to isolate and assess the influence of kinship on the system of social relations in Esperanza. It tends to fuse with other factors (analyzed in later chapters) such as neighbors and *compadrazgo.* But there is, perhaps, one thing that isolates kinship from these other two factors. In Esperanza, people say that with *familia* (kin) you can have more *confianza* (trust) than with *compadres* or neighbors. Don Paco put it this way: "Well, to have kin is a very beneficial thing, because in case one sees kin in need, one is obliged to help them before helping anybody else." Kin are first and then come others. With *compadres* there is *confianza,* too, but it is of a very different nature. This *confianza* is more restrained, more formal in character. With a *compadre* there is always the element of *respeto* while with kin (*familia*) the tone of the relationship is less restrained. People openly state that they would rather have a fight with a kinsman than with a *compadre* (cf. Pitt Rivers 1958). "When one is dealing with a *compadre,* it is a very sacred thing. Not everybody can be a *compadre,* one must choose a person who has good discipline."

It is possible to have *confianza* with neighbors, but it is superficial, more restrained. "They are *vecinos* (neighbors) but they are not kin, they do not give us blood (*no nos dan sangre*)," informants stated.

These are the distinctions that people make, and that give kinship its special character. There is less formality and more intimacy in kinship relations than in neighbor and *compadre* relationships. You can trust kin more because it is a thing of blood (*cosa de sangre*), a given thing.

In certain situations kinship becomes especially relevant. In cases of sickness, death, financial misfortune and the celebration of marriages and baptisms, kin are supposed to give active assistance. If there is a sick person, it is the duty of kin to look for the doctor or bring the person to the hospital. If somebody dies, they are expected to make all the arrangements for the funeral. If there is some financial misfortune they must give their help. Siblings will be expected to participate more actively and with more interest than first and second cousins, as they are nearer to Ego. At another level one of our informants stated: "Grandparents are important, because if the parents are missing, they can take charge of the children." And again: "The importance of siblings, when you live in a united family . . . that lives well . . . is that they help in case of need (*necesidad*). They are the persons *nearest* to you, the siblings." "When uncles (and nephews and nieces) and aunts are near, we ask them in cases of need, if siblings and the rest of the family are not available." "The importance of cousins is that first cousins are sometimes like real siblings."

But recent events have somewhat modified this situation. At the beginning of this chapter, we mentioned the fact that many people have migrated to the town of Arecibo or to the United States. People say that *Esperanza se ha vaciado* (Esperanza has been emptied) and that now almost everybody has kin in town. It follows that people have fewer relatives (kin) in the area. All the people with whom we were able to discuss the matter readily make a verbal list of the kin who had gone either to Arecibo or to the United States.

The result has been that there are now many situations where kin are not available in case of need, either because they are totally absent from the area or live too far away. In cases like this, neighbors or *compadres* come into the picture. The case of Severo is a typical one. Severo and his son, Urías, were two Negro laborers who lived in an old hut. Severo, a very old man of ninety-five, was chronically sick and always in bed. They had neither kin nor *compadres* in the area, and when Severo died the nearest neighbors took charge of everything until he was finally buried, and even started and finished the *novenas* (see chapter on religious and supernatural practices). When we asked why they did it, they said that this was the duty of good neighbors.

In many places in Esperanza, people said: *"Aquí somos como familia"* (Here we are like kin), when speaking about being neighbors. The same thing happens with *compadrazgo* and *compadres* are considered *casi familia* (almost kin).

The extent to which kin are in contact with one another, apart from the special occasions which bring them together, depends on the distance they live from each other. The sons of Alfonso, who lived very near, used to go to his house almost daily to check if everything was all right. But Ricardo and Patricio, two brothers who lived something like a mile and a half apart, used to see each other less frequently, perhaps once a week, except in emergencies.

People recognize that this element of *confianza* between kin is different from that between neighbors (or *compadres*), and they react accordingly. They say: *"Hacemos lo que podemos en lo que llega la familia"* (We do what we can until the kin arrive).

Affines

People in Esperanza classify affines as kin but they distinguish between kin by marriage (*parientes políticos*) and kin by blood (*cosa de sangre*). Relations between affines are permeated by respect and harmony. They are expected to avoid conflict even more than blood relations. There is more restraint, less intimacy and cooperation between affines than between consanguineal kin (see Chap. 9 on the relations of Genoveva and Miguel throughout that conflict).

Relations between affines are perceived as more distant than relations between kin by blood. Genoveva put it this way: "Here we give more importance to kin (*parientes*) by blood or direct kinship. We judge affines through tolerance (*tolerancia*) or education or understanding (*entendimiento*) but they never come to be so close as direct kin" (see Fig. 3 for affinal kinship terminology).

This situation is in some cases modified by actual social intercourse. The case of Juan and his mother-in-law (*suegra*) Victoria is a good example. We have seen Juan joking with her, although he always addresses her by the term *usted* that implies respect. She is older than he (Victoria is in her seventies and Juan is in his fifties) and addresses him by the term *tú,* that in a situation like this implies trust. Victoria has lived for many years in Juan's house, and relations between them appear to be excellent. It is to be expected that relations between them were not like this when they first came into contact, although we cannot document it.

It is probable that relations between many affines are formal and restrained at first, but that with experience and contact through the

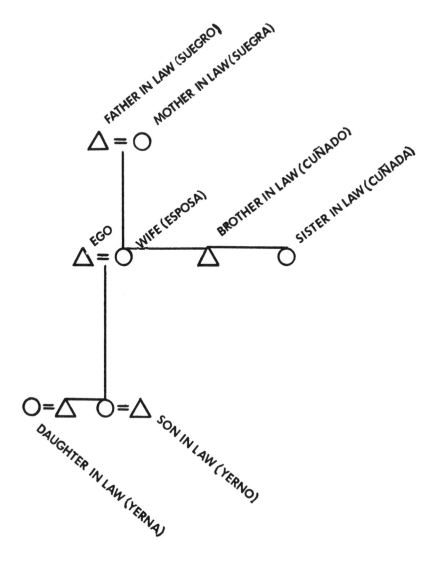

KINSHIP TERMINOLOGY

(AFFINAL)

Figure 3

years the relationship becomes less formal in character. Our general impression in Esperanza is that this is so, especially in the case of affines who live under the same roof or who meet often.

But even with this the relation remains different from kinship by blood. The son-in-law (*yerno*) can joke or feel somewhat at ease with his father-in-law (*suegro*) and mother-in-law (*suegra*) on some occasions, but there is always some sense of distance between them. The relation with both is based on *respeto*. The significant difference from consanguineal kinship is that while the relation with one's parents in Esperanza is based on respect, there is also an element of affection in it, particularly in the case of the mother. One respects one's mother, but one loves her more. The affective element predominates over respect, a situation that is impossible in the case of affines. One may come to like them more as affines, but love them not as consanguineal kin. The situation is similar with a brother- or sister-in-law (*cuñado o cuñada*). They are or could become like siblings (*como si fueran hermanos*) but will *never be* siblings. They are not a thing of blood (*cosa de sangre*).

Terms of address between affines take into consideration age and sex. An older affine addresses a younger one by the term *tú* while the younger addresses him by the term *usted*. Affines of the same generation or similar age use the term *usted,* but if they get along well could use *tú*.

There is a tendency for relations or cooperation (based on *respeto*) to be established between affines. Inquiries about *compadrazgo* in fifty households revealed that out of fifty-three *compadrazgo* relationships between kin (consanguineal and affinal) twenty-one were between affines, and twelve of those twenty-one were between brothers-in-law or sisters-in-law.

Compadrazgo involves an element of respect but it also involves an element of cooperation. The element of respect is perfectly consistent with the same element present in the affinal relation, while the element of cooperation adds a new element in the relation between affines. Respect is seen as the essence of affinal relations in Esperanza, while cooperation is seen as the essence of consanguineal kinship. Through *compadrazgo*, affines come closer than kin as they are formally required by the relationship to cooperate. The fact that most of the affines who become *compadres* are of the same generation or similar age range follows the formal rules of *compadrazgo,* which require equality between the parties, as *compadrazgo* is a symmetrical relation (see Chapter 10). In the same way that siblings enter into *compadrazgo* relations to introduce the element of respect into their relationship, so affines enter the relation looking for the other element: cooperation. *Compadrazgo* offers both elements at the same time without any inconsistency.

Kinship and Inheritance

Condensed from *Leyes de Puerto Rico Anotadas* (1955), the general principles of inheritance are briefly as follows: when a man or a woman dies his (or her) valuables are divided in three equal parts called the "legitimate" (*legítima*), the "best" (*mejora*) and the "freely disposable" (*libre disposición*). The "legitimate" part must be divided equally among the children. The "best" part can be divided or apportioned among children as the dead man wished, and a third of this part goes to the wife. The "freely disposable" can be distributed in any way that the dead man or woman wanted. These principles apply to any type of inherited item, either movable or immovable.

What happens in reality is a little different, and to some extent is affected by the size of the inheritance. Our informants told us that when the inheritance was large this led to some disputation between heirs, but that when the inheritance was small there was not usually any fighting. In a case where people have the expectation of inheriting some 10, 20 or more acres, disputes arise more easily about what constitutes each heir's part. With a farm of 10 or 20 acres one can manage to live off the land in Esperanza.

With small inheritances the situation changes. Heirs know that if they divide a farm of 8 or 10 acres among five or six of them they will each get a very small plot indeed, and one cannot make one's living solely out of a small plot. The usual arrangement, informants told us, is to leave the land undivided. Some of the heirs will emigrate either to the United States or to Arecibo.

In both cases the process is one mainly involving siblings and the surviving spouse. Each sibling wants a part in the inheritance, but at the same time they also have to share with the father or the mother. When the mother is the survivor, the children usually let her take more than a third of the *mejora* inheritance if she wants, to avoid any conflict. They also manage to help her, especially the men, to operate and cultivate the land. This was the case between Teodoro and his mother. She had a plot of some 10 acres and Teodoro helped her at regular intervals. He himself lived as a squatter on the land of one of Esperanza's biggest landowners.

Another type of arrangement, if the plot is too small to be divided, is for the mother to emigrate to town and perhaps for one or two siblings to do the same. The property title of all the land is written in favor of the mother, and one or two siblings remain and operate the plot in Esperanza and give their mother a percentage of any income or produce.

With the big farms, the problem, as stated before, is somewhat different. But the actors are the same and the principles practiced similar. Perhaps, as the Armando-Atanasia case in Chapter 9 illustrates, the expectation of a good piece of land leads to more conflict.

The siblings in principle are equal, but only partially. The "best" and the "freely disposable" parts create the seeds of conflict between them, and can also draw the surviving parent into the same situation.

Most of the time an attempt is made to keep the parent out of the conflict, as to fight with one's parents over property or inheritance is to rebel and to violate the respect they are always due. People prefer to wait until the person dies rather than violate the moral norms of parental respect.

The same, although perhaps with less intensity can be said for the competing, potentially conflicting, situation in which siblings find themselves in the matter of inheritance. Very rarely does a dispute come out in the open. Atanasia and Armando's (Chap. 9) subtle way of handling their conflict illustrates this clearly. With a small inheritance, siblings tend to disperse, preventing any dispute, and a compromise is arrived at. With a big inheritance, siblings accept provisionally the part allotted to them while the fight goes on in subtle ways. Jorge, Armando's half-brother, mentioned in the Atanasia and Armando case, has been fighting in this manner with Armando for years, but he is always careful not to provoke an open break.

Range of Kinship

It is clear that both sides of a person's kinship framework become relevant when kinship is reckoned; no discrimination is made between the paternal side and the maternal side. When one uses the term *parentela* (kin) both sides are implied. This extends in theory as far back as the great-grandparents, but in practice only to the grandparents, as few people can remember their great-grandparents.

The bilateral character of kinship in Esperanza provides each actor with a whole gamut of kin that can *sometimes* include more than fifty or sixty individuals, although this is non-exceptional. People state, *"Yo tengo familia regada por todo el barrio"* (I have kin all over the *barrio*).

This statement emphasizes bilaterality. The people are conscious that they have fewer kin available than in the past.

Every member of the social system of Esperanza comes to know and to interact with this kinship framework, created by the marriage of his father and mother, his brothers, sisters and children. One is fully conscious of this whole configuration and in that sense it is real, even if it cannot be considered a corporate group, because one has to take it into consideration in the whole process of social intercourse, inside and outside Esperanza. Kin are kin both in a jural and in a moral sense.

A farm with corn in the foreground, plantains in the left, the farmer's house in the center, and the tobacco shed to the right of the house.

CHAPTER 9

Conflict Between Kin: A Case Study

In this chapter, we describe and analyze in detail a dispute between siblings. The case is rather detailed and at times it may seem confusing, but we believe that to fully understand the subtleties of the system, especially the kinship system, the detail is essential. In this way, many of the principles discussed in the previous chapter on kinship, especially those related to siblings, can be seen in operation. The analysis that follows attempts to summarize the salient features of the case. We are also able to observe such other aspects of the system of social relations as class (based on prestige) and the overall theme of harmony and solidarity, so pervasive in the social life of Esperanza.

One of the most outstanding features of the dispute is perhaps the number of actors that participate, directly and indirectly. We have focused our attention on the four principal characters: Genoveva, Miguel, Armando and Atanasia. Our account is based on the actors' statements, on our own observations and on whatever other information we could gather. There are some gaps in the information. For instance, we were not able to wait for the decision of the surveyor, simply because we had to end our period of fieldwork. The account is therefore incomplete. But enough information was collected for a coherent picture to emerge.

The story is in itself representative of Esperanza; the norms operating in the Atanasia-Armando dispute are typical of all the members of the community, when they operate in similar contexts. In that sense they are independent of social class; a group of siblings at any socioeconomic level would act in a similar way.

The main personalities involved are: Genoveva and her husband Armando, who are also second cousins, Atanasia who is Armando's sister (and also Genoveva's second cousin), and Atanasia's husband

Miguel. Genoveva, the youngest, is in her early forties; Atanasia, the oldest, in her early fifties. The rest of the actors involved will be mentioned as they come into context.

The case study starts in November 1962. In that month Genoveva told my wife that Atanasia had written a letter to Armando, her brother, from the United States, where she had been living for a long time. Atanasia had left Esperanza when she was about twenty-five years of age and met her husband, Miguel, in the United States.

This letter said that the land where Armando and Genoveva had constructed their house was the property of Atanasia, and that Armando and Genoveva had then constructed it on land that did not belong to them. Genoveva emphasized the fact that the letter was written in strong language and told my wife not to tell anybody about it. Genoveva explained some of the details of the problem. She stated that Armando's and Atanasia's father had left them a piece of land to be divided in equal parts, but that the line of division was not specified in the will. The size of the whole plot was 22 acres to be divided in two equal parts of 11 acres each. When they were trying to decide where to build their house, Armando asked Genoveva where she wanted it. Genoveva chose the site, stating that she wanted the house in a place near other houses, as she was afraid of staying alone in a solitary spot. She also emphasized that this was the only criterion she used in the selection of the site. This site is now claimed by Atanasia as her property.

Genoveva said she was almost sure that the wife of Herminio, a brother of Armando and Atanasia who lives in the United States, might have told Atanasia that Armando and Genoveva had built an excellent house in Esperanza. Genoveva thought that this may have prompted Atanasia to write the letter.

After this, Armando wrote a letter to his sister Atanasia explaining his position. Genoveva did not give details of Armando's letter and finished by saying that Atanasia did not answer Armando's letter.

After this event, and for a few months, things remained quiet. Then in February, 1963, Miguel, Atanasia's husband, arrived in Esperanza. This visit was not unexpected as rumors about it had already been heard. Miguel was invited to stay at Armando's house but he refused and stayed at the home of some paternal cousins of Atanasia's in Esperanza. In his first visits to Armando and Genoveva, Miguel never mentioned the dispute over the land in an open manner, and only suggested that the problem should have been discussed sooner. But he did not force the issue and most of the time he emphasized the social character of his visit. At the same time, Miguel declared that he was interested in land, and that he was looking for some farmland to buy.

But out of all this no direct confrontation or discussion emerged. During this period, Genoveva said one day to my wife that she could not understand why Atanasia had started all this dispute after they (Armando and Genoveva) had built the house and not before, and that some kind of agreement could have been arranged.

In April, Atanasia arrived in Esperanza and joined her husband at her cousin's home. She declined at first to stay in Armando's home but within a week she went there, without Miguel, and stayed a few days.

Atanasia had many kin in Esperanza, and one of the first things she did was to visit them. On April 20, she paid a visit to her half-brother Mayito, and then to the home of Jorge, another half-brother. Jorge lives on and works a plot of 7 acres owned by Armando.

Jorge exchanged this plot for one which he owned and which was near to the road. Jorge complained that Armando made the exchange with him many years ago and without any legal or written documents, and that if he died his children and wife would lose everything. Jorge concluded, "I do not know what is happening in Armando's mind." Jorge's wife stated that some people had advised them to take the case to court. Atanasia told them not to do that because they had to remember that they were kin, and kin do not fight.

All this time all the parties avoided a direct confrontation. Atanasia told her cousins that she would not return to town (Arecibo) until she solved this problem, but to Armando and Genoveva she said nothing about this, limiting herself to the discussion of other matters.

During this period Atanasia and her husband stated that they were planning to build a house in Esperanza, but that they had not agreed on the location. Atanasia had another plot of 12 acres in a different part of Esperanza, and sometimes she thought of building the house on that plot. She inherited this latter plot from her mother, who was also Armando's mother. She thought that perhaps the other heirs (her brothers and sisters: Herminio, Rosalía and Armando) would sell their part to her. For this plot of 12 acres there were four heirs including Armando.

Miguel, Atanasia's husband, used to work as a mailman in the United States, but retired that year. He had a pension from the United States government and planned to live in Esperanza.

At this stage Atanasia told my wife the following: she had rented her portion of the plot in dispute to Armando many years ago. It amounted to 11 acres. At first Armando paid the rent regularly, but later he failed to send any money in payment for the use of the land. She added that Armando made his money by "hard work," but that he also used the land of his brothers.

At the end of April, things began to clarify a little and a surveyor came to measure and later divide the land. He was brought in by Atanasia. During this same period Genoveva and Miguel had a small discussion. Genoveva asked Miguel what would happen if the surveyor decided that Genoveva and Armando had built their house on Atanasia's plot, and what would Atanasia and Miguel do before the "fight" started. Miguel stated that he did not want to "fight," and that all they wanted was a plot equal to the one that Armando had, and with the same advantages: good location, level land, and so on. Miguel also emphasized the fact that he had to be in agreement with his wife. Miguel finished by stating that Atanasia and Armando were siblings, and siblings do not fight; that he wanted peace and harmony.

That same day Atanasia made the comment to her cousins that if Armando started making trouble, she would tell him to keep everything to himself and that she would return and stay in the United States.

A few days later Armando told Atanasia that he was going to sell a cow in order to find the money for partial payment of the surveyor's fees. The rest was going to be paid by Atanasia. That same day Reinaldo (half-brother of Armando and Atanasia) told Atanasia he was interested in the other plot (the one she had inherited from her mother) and was willing to buy it.

On the last day of April, we had a conversation with Armando and Genoveva. Armando tried to convince us that he was not as rich as people in Esperanza said he was. He described to us how he bought a farm and how he was forced to borrow money from a bank in Arecibo to be able to complete the transaction. According to his information he was also forced to mortgage his house and land during this financial operation. He was very careful to state that the part of the plot that belonged to Atanasia had not been mortgaged or tied in any way, and that he was not in the habit of handling land that was not his.

Armando Speaks of His Father

He also spoke of his father, describing how he used to have four "wives." According to him, his father preferred Armando's mother and her children and visited them daily. His father did not sleep in the houses of any of his wives and had his own independent place.

A few days later Miguel requested our services as mediators in the dispute. He wanted us to be present when the results of the surveyor's work were brought in. While making this request, he went into some of the details and arguments. He said that Armando was trying to make a fool of him in the same way that he (Armando) had made a fool of some of his own brothers in the past. According to Miguel, Armando considered him a stranger, and avoided him every time he came to discuss the case with Armando. Miguel added that Armando always sent Genoveva in his place. He said it was his moral duty as a husband to protect his wife's interests. He argued that Armando was trying to deceive him by including in the land a piece that was not part of the inheritance, but which Armando had bought from another person to suit his own purposes.

Miguel explained that by adding this piece of land one-half of the plot became a little bigger, and if cut in half near that piece, Armando's house would not fall in the part belonging to Atanasia.

He concluded by stating that Armando owed them more than $1,000 in unpaid rent from that part and was always saying things were bad as an excuse for not paying his debt.

During that same week, some cousins of Miguel came to Esperanza to visit him and Atanasia and to look over some farms with the intention of buying. They spent some five or six hours in the *barrio* and went to take a look at Atanasia's plot near Armando's house. Apparently, Miguel was taking advice, as these kin were experts on farms.

Some weeks later we were speaking with an old resident of the *barrio* named Isidoro, and he indicated that the land when inherited was always divided into equal parts among the heirs.

Atanasia revealed that Armando and Miguel had reached an agreement a few weeks before about the payment for the surveyor's services. Each party would pay for the measurement of his plot. But Atanasia also stated that before they reached this agreement they had a very acrimonious argument, because Armando had tried to include in the measurement the adjacent piece of land mentioned by Miguel, not belonging to Atanasia's plot, but which Armando had bought privately. After lengthy discussion, however, they could not reach any agreement with the surveyor, because the price he quoted was too high for them.

Atanasia said she loved her brother Armando very much, but that if things reached a certain level, she was willing to use dirty language in dealing with him.

Genoveva and Armando, a few days afterwards, told us about plans Armando had for establishing a mechanized dairy. According to them, the government had loaned Armando $17,000 for that enterprise and for building a farmhouse. Armando and Genoveva told us that they were considering the possibility of establishing the dairy outside Esperanza and that the land Armando had in Esperanza might be sold. But the issue seemed a little obscure, because Genoveva told a certain Meleto that the loan had been approved, while Armando told Isidoro, father of Meleto, (both of them residents of Esperanza and friends of Armando and Genoveva) that the government was still considering the matter.

A few days later Genoveva spoke with us again. She was of the opinion that Miguel was acting a little queerly and suggested that perhaps he was somewhat out of his mind. She continued speaking about the dispute. She stated that Miguel had the impression that Armando was going to buy Atanasia's part in the land and that he (Miguel) was angry with Genoveva and Armando because they had not made any offer to buy. Genoveva added that when Atanasia and Miguel bought a house in the United States, Armando loaned them $1,500 which he never asked Atanasia to repay because she was his sister. Last year Atanasia and Miguel repaid the loan. Armando, according to Genoveva, never acknowledged the payment because "he is like that always," and not because he was angry with them or anything like that.

She added that the house they had built did not lie in Atanasia's plot, because the will does not specify an exact dividing line, and they had built the house at the midpoint so as to avoid that problem. She added that Miguel said that the piece added by Armando was a rectangle and not a triangle (as stated by Armando and Genoveva), and that Miguel argued that way to prove that the house was situated in Atanasia's part. Genoveva and Armando had built the house in that place without any ill intention, and the main reason was that it was a site near other houses. Genoveva did not want to build it in a solitary place as at this time Armando was always out of the house, and she was alone a great deal of the time. They had built this house with small resources, and they were forced to borrow money to finish it. They spent as little money as they could in the construction, and with some that was left over, they were able to pay some debts. Genoveva also said that if Atanasia and Miguel wanted it, Armando would sell the house to them.

Genoveva spoke about another possible solution to the dispute. She said that if the surveyor decided that the house was not (as she expected) in Atanasia's part she and Armando were willing to transfer part of Armando's plot to Atanasia and to exchange the piece that Armando added (according to Atanasia and Miguel) for a part of Atanasia's plot. But Genoveva said that the biggest obstacle to this solution lay in the fact that Armando had applied for a loan to the government and this type of arrangement would delay the establishment of his mechanized dairy, as the land was given as a guarantee in the request for the loan.

Genoveva added some comments about Miguel. She said that he was a queer person, who liked to exaggerate things and followed the letter of the law strictly. She insinuated the possibility of Miguel's being an emotionally maladjusted personality. According to her, he had had some trouble in his job as a mailman in the United States as a result of his nervous disposition. She complained that Miguel was always examining all the documents in the dispute in detail.

Genoveva said that she and Armando did not have an exaggerated interest in the matter, and that they wanted to avoid any disputes between kin. She went on to say that one of her brothers had been operating, for many years, a farm in which she was a coheir, but that she loved her brother more than the inheritance. If she at any time needed anything she would simply ask her brother, but only in case of real need.

She concluded by stating that Armando made his money by hard work, and that people tended to forget that aspect. She said that Armando was also very lucky in his financial dealings. He had bought a farm for $35,000 many years ago, and the farm was worth $100,000 today. He had also bought a house plot in Arecibo for only $5,000, and the plot was worth $11,000 at the present time.

That same day we met Armando again, and he commented that his siblings did not love him because he had made his money by hard work while they were doing other things, which he did not specify. He finished by saying that his mother "had opened his eyes."

Six or seven days after this, Atanasia and Miguel declared that a surveyor would be coming very soon to measure both Atanasia's and Armando's plot. They also announced that they had placed an advertisement in the newspapers offering Atanasia's plot for sale or rent.

Improper Behavior Between Kin

Atanasia also made some comments about her half-brother Ceferino. Ceferino, according to Atanasia, had a "black heart." He was building a house in Spain with the money he had made "with the sweat of the poor." Atanasia said that Ceferino loaned $1,500 to his half-sister Margarita (also half-sister of Atanasia) but had insisted that Margarita give him the mortgage and property title to her house. Later he asked her to pay the money back since he needed it to get married. Consequently, Margarita had to borrow from an unlicensed money lender at a high rate of interest to be able to pay him. Atanasia criticized Ceferino for demanding the payment of the money from his half-sister without consideration for her financial situation.

Atanasia also described a similar dealing between Ceferino and a cousin named Teodoro. Teodoro had a farm in Esperanza, and he had been in a very critical financial situation. He borrowed money continually from Ceferino until he owed him $13,000. Ceferino demanded payment in full but Teodoro could not satisfy that requirement, and he lost the farm when Ceferino took him to court. This was severely commented upon by Atanasia as improper behavior between kin.

Atanasia returned to the theme of the dispute with Armando. She said that she had not consulted Armando before placing the advertisement in the newspapers as it was not "his business." She also said that Miguel had visited Armando and had announced that some "engineers" were coming, including a nephew of Miguel's, to measure the plot. Later that same day, Atanasia and Miguel paid a social call on Armando and Genoveva, but the subject was not mentioned.

The following day, we had a conversation with Miguel. He mentioned that the plot measurement was going to be delayed because the "engineer" and Miguel's nephew could not come as they had previously announced.

Miguel referred to the other plot that Atanasia had inherited from her mother and declared that he and Atanasia were planning to build a house on it, but that they had to buy the portions belonging to the other siblings if they were willing to sell because they (Atanasia and Miguel) wanted more space. Miguel also stated his previous intention of selling the plot involved in the dispute. He emphasized the fact that all these were provisional plans and as such could be changed.

He stated that a family had built a house on this other plot and that Armando had given them permission to do so many years ago. Miguel had discussed this matter with the family and asked them what they were planning to do, as the land did not belong to them. He told this family that if he sold the farm, the decision would then rest with the new owner.

This same day, Atanasia told my wife that she wished that all this business had finished as she was tired of it all already.

Two days later Atanasia and Miguel made a trip to Camuy, a nearby town not far from Arecibo. They had heard about a construction firm that was building low-priced houses, and they wanted to inquire about the cost of building a house in Esperanza. But Atanasia was still undecided and did not know if she was going to settle in Esperanza or any other place in Puerto Rico, or if she was going to return to the United States and remain there.

When we met Genoveva two days later, she told us she was under the impression that Miguel had been making inquiries in Arecibo and in the capital (San Juan) about Armando's financial position, trying to check if it was true that he had not mortgaged Atanasia's land when applying for the loan.

A few days later in the same week, while we were going into town in a *público* (cars that carry passengers from Esperanza to Arecibo for a fare), Tano the driver inquired about the plot Atanasia was selling. When he heard that Atanasia was selling at a price of $750 an acre he commented: "Such a high price for that bunch of stones." Moncho, a butcher, asked if Atanasia was going to settle in the *barrio*.

Miguel was absent from the *barrio* for two days after this incident. When he returned in the early evening hours, we were told that he had been in San Juan. It came out that he had been looking for someone to survey the land, and he announced that they were coming the next day to do the operation. Miguel also stated that he wanted to seek a loan from the government to build a farmhouse on Atanasia's second plot, and he showed us the documents that he was preparing. But he was quite pessimistic about the prospects, since, as he said, he was not a professional farmer, and the government would probably not grant him the loan because of that.

This same day, Atanasia told my wife that she was planning to return to the United States because her married daughter Lulu was going to give birth to a baby, and she wanted to be there to take care of them. She said that she did not know what plans Miguel had, if he was going to stay or to return to the United States.

The surveyor and his assistants came the next day to start measuring the land and spent the whole day with Miguel working on the job. Atanasia told my wife that they quoted a price of $400, which she considered excessive.

When they started work in the morning, Miguel asked Armando if he would help the surveyor as he knew the points of reference (landmarks, etc.) better than anyone. Armando said he was too busy and had no free time. Miguel then asked Armando's son Armando (named after his father) if he could help, but the answer was the same; he was also too busy and could not spare a minute. The surveyor and the assistants then said that they did not need anybody's help and started on their own. Miguel remained there all day and came home in the early evening hours. He said the whole operation would take five or six days as the surveyor had to verify and certify the information and draw up the documents.

In the evening, Atanasia told us that Armando's request for a loan for his dairy farm had been refused on the grounds that he had rented part of his land to other people.

Later in the week, Atanasia told my wife the following: her father (who was also Armando's father) had had plenty of land in Esperanza, although she could not tell the amount. He was always buying more and more land as at that time it was cheaper than today, as low as fifty cents an acre. Atanasia also said that he had plenty of money in a bank in San Juan. When he died, Ceferino, whom we mentioned earlier and who was the eldest sibling, and who knew that their father had this money, managed to get hold of the money, using the services of a lawyer. Atanasia did not give details, but she emphasized that Ceferino got hold of all the money and did not share any of it with any of his siblings (full or half).

This same day Miguel had been all day with the surveyor working on the plot. Somebody asked him if Armando had helped them. Miguel said he had not, but that they did not need his help.

A friend paid a very short visit to Genoveva at this time and Genoveva added some details as to how the dispute was going. She said she and Armando were going to dismantle a big barn they had constructed near Atanasia's plot, if it was found they had constructed it on Atanasia's land. She also said that she and Armando had offered their house to Atanasia and Miguel for sale, but that Miguel said they could not afford to pay the price they were asking for it. Genoveva was of the opinion that Miguel and Atanasia should construct their house on the plot in dispute, and not on the one that Atanasia had inherited from her mother, as this was too isolated. But she added that if Atanasia and Miguel wanted to buy Armando's part of that inheritance, she would have no objection to Armando's selling it and would tell him so. Genoveva also said that Atanasia was an excellent housewife and a good cook.

The next day Miguel told my wife that the surveyor and his assistants were working on the plot but that he had not been there. He added that the whole operation would take some time because the "engineer" had to study the whole problem in detail.

After this Miguel made another trip to San Juan, but did not tell anyone the purpose. The only indication that it could have been related to the Atanasia-Armando dispute was the fact that he declared before starting that nobody should tell Armando and Genoveva about this trip.

The same day Atanasia told my wife that she was planning to visit Armando and Genoveva. She had not visited them for some days and thought they would think she was behaving in an improper way.

A few days later Miguel returned from San Juan, but then he and Atanasia went to Adjuntas, a town quite far from Arecibo and Esperanza, to visit Miguel's kin. Adjuntas is Miguel's birthplace. In the meantime, the surveyor and his assistants finished the fieldwork, but declared that now they had to work on the drawings and maps.

Atanasia and Miguel came back from Adjuntas a few days later. That same day, in the early evening hours Genoveva (with her children) paid a short visit to Atanasia and Miguel. It was purely a social call. She had killed a pig and wanted Atanasia's help (Atanasia is an excellent cook) in preparing it. Miguel and Atanasia went to Genoveva's home, and late that night Genoveva and her children accompanied Miguel and Atanasia to the place where they were staying. Apparently the dispute was not mentioned nor discussed as this was entirely a social occasion.

The following morning Miguel visited Armando to inquire about the surveyor and his work and was told that they had said they were in the last stages of the work.

That same day Atanasia declared that she would very soon have to return to the United States, and that a cousin was planning to go with her. Atanasia also said that a few days before Armando had told Miguel humorously that if he (Armando) had had the opportunity of following a profession he would have liked to be a boxer.

While waiting for the results of the survey, Miguel took long strolls around Esperanza. It seems that during one of these strolls he met Enrique, a merchant. Enrique was interested in Atanasia's plot, probably from a commercial point of view. Enrique had a store in Esperanza, but he did not own the land or the building. Enrique and Miguel also discovered that they had one thing in common: both were Spiritualists and they made a visit to a nearby center together. After this Enrique and Miguel met quite often.

One day Atanasia made the comment that she loved Armando very much and that he was the brother she preferred. She would not like to lose him, that is, to have a break with him. She concluded by repeating her desire to return to the United States.

One day later, Atanasia made a trip to Arecibo, where she stayed at the house of her half-sister Margarita, who was also planning to join Atanasia on her trip to the United States. She remained there for a few days. While she was in Arecibo, Miguel made a trip to San Juan and stayed there for two days. In the meantime, Atanasia bought the ticket for her return trip to New York. Her married daughter was going to have her baby in a few days and Atanasia wanted to be there to assist her.

After buying the ticket, Atanasia returned to Esperanza to the place where she and Miguel were staying. Miguel had already returned from San Juan. That same day, Miguel visited and talked with Armando. Later that night Miguel and Atanasia were busy examining the docu-

ments of the land dispute, and Atanasia seemed more angry than
Miguel, although we could not find out why.

A few days later, Atanasia told us she did not know what Miguel
had decided in relation to a house they owned in the United States,
whether to sell it, rent it, or follow another course. She also said she
thought that perhaps Armando was really in a bad financial position,
because he had his children in school and had been forced to borrow
money in the past. In contrast to a few days earlier, she seemed more
sympathetic toward Armando.

Some days later we paid a visit to Armando and Genoveva. Armando
was busy with his cows, but we were able to talk for some time with
Genoveva. At the beginning, Miguel appeared and remained for a few
minutes. Genoveva and he did not mention anything about the land
dispute, but after Miguel left, she talked about it. She began by stating
that the surveyor had finished his job and added that Miguel was wrong
in his argument that she and Armando had constructed the house in
Atanasia's plot. She said he was angry with Miguel about this problem
because he made her lose her patience. She thought that Miguel was out
of his mind and felt sorry for Atanasia who was a noble person and an
efficient housewife, and who did not like to engage in a dispute over
land. This was perhaps because she had plenty of land, Genoveva commented. If Armando wanted, she said, he could win this dispute very
easily, but that he did not like disputes either, especially with kin.

Genoveva added that the property titles and all related documents
were ready and that Miguel could do as he pleased. This comment was
heard by Armando, who was working nearby, and he interjected, "He
cannot do as he pleases, he can only take what they are entitled to."

Genoveva said that at the start of the dispute she was very angry,
but that she did not feel that way any more. She stated that Armando's
kin felt a great deal of affection for her. At this moment a niece and
her husband came to visit Armando and Genoveva.

We remained and after the niece and her husband had left, Genoveva
added some more comments. We had remarked that people in Esperanza
had the ability to tell a lie in such a way that one could believe it to
be true. Genoveva said that this was true and that Miguel in his strolls
around Esperanza had believed many of the lies that people had told
him. She was trying to make the point that Miguel was naive. She also
said that people in Esperanza came to her and said that other people
were telling Miguel that the land near Atanasia's plot was part of
Atanasia's piece and Miguel "swallowed" all this.

Genoveva said she was very angry with Miguel because he was trying
to change the opinion of the people of Esperanza about them (Armando

and Genoveva) with false rumors, instead of examining documents and information. She added that Atanasia was very intelligent, but that Miguel's idea that he was intelligent was only an illusion on his part.

She and Armando had examined their documents relating to the land in dispute, she said, and they had found that the piece Atanasia and Miguel said Armando had added to Atanasia's plot was on the other side of the road and as such was a separate piece from Atanasia's. This fact pushed the dividing line away from Armando's house, and so Atanasia and Miguel were completely wrong in stating that they had constructed the house on Atanasia's plot. She said that they had given these documents to Miguel to examine and that he had been forced to admit that she and Armando were right on this point.

Genoveva also told us a little about Armando's father, Eleuterio. He had four "wives" called Teresa, Isolina, Beatriz and Amanda; he had had children with each one of them. He had provided a separate house for each one and her children and never lived with any of them in the same house. He always lived with his widowed mother in the main house, and the children he had by Isolina (among them Atanasia and Armando) lived with them. When Armando's father died, all these children received their inheritance. Armando and Atanasia received land as theirs. Other children by other "wives" received their inheritance in money.

The children of Teresa were the youngest of them all, and being under twenty-one years of age were minors and not adults according to the law. Their inheritance was placed under the supervision of Armando, who became what is known in Puerto Rico as a "tutor." Ceferino, another half-brother of Armando, was also named a "tutor" of these children. They had to take care of the inheritance of Teresa's children until they reached twenty-one.

A few days later Atanasia announced that she had everything ready to return to the United States, and that she was leaving for San Juan, from where she would fly to New York. This same day Armando's daughter paid a visit to Atanasia and spent some time with her.

One or two days before Atanasia's trip to the United States, Genoveva met a cousin. She stated that Atanasia was a "good" person, but that Miguel was a bad one. She added that perhaps he was also good, but that he was full of revenge because Armando's house was not on Atanasia's plot, and he had come all the way from the United States just to prove that point. Genoveva said she was very angry about what they had tried to do to Armando, because he was an excellent person, very humble. She stated that they had won the case but that in spite of this, Miguel continued the examination of documents trying to prove the opposite.

One day while Genoveva was speaking to my wife, and away from home, Atanasia went to say good-bye to Armando, who was alone in the house. She later said that this was the only way she could speak to her brother because Genoveva did not give her the opportunity.

Atanasia told Armando that she was returning to the United States, and that the dispute was at the same point as when she first arrived. Armando replied that it was going to be solved very soon. Atanasia told him that Miguel was in charge of the problem. She asked Armando if he intended to rent or buy the plot, but he replied that he could not do either due to his lack of money at the moment. Atanasia told him that she was asking him this because he had preference over anybody who wanted to use, rent or buy her plot. Then she embraced and kissed him and wished him good luck in his activities. He replied by wishing her well. Returning to where she was staying, she met Genoveva, who asked about her daughter. Atanasia did not mention her visit to Armando nor did she say good-bye to Genoveva.

This same day a man came to inquire about the advertisement Atanasia and Miguel had placed in the newspaper. He wanted to rent the farm and was willing to pay $400 a year for its use, but nothing definite was decided.

The following day Miguel and Atanasia made a trip to San Juan. He was not going with Atanasia to the United States but went only to say farewell. Two days later he returned alone to Esperanza. He said his wife was going to the United States that same day.

Miguel went to Arecibo later in the week, but before leaving he said there was a chance that he might continue to San Juan. The same day he returned to Esperanza.

Miguel was becoming very impatient as the surveyor had evidently not finished his work, which would demonstrate who was right. He told us he did not know yet to whom the land where Armando had built his house belonged. He added that it would be best if the decision favored Armando and Genoveva, because that would prevent further problems and disputes.

Miguel was so impatient that he called on the bank to cancel the payment of a check he had given the surveyor, in the hope that the man would expedite the job if he wanted to be paid in full for his services.

The next day, when the surveyor had not come, Miguel said he was thinking about the possibility that Genoveva might have bribed him, and that this was the cause of his delay. He said that Armando had not paid one cent to the surveyor, and that finally he (Miguel) would be obliged to pay the full amount of $400. He also stated that the surveyor had not even paid his assistants. Some weeks later, Miguel went to stay with some kin in San Juan, where we left him at the end of our fieldwork.

Analysis

The dispute is mainly among four persons, Armando and Genoveva (husband and wife and second cousins), Miguel and Atanasia (husband and wife). Figure 4 shows all the actors involved. Atanasia and Genoveva are second cousins, and are related through affinal ties. Another relevant point is that all the main contestants are more or less in the same age range, and this implies a certain equality in the relations between them. Here we do not find any person who could exercise some degree of authority based on age over all or some of the individuals.

The fact that Atanasia had been living for some time in the United States reflects the situation that Esperanza is not a closed society, and that even long-term emigrants do not sever their ties with the social system from which they had come. The fact that Atanasia had some land in Esperanza and that she was always interested in its status indicates that she had not cut her ties with her birthplace and that there was a possibility that she might return and settle there again.

When Genoveva and Armando received the letter about the land, they were placed in a difficult position. Sooner or later Atanasia and Miguel would come to Esperanza to settle this problem, and the whole matter would have to be discussed. Genoveva and Armando had quite a high reputation and prestige in Esperanza, the place where they had lived all their lives and where they were considered members of the upper class. They were also members of the old families, so they had everything to lose in case the dispute came out in the open, and it could be proved that Armando and Genoveva had done anything improper. That is why Genoveva asked my wife not to tell anybody. However, Genoveva immediately started to explain, so that if the word got around, people would come to realize that she and Armando had not done anything morally reprehensible. She emphasized the fact that the dividing line had not been specified, and also that she wanted and had the house built in a place where she was not without possible protection and company. This was intended to show that they had a "clean" reason for doing things that way. If it happened that the house had been built in Atanasia's plot, the declared motive would help to mitigate the act on grounds of moral "cleanliness."

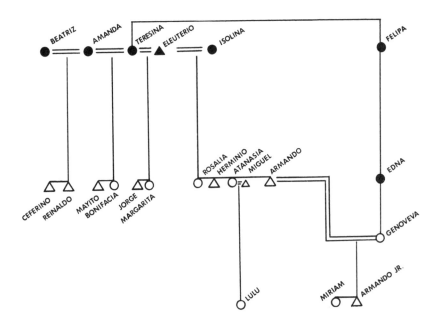

ACTORS IN THE DISPUTE

Figure 4

Genoveva also remarked that the letter was written in strong language which suggests that the dispute had been going on for some time. This kind of language is used only as a last resource, when all the others have failed.

Armando and Atanasia's father, by not specifying the dividing line was also planting the seeds of the problem. Perhaps he thought that because they were full siblings they would not engage in a fight and would solve the problem in a peaceful way. The father was not altogether wrong in his judgment, if he had this in mind, as the constant avoidance of a direct confrontation between Armando and Atanasia all through the dispute testifies. Never during the whole dispute did they engage in any direct discussion of the land problem. Later in this analysis we will amplify this item.

One aspect of inheritance rules is especially relevant to understanding the problem. In Puerto Rico, and in the specific case of Esperanza, it is the rule that equality must be observed in the proportions in which heirs receive an inheritance, regardless of sex. The result is that Atanasia received exactly the same share of her father's inheritance as Armando.

When Genoveva said that perhaps the wife of Herminio, a brother of Armando and Atanasia, might have told "the story" about the house, this implies that kin (in this case siblings) maintain some sort of contact, in spite of distance, either by personal visits or by letter. It is revealing that Genoveva did not say that it was Herminio, but his wife; perhaps she did not want to start a fight here among Armando, Herminio and Atanasia. By stating that it was his wife, Genoveva avoided breaking the harmonious relation that should prevail among siblings, and at the same time guarded herself from being accused of disrupting them.

The next stage of the dispute takes us to the beginning of the confrontation. Atanasia's husband arrived in Esperanza and made the first contacts with Armando and Genoveva. It is interesting that it was the husband and not the wife who started the proceedings. Right from the beginning, we can see that Atanasia did not want to engage in a direct fight with her brother. Armando seems to have reciprocated by "delegating" the role to Genoveva. The result was that the two persons not related by consanguineal kinship ties came to take the active and explicit roles in the dispute.

When Miguel arrived in Esperanza he was in a conflict-ridden situation. The motive of his visit had been to open discussion on the dispute over Atanasia's and Armando's inheritance. But at the same time he was visiting and coming into contact with affines, with people toward whom one should behave in a respectful manner. The solution Miguel found was ingenious. By staying at the home of Atanasia's cousins he avoided being in direct and daily contact with Armando and Genoveva, and so this physical distance could prevent any unplanned open conflict between the persons involved. But this was also in a sense a declaration (very subtle indeed) of war. By refusing to stay at Armando's house, Miguel made it known that a situation of conflict existed and that discussion sooner or later was going to take place. By stating that he was interested in land matters and by hinting that the problem should be discussed, Miguel took the first real steps in the dispute. But at the same time by making the first visits social Miguel was also making it clear in an indirect way that the issue could be discussed in a peaceful manner.

Armando and Genoveva acted in a similar way, although it must be noted that by this time Armando had already delegated the initiative to Genoveva. But they fulfilled their roles as good kin and hosts by inviting Miguel to stay in their house. Nobody could now say that they had behaved in an improper way toward an affine; it was he who refused. At this stage it seems that the temperature had not yet risen. This is reflected in Genoveva's statement that she did not understand why the issue had been raised after the construction of the house and not before, and that some kind of agreement could have been reached. Perhaps she was lamenting that she would have to engage in a dispute with people with whom she disliked having to fight.

Atanasia's arrival a few months later signified that she and Miguel wanted to accelerate the discussion and resolution of the dispute. But immediately after she arrived in Esperanza, the strength of kinship norms made things more difficult. The value of nonconflicting relationships between siblings (full and half-siblings) came to the fore, and Atanasia did not directly confront either Armando or Genoveva. It is very revealing that Atanasia was practically forced to engage in a whole round of visits to her kin in Esperanza, especially the visiting of her siblings. If she had not done this, gossip would have started among them, labelling her as a "bad" sister. The invitation she received from Armando and Genoveva to stay in their house was the prime example. Here she was in a dilemma similar to the one that Miguel had been in when he first arrived. By staying for a few days without Miguel, she achieved two goals: she made it clear that there was a dispute to be solved and at the same time acknowledged her affection and kinship ties with Armando (and Genoveva) and also her desire that a peaceful solution should be arrived at.

Atanasia's desire to avoid a conflict with Armando was exemplified in her visit to Jorge, half-brother of Armando and herself. When Jorge told her about his conflict with Armando, and Jorge's wife said that some people had advised them to take the case to court, Atanasia urged that they should not do so because they (Armando and Jorge) had to remember that they were kin and kin do not fight.

The two parties involved in the dispute took some time in making the first approaches toward the discussion of the land dispute. For more than a month, Miguel and Atanasia engaged in other activities while Armando and Genoveva were just waiting. The interest Atanasia and Miguel showed in building a house in another part of Esperanza was perhaps an attempt to evade the problem and to see if a way out could be found without conflict.

Things started moving a little when the first surveyor came. It was really a move by Miguel and Atanasia to force Armando and Genoveva into initiating the discussion of the dispute. It was at this stage that the first discussion and confrontation between Genoveva and Miguel took place. Genoveva seemed interested in trying to clarify the position of Atanasia and Miguel. This was done in a very subtle way, by creating an imaginary situation. Genoveva asked what would happen if the survey proved that Genoveva and Armando had constructed their house in Atanasia's plot: what they would do before the "fight" started.

Miguel answered by reaffirming the value of the nonconflicting relationship between siblings. He said that Atanasia and Armando, as siblings, were not going to engage in a fight as that was a very improper thing to do. He appealed also to the harmony among all the parties by stating that he too did not want to fight. By stating that he and Atanasia wanted a plot with the same advantages as Armando's, he was making it clear that he was not imposing an inequitable demand on Armando and Genoveva, but that all they wanted was a fair settlement. For the time being, Miguel had avoided any open conflict.

This is one of the outstanding characteristics of the dispute. All the actors involved did their utmost to prevent any open break. Armando and Atanasia, the persons most directly involved in the land (they are the owners), avoided any direct clash and instead delegated discussion to their mates. Miguel and Genoveva in their discussions always made known their opinions in very subtle ways, as if they were concerned not to create a grave and open conflict.

When they wanted to vent their hostility toward one another, they always resorted to talking to another person not involved in the dispute. When Atanasia spoke about Armando's failure to pay the rent of her plot for some time and insinuated that perhaps Armando's dealings with his brothers' land were not so clean after all, she was speaking to neutral observers, her cousins, and Atanasia knew from experience their desire to stay as neutral as possible. In point of fact, the place where

Atanasia and Miguel were staying came to be a sort of neutral ground. Here Atanasia and Miguel could plan and discuss without being molested. Even Genoveva and Armando came there sometimes on visits of a purely social character. They did not show any hostility or resentment toward these cousins at any moment.

Armando's behavior during the whole dispute seems to have been the most intelligent. His tactic was to wait for Atanasia's and Miguel's movements, and then he would say as little as possible and always in a very subtle way. When Atanasia and Miguel announced that a surveyor was coming up to measure the land and to determine the boundaries, they spoke with Armando about dividing the costs of the surveyor's services. His remark that he was going to sell a cow to pay his part of the costs was a piece of intended irony; he wanted to tell Miguel and Atanasia in an indirect way that he was not as rich as they thought. At the same time he was making a joke and that would help to avoid "explosions." In this way Armando was maintaining peace.

At the same time, Armando was very clear in his intentions of making it known that his dealings had been on the proper side and that there was nothing improper in his use of Atanasia's plot. He told us that his financial position was not as good as many thought, and that he was paying several loans he had been forced to take out. He also made the statement that Atanasia's plot was free from any financial charges and that he was not in the habit of making "dirty" deals, especially with land that was not his. He also reinforced this attempt at enchancing his reputation by stating that his father preferred his mother among all the "wives," and that he (Armando's father) visited his mother (Armando's mother) and his children daily.

Armando's tactics exasperated Miguel. Miguel wanted to discuss the matter with Armando, but Armando continually evaded him. Miguel's remark that Armando considered him a stranger could be interpreted as follows: Armando considered the dispute to be basically between him and Atanasia, the two people related by close consanguineal ties. They had inherited this land from their father, and it was up to them to clarify the matter. When Miguel tried to enter the "inner circle," he was rebuked by Armando, who evaded him and instead sent Genoveva, who was in a position similar to Miguel's. Miguel counterattacked by justifying his close interest in the dispute. He emphasized his role of husband, and stated that the husband should protect the interests of his wife.

Miguel's position was the most difficult of the four persons involved in the dispute. In a very real sense he was a stranger. Genoveva, Armando and Atanasia had been born and reared in Esperanza and had known each other for a very long time. Genoveva was second cousin to both Atanasia and Armando, her husband. This kinship tie with Atanasia could explain to a great degree the lack of hostility between them; Genoveva sometimes even praised Atanasia, and Atanasia reciprocated by trying to avoid any hostility. The consanguineal kinship tended to unite Armando, Genoveva and Atanasia *vis à vis* Miguel. Miguel had been born in a town quite far from Esperanza, and he met Atanasia in the United States. He had made one or two visits to Esperanza with Atanasia, but his contact with Armando and Genoveva had been minimal. In the light of all this, Miguel's remarks make sense. When he requested our services as mediators he was perhaps trying to gain some support. By having an impartial observer he was thinking that he could have a person who would not be hostile to him, and this could strengthen his bargaining position.

The additional piece of land that Miguel and Atanasia accused Armando of adding illegally to the land to prove that his house was not built on Atanasia's plot was the issue that precipitated the first open fight between Armando and Miguel. In a conversation in which Genoveva also intervened (but not Atanasia) Armando and Miguel reached the agreement that each one would pay for the cost of the survey that pertained to his plot; Armando would pay for the measurement of his and Atanasia for the measurement of hers.

But the moment the piece of land was mentioned, the dispute broke out in the open. Armando tried to include the piece as part of Atanasia's plot, but Miguel replied that it did not belong there. After a long and heated argument the issue remained unclear, each party reaffirming his position.

At this stage, Atanasia said to my wife that if things reached a certain level (and in spite of loving her brother very much) she was willing to use "dirty" language with him. She was here torn between backing Miguel's position and her love for her brother. That was why she stated that she was willing to use "dirty" language with him in spite of loving him as a brother. She was saying all this, not in the open, but as a way of relieving tension and hostility. The role of sister demanded that she should avoid conflict and show her love for her brother. That is why she made the conditional statement "if things reach a certain level."

In the next stage, we find Genoveva acting out her role while Armando remains in the background. It is noticeable that Genoveva's attack was concentrated fully on Miguel and made no mention of Atanasia. She attacked Miguel on several grounds. For one thing, she stated that Miguel was perhaps a little crazy and as such was not responsible for his acts. This argument is interesting, because if accepted, then here would be no reason for being angry with Miguel, and hostility towards him could be avoided. Genoveva brought forward this argument many times during the dispute and elaborated on it, trying to prove that something was wrong with Miguel's mind. The idea was to make him an object of pity and not of hostility.

Even in the middle of the most heated arguments, Genoveva tried to arrive at some sort of peaceful solution. Her constant, if contradictory, repetition of the theme that they had not built the house on Atanasia's plot and that if by mistake they had built there, it had happened in good faith, was an attempt to prevent an open break. At the same time that she accused Miguel of being angry because Armando was not offering to buy Atanasia's plot (as she thought Miguel expected), she was stating that they had built the house at a middle point so as to avoid the problem of later finding out that they had built on Atanasia's plot. The offer to sell Armando's house to them was basically along the same lines, demonstrating good will.

Another comment by Genoveva was very revealing. She complained that Miguel was following the "letter of the law" too strictly and that he was not behaving "as kin should." This is crucial, because it reveals that even though Miguel was to some extent a stranger, he was also the husband of Atanasia and so was an affine who should be treated as kin. She was suggesting that he should start behaving as if he were. Genoveva was also referring to Atanasia, but in an indirect and very subtle way. When she referred to the fact that one of her own brothers had been using a piece of land that belonged to her by right of inheritance and that she did not claim anything, Genoveva was suggesting that as the proper behavior between siblings and kin. If she behaved in a disinterested manner, why could not Atanasia and Miguel follow her example? When Armando made the comment, a few days later, that his siblings did not love him because he had made his money by hard work, his message was the same as Genoveva's, that relations between siblings (and also in a more general way, between kin) should be based on harmony and solidarity.

This same theme was later taken up by Atanasia. Her story of her half-brother Ceferino is an example of how a brother (and sibling) should not behave. He had behaved like a businessman and not like a brother. Instead of demonstrating love for his sister Margarita, he had treated her like a client. In the more general category of kin, he had mistreated his cousin Teodoro in a similar way. Atanasia was implying that Armando should not behave like Ceferino.

At this time Atanasia and Miguel had placed an advertisement in the newspapers announcing that Atanasia's plot was for rent or sale. The fact that neither she nor Miguel had told Armando about it could be interpreted as an act of hostility toward Armando and Genoveva, as Atanasia said that it was not Armando's business. But it can also be interpreted in another way. The sale or rent of the plot looks like a strategic retreat on the part of Atanasia and Miguel. If they wanted to sell or rent, it meant that they were not so attached to the plot. It takes time to sell or rent land in Esperanza, and this gave them a breathing space to search for a solution. The proposal to sell or rent also meant that they did not, after all, want to build a house on Atanasia's plot. They implied that they did not want to live near Armando and Genoveva and in this way were willing to *avoid* a dispute. The refusal to live near her brother had a dual meaning: it meant hostility but it also meant that she wanted to avoid (by physical distance) any dispute.

We found all the actors constantly trying to avoid any open breach. Even at the moments of more violent contact, both sides emphasized that harmony and solidarity should be maintained. The values of kinship (consanguineal and affinal) were showing their strength.

Another way in which Miguel and Atanasia tried to avoid an open conflict was by announcing plans to build a house on the other plot about which there was no dispute. Armando and Genoveva went along with these plans by stating that Armando was willing to sell them the plot he had near the one belonging to Atanasia so they could have more space. In this way attention was being diverted from the plot in dispute to the plots where no dispute would emerge.

It was at this time that Miguel made a mistake in terms of the norms prevailing in Esperanza. The family of squatters that was living on this second plot had been given permission by Armando to build a house there. Miguel demonstrated that he was completely ignorant of the manner in which these matters are handled in Esperanza. He and Atanasia wanted to tell this family that they should move from Atanasia's plot. The proper way in Esperanza is to tell somebody else that you want them to move; in this way, by an indirect chain of communication (in the same way that gossip operates), sooner or later somebody will tell them. When you are able to verify that they know it, then you can start another indirect approach. You start the rumor that you would like to talk to them; in less time than might be imagined, they will come to know this and will visit you. Miguel did not follow this procedure; instead, he went straight ahead and paid a visit to this family. He spoke to them directly about leaving. Later on, we heard disparaging comments by many people in Esperanza criticizing Miguel's action in very negative terms; most people thought that he had behaved without any consideration (*consideración*) toward this family. People who behave toward others without consideration are graded low in moral terms in

Esperanza, and Miguel was not aware of all this. Without knowing it, he had given Armando and Genoveva a few points in their favor, as Armando had never behaved in this way with squatters or with his family.

The selection of the surveyor was another matter that brought some difficulties. The role of the surveyor in this case came to be the role of judge. He was going to be the person who would decide who was right.

The first one was rejected because he asked too much for his services. The second was employed and was the one who actually made the survey.

At this point Atanasia announced her intention of making a trip to the United States, with the declared purpose of being near her married daughter when she gave birth to a child. This step can be interpreted in two ways: Atanasia's duty as a "good mother" was to be near her daughter and take care of her (a value perfectly understood in Esperanza) in this critical moment. It was also a way by which Atanasia expressed her desire to retreat and leave the rest of the "fight" to Miguel. She had so far avoided any active participation during the dispute, but now that it appeared that it was going to take still longer, the help needed by her daughter offered the necessary excuse. But she did not announce her trip openly, instead she told only a few people, mostly her cousins. She did not want to appear (especially to Genoveva) as if she were beating a retreat.

The incidents involving Armando, Miguel and Armando's son are worth examining in some detail. Miguel requests Armando's help to trace the landmarks. Armando resorts to his tactic of evasion. By saying that he is too busy, he is telling Miguel that he does not like the idea of the survey and that if Miguel wants to he can go ahead on his own. Here Armando is being hostile to his brother-in-law in a short quick manner. By evading and ignoring him, he has evaded a long confrontation that could lead to a severe breach.

When Miguel requested help from Armando's son, he got the same answer. Evidently Armando wanted to demonstrate that all the family was united in the issue. If the son helped the surveyor and Miguel, he would have shown some disagreement with his father (at least in the eyes of the people of Esperanza, who state that a son should do what the father does and should back him always). By doing exactly as his father did, they offered a united front. Miguel, by asking the son after Armando had refused, was (whether he knew it or not) attempting to violate this unity.

A few days after this incident, we find the theme of unity and harmony operating again. Atanasia commented that she was planning to pay a visit to Armando and Genoveva. She had not visited them for some days, and she wanted to make clear that in spite of the dispute harmonious relations should be maintained. A few days after Atanasia had said this, Genoveva made a social call on Atanasia and Miguel. She had the perfect excuse: she had killed a pig and wanted the help of Atanasia (who is an excellent cook) to prepare it for roasting. She also took advantage of inviting Miguel to accompany them. As the occasion was only a social one, the dispute was not mentioned. All enjoyed themselves and the harmony between the actors involved had been reinforced by Genoveva's and Armando's friendly gesture.

A few days later, Atanasia revealed in a very explicit way the value of siblingship and harmony. She declared that Armando was her preferred brother and that she would not like "to lose" him and that her next move would be to return to the United States.

The work of the surveyor and the final decision had not arrived before we left Esperanza. While we were still there, both sides claimed that the survey had been finished, and that the decision had favored them, but when we inquired from them no details were given, and the surveyor kept coming and checking.

While they were waiting for the surveyor's decision, the "battle" went on. We had ample proof of this in a visit we paid to Genoveva. She began by repeating the theme that they were on the right side of the dispute and by telling us that the surveyor had arrived at a decision in their favor, though she did not give further details. She then made the familiar comments about Miguel being out of his mind, but said that Atanasia was a noble person and a very efficient housewife. Genoveva said then that she did not like to engage in disputes over land, especially with kin. She seemed so certain of having won that she added that now Miguel could do as he pleased. Here Armando made one of his few comments by correcting Genoveva and stating: "He cannot do as he pleases, he can only take what they are entitled to."

They were here mixing two main themes: their desire to avoid a dispute and the fact (from their viewpoint) that they had always been in the right in the dispute. It seemed as if they were saying that all this could have been avoided from the start if Atanasia and Miguel had been more careful. The interesting thing here is the fact that Miguel was always the direct object of any hostility that Armando and Genoveva showed. It was as if Armando and Genoveva had diverted any hostility they felt toward Atanasia in the direction of Miguel. They had apparently defined Miguel as a "stranger" and "outsider." He did not "belong" to Esperanza; Atanasia, Genoveva and Armando "belonged," and this fact of common origin seems to have made a big difference. Genoveva avoided any negative comments about Atanasia, and Atanasia made few comments about Genoveva. Hostility was concentrated between Genoveva and Miguel, with Armando in the background.

Armando and Genoveva also showed some concern about "public opinion" in Esperanza. They were angry at Miguel because (according to them) he had spread false rumors about Esperanza, trying to demonstrate that Armando and Genoveva had behaved in an improper way in their land dealings. Armando and Genoveva are descendants and members of the old families of Esperanza, and they have to observe the norms of proper behavior if they want to maintain their prestige in the eyes of the community.

Genoveva then told us a little about inheritance patterns in Esperanza and about Armando's father, who had had children with each of his four "wives," and when he died, had provided an equal share of inheritance for each child, the customary and legal pattern in Esperanza (and Puerto Rico). It also shows to some extent a sense of parental responsibility on the part of their father.

The role of the elder brother as "father substitute" practiced in Esperanza appears here, when the older siblings Ceferino and Armando became the "tutors" of the inheritance of some of the children who were not yet of legal age. They were acting as protectors, a role usually performed by one's father.

The last stages of the dispute (up to the point where we were able to follow) can be summarized as follows: Atanasia made her trip to the United States, implying her desire to avoid conflict. The manner in which she avoided Genoveva and managed to say good-bye to her brother was a way of expressing her love for him while at the same time making it clear that some hostility emanated because of the dispute. Atanasia did not want an open break with her cousin Genoveva; but she was also an affine and they were enemies in this fight. Perhaps Genoveva understood Atanasia's tactics and give tacit support by keeping silent. It is very revealing indeed that Genoveva, in this last stage, praised Atanasia and added the comment that *perhaps* Miguel was also "good." We do not have the proper documentation, but the atmosphere during these days seemed one in which Miguel and Atanasia were making an "elegant retreat" (*retirada elegante*) with Armando and Genoveva feeling that they had won the case and allowing Miguel and Atanasia to retire from the "battlefield" without loss of face. Miguel remained in Esperanza for some months and after a few attempts to prove the correctness of his arguments left Esperanza and went to stay with some kin in San Juan, some 80 miles from Esperanza.

Theoretical Implications

The whole dispute has implications which transcend its peculiarities. It activates the kinship framework and shows the relationships between the system and economic factors such as property. The general principles of inheritance discussed in the chapter on kinship operate in this case. The principle of the equivalence of siblings in inheritance matters emerges clearly: Atanasia and Armando act as equals. But the process of migration, another regular feature of Esperanza, had created, accompanied by other factors, the line of stress. Atanasia did not stay in Esperanza, like many other *esperanzeños,* and had moved instead to the United States, to the city of New York. In the meantime, Armando established himself in Esperanza as a farmer. As such, he needed land. From the information we have from the case we can see him manipulating the principles of kinship structure to get control of more land. His manipulations show that he is aware of the formal relevance of the rules of kinship and its relation with inheritance. In almost all societies, kinship regulates to some extent the transmission of property. This regulatory function assumes, in our case, the level of a categorical imperative; it is never questioned. The case thus demonstrates that kinship is a living and active force, and that the rules discussed in the chapter on kinship are not the creature of the anthropologist's imagination.

This case also shows in a broad manner the ways in which migration has altered or modified some of the aspects of social organization. The first thing is that migration "opens up" the community and extends or distributes people over a wider territory. The convergence of kinship and some degree of territoriality is broken. The case of Atanasia (living in the United States) and Armando (living in Esperanza) demonstrates this in a very clear manner. In their childhood and youth they lived in Esperanza, as did Genoveva, and there was some kind of interaction over a regular period. Later they dispersed. In this respect, one is reminded of the modifications in the developmental cycle of the family brought about by migration.

The Relationship Between Migration and Territoriality Demonstrated by This Case Study

The movement out of the community is not simply that. People do not just disappear forever. The outward movement of human beings does not cut them off completely from their community of origin. People keep an interest in their communities: they write, return for short visits, or return in their later years to spend the rest of their lives in the land of their birth (Hernández Alvarez 1967).

The strength of territoriality is revealed by the fact that the outward movement can be converted into what Hernández Alvarez calls a "return movement." This has in fact been taking place in Puerto Rico for the last two or three years. More Puerto Ricans have been returning to the island than moving to the mainland according to the "Junta de Planificación de Puerto Rico" (1970).

A large part of the people who return to Puerto Rico are almost middle-aged or older. This indicates that, if married, they are in the middle or last stages of their developmental cycle, as individuals and as members of a family. Hernández Alvarez comments on this and makes the interesting point, based on careful research, that the inhabitants of the recent private housing projects in the metropolitan area in San Juan, are in great part returnees. They are basically older couples with no children, as their offspring have already married and settled on their own. Speaking about these groups, Hernández states:

The median age figures were fairly consistent between the sexes in each residential category. Both males and females living in urban areas were older than migrants settling in rural farm and nonfarm areas. Within urban categories, migrants living in metropolitan areas were older than those residing in smaller cities; the oldest groups were residents of middle and upper middle-class suburbs in San Juan (1967:50).

There is certainly a parallel trend here with the case under discussion. Atanasia and her husband Miguel are in the last stages as members of a family unit. All their children are married and living in the United States. When they started thinking about Puerto Rico and their return they considered settling in Esperanza, among other places. This was the beginning of the conflict. They needed a piece of land where they could build a house, and the land inherited from Atanasia's father could well be this piece of land. The lot was situated near the road, an excellent place for building a house. The condition of being in the last stages of the family cycle plus the need of land was, then, the precipitating factor. The conflict between Atanasia and Armando can then be seen as a variant on the process of "return migration" that is taking place in the Puerto Rican society, and we may add, in other societies as well (see Lopreato 1967 on Italian society). Instead of viewing the migrating process as a thing in itself, it is viewed here against a more general background and closely related both to the individual's life and to the family developmental cycle.

The conflict also serves to generalize on some trends that are developing in many societies and which have been called or described by many labels, like "modernization," "urbanization" and so forth. Returnees from metropolitan countries, as the work of Hernández Alvarez demonstrates for Puerto Rico, exhibit a system of values which have become different from what we would call the traditional one. When they migrated originally they came from an agricultural society in which they had a certain relationship with the land and related activities. They, in the metropolis, got accustomed to living in an urban setting and practicing an urban occupation. Our contention is that the attachment to traditional values acquires a "romantic connotation." People have been "urbanized" but they still practice the "ritual of tradition." They want to return to the fatherland, but the relationship with the place of origin has been altered. They do not want to be farmers, they want to recapture the positive values of an agricultural society, but to practice the values of an urbanized one. The essence of the change can be thus stated: the people who still practice the values of an agricultural society have a productive relation with the land; it is an active relationship. Land is seen as a vital productive factor. People do not only live *on* the land; they live *from* the land. Return migrants do not appear to have this kind of attitude or relationship. They want to live *on* the land, but do not approach it as a productive factor. Their relationship is strictly passive, receptive. The fact that most of the return migrants settle in the new Puerto Rican suburbs adds force to our argument. The contrast between Armando, a farmer, and the return migrants fits well within a broad framework that is not limited to Esperanza. It is part of a broader process taking place in societies undergoing radical transformations (Hunter 1969). Migrations bring in new values and, these, confronted with the old ones, create or contribute to the stress. We see three main factors involved: kinship, migration and land. In the past, in the traditional society, the second factor was missing. The relation between kinship and land was of another nature.

Typical topography of a farm, showing the farmer's house, a shed, and the division of the different areas.

CHAPTER 10

Compadrazgo

The system of relationships known as *compadrazo* is one of the main mechanisms that regulate interhousehold relations in Esperanza, together with other factors such as kinship and neighborhood. *Compadrazgo* involves a series of actors. Ideally these should include two married couples, a child, a priest and God. This is not an absolute requirement, but is preferred. One of the couples are the parents of the child. They wish to have their child baptized, but the church requires two godparents (*padrinos*) of opposite sex, to be present and to take the main part during the ceremony. The *padrinos* also have to pay the church fee and, according to the church, must act as moral and religious supervisors of the child for the rest of his or her life. It is the duty of the child's parents to find persons to act as godparents.

These are the formal aspects of establishing the relationship, and only after the baptism is finished is the relationship fully established. The parents of the child and the godparents are now *compadres*. The peasants understand the formal aspects of the relationship, and they go through the ritual and observe all the rules. But the original religious meaning of the ritual and of the relationship has been reinterpreted, a whole new set of meanings and functions has been added, and certain parts of the relationship have been established at the expense of others.

According to informants and based on our knowledge of Esperanza, *compadrazgo* is both an intraclass and interclass affair. Inquiries made in forty-seven households revealed that out of 132 *compadrazgo* relationships, 69 were between persons of the same class and 63 were between persons of a different class. The peasants emphasize that it is the duty of the child's father to find the godparents (*padrinos*). Informants state that potential godparents must have (ideally) the following character traits: respect, humility, responsibility. To insure that these virtues are present, the persons selected must have been known by the child's parents for many years. The father goes to them, talks with them and asks them to be the godparents. They must reach some kind of agreement as to when the ceremony can be held, as it requires some financial resources on the part of the child's parents. It is they who pay for everything that is bought for the party that follows the ceremony. The church fee is paid for by the godparents.

Of all the relationships that are established at baptism, that between *compadres* (cofathers) is the most important and relevant (cf. Mintz and Wolf 1950). The one established between comothers (*comadres*) recedes into the background, and so does that of godparent and godchild. We do not imply that they fade and disappear, but only that compared with the one established between *compadres* their relevance or the social system is minimal.

The way in which people in Esperanza characterize the relation between *compadres* is the starting point for an understanding of it. If one inquires into the rights and duties of *compadres,* the same main themes appear again and again. The words "respect," "help," "love" and similar ones are the stereotyped answers that are repeatedly heard.

There is an emphasis on unity, solidarity, cooperation, help, in all the areas of social intercourse. Once two people are *compadres,* they are bound reciprocally by the system in this way. If a *compadre* is sick, he must be visited by his other *compadres,* and usually the *compadre* when he arrives at the place, formally states that the purpose of the visit is "to see if he can be of any help" (*si puede ayudar*). If something happens to other members of the family, it is also the duty of the *compadre,* if he comes to know about it, to offer his help. If somebody in the family dies, it is expected that *compadres* will be among the first to arrive and start helping. If you need someone to help you on the farm, at least for a short time, you ask a *compadre* to help you, because you know that it is difficult for him to refuse. If there is a fight, and you see a *compadre* in there "making trouble," it is your duty to dissuade him and take him home. If in the course of this he insults and strikes you, you cannot hit him back because he is your *compadre.* *Compadres* should help each other in every possible way; this is the general norm. Competition and conflict are barred in the *compadrazgo* relationship, and to introduce such elements would be to offend against the essential character of the institution. This general pattern of *compadrazgo* in Latin America has also been observed by Mintz and Wolf (1950) and by Willems (1962) among the Portuguese peasantry.

The initiation of the relationship between two men (or women in cases of comothers) is signified by the change that occurs in the terms of address they use between them. From then on they have to address each other by the term *usted* that implies respect and harmony in their relations. The use of the first name alone is forbidden, and they have to state first the relationship (*compadre*) and the name, with the use of *usted*. The godchild, every time that he or she sees the godparents, must ask for their blessing, which goes like this: the child says to the godparent, "Your blessing, my godparents" (*Bendición, padrino*), and the godparent answers, "May God bless you" (*Que Dios te bendiga*). Willems (1962) reports the same pattern in Portugal.

Theoretically, almost anybody can be a *compadre,* but the rules imposed limit the number of candidates. There is the also implicit requirement that he has to be an adult, as he must be able to act as moral guardian (at least in theory) and deputy father (though that seldom happens) of his godchild. With the identification made in Esperanza between adulthood and marriage, it is not surprising that most godparents are married.

Close kin can become *compadres,* but they should be of the same generation, as *compadrazgo* implies equality between the parties. It ideally excludes parents and children, uncles and aunts (if age and marital status levels them, they can and *sometimes* do become *compadres* with nephews and nieces) and grandparents, but it permits siblings to become *compadres* (and *comadres*) to one another.

The Function of Compadrazgo

Compadrazgo is one of the mechanisms that establish and regulate relations between households in Esperanza. The establishment of the relationship is channeled mainly through the ritual of baptism. We stated before that the relationship between *compadres* (cofathers) is the most relevant and important relationship that comes out of baptism, that of godparent-godchild having been relegated to a mere mutual acknowledgment when they meet. The relationship between *comadres* has not receded so much into the background as that between *padrinos* and *ahijados* (godparents and godchildren); but compared to relationships between cofathers, its everyday relevance is small.

There is a series of activities that are channeled through the framework of *compadrazgo,* and which are seen as the purpose *compadrazgo* is expected to perform. We asked a sample of peasants to enumerate the purposes and goals of *compadrazgo*. It was relatively easy for them to do this. They mentioned the religious aspect (acting as godparent of child), the moral aspect (the regulating of behavior), and the quasi-economic aspect (helping *compadres* and *compadres'* families). *Compadrazgo* thus covers a wide area in the field of social intercourse.

Of all these goals, the quasi-economic and moral aspects are the most important. This was emphasized by all our informants and corresponds closely to our own observation of the institution. These two areas of the relationship are also permeated by a tone of cooperation and harmony. Not even the fact that *compadres* can and do borrow money from each other can obliterate this. If one *compadre* does not repay a debt to another one, mechanisms are available that exert pressure in an indirect way. *Compadres* are forbidden to clash one with the other directly, so there is no direct confrontation on the issue. Perhaps one of the women of the house would mention it during a visit to the other household, or somebody else might do so. It is in this way that the debt might in due course be repaid. Another mechanism that eliminates conflict is used by most of the people who, when lending money, tell their *compadres,* "Pay that back when you can." This removes all direct and immediate financial obligation, and if he has not paid it back after a long time it is understood that he has lacked the means to do so. Alternately, if a man lends money to a *compadre* who fails to repay it for a long time, and the lender wants his money back, his solution is to borrow money from his debtor and in this way he recovers the debt owed to him without creating any conflict. Pitt Rivers, in his account of *compadrazgo* in Spain, states, "For this reason the *compadre* is the person *par excellence* from whom to borrow money. He cannot refuse to lend, nor can he refuse to pay" (1958:430). This does not apply with the same strength in Esperanza. People seem to hesitate to borrow money from their *compadres,* saying, "Money can bring disputes."

This theme of harmony and cooperation is indeed the whole basis of the system: "With kin you can fight because they are kin, with *compadres* you cannot fight because they are *compadres*" is what people say when trying to define *compadrazgo*. *Compadres* are bound by a whole system of social control based on respect and consideration, and there is even a semblance of avoidance relationships. They should not make "brutal" jokes nor engage in heavy drinking together, as there is the chance that they may get drunk and violate the norms by fighting and insulting one another.

Compadrazgo, then, has the overall objective of promoting harmonious social intercourse and quasi-economic cooperation between the households concerned. Ties between households are constantly increased each time a child is baptized.

Compadrazgo, Kinship and Neighbors

Compadrazgo tends to fuse with kinship (consanguineal and affinal) and neighborhood to create a more complex system for regulating and promoting relationships at the interhousehold level. Willems (1962) found a similar situation among peasant families in Portugal.

We asked the heads of fifty households to name four *compadres* they had within the *barrio* limits. After they had named them, we asked how many of them were relatives. Then we asked how many of the four *compadres* were close neighbors (Table 10.1). Out of a total of 187 such relationships, 130 were with neighbors and, more important, *close* neighbors. So it can be stated that close neighbors have a marked tendency to become *compadres,* and to become bound by the rules of the system. The same tends to happen with kinship, but to a lesser extent. Out of 187 *compadrazgo* relationships, 53 were with kin, either consanguineal or affinal. Table 10.2 describes these in some detail.

Table 10.1—Relationship Between *Compadrazgo*
and Neighborhood

Number of *compadres* — 187

Compadres who were kin — 53

Compadres who were close
neighbors but not kin — 130

Compadres about whom
above information was
not available   — 4

Table 10.4 confirms that *compadrazgo* is a relationship that implies a degree of equality between the parties. Informants and all people of whom we inquired always stated that only people of adult status could become *compadres*. They also stated that they became *compadres* with their kin to respect each other more. Most of the kin are of the same generation as the informant: brothers, sisters and cousins. Only a handful of *compadrazgo* relationships are with members of older generations, and then it is with the uncles and aunts. *Compadrazgo* ties seem to be forbidden between members of the same elementary family while under the same roof and with the status of minors. It is only when siblings reach adulthood through marriage and establish independent households that *compadrazgo* affiliations begin to be established. The affinal relatives, to give more force to our argument, are of the same generation, most of them being brothers-in-law.

The three factors then fuse to some extent. Neighbors tend to be

Table 10.2—Categories of Kin (Consanguineal and Affinal)
with Whom There Existed *Compadrazgo* Relationships

Category	Number of Relationships	
Consanguineal Kin		
Father	0	
Mother	0	
Brother	16	
Sister	2*	
Grandparents	0	
Uncles and Aunts	3	
Cousins	10	
Son	0	
Daughter	0	
Nephew	1	
Niece	0	
	32	Total
Affinal Kin		
Categories unspecified	21	
	53	Grand Total

*The husbands of these two sisters were also named as *compadres.* They are included under "affinal kin."

compadres. Kin also tend to be *compadres.* Sometimes kin are both neighbors and *compadres.* The operation of all these factors gradually interrelates some households with others, though, *not all* households are related to *all* of the others. But the framework exists and influences behavior with the main themes of cooperation, respect and harmony. The ideal conception of a good *compadre* is very similar to the ideal of a good neighbor and a good sibling: respectful, humble, cooperative and considerate. When these characteristics merge, relations between households become stronger.

CHAPTER 11

Marriage

In Esperanza we find three types of unions, two of which we can classify as legal. There is religious marriage (mainly Catholic) and civil marriage. Both types have legal sanction. There is also consensual union, which does not have legal sanction, but neither does it entail full moral condemnation.

Civil Marriage

Civil marriage is defined in Esperanza as marriage in "front of the judge," as marriages of this type are officially performed by a judge in the town of Arecibo. Numerically speaking, it is practiced by only a minority. In a survey of 133 married people, only 10 had been married by the judge, 115 by the Catholic priest and 8 were living in consensual unions.

People who intend to have a civil marriage follow the customary patterns of courtship, the wedding and then the establishment of the independent household, just as in the other form of marriage. The man first makes his intentions known to the girl of his choice. This could happen in a direct way (at a vigil, for example) or in an indirect one (through a letter). If the girl answers in the affirmative, and if he is serious, he will talk with the girl's father to see if he has any chance of being approved. It is here that the father's role becomes the crucial one. He can end negotiations by saying no, as he is the one who has the last word in relation to this issue. This is usually avoided because the father and the boy will explore the possibilities in advance through indirect channels, so that when a boy goes to talk with a girl's father he already knows that the mission will succeed. This prevents embarrassment for all the parties involved.

After getting the father's approval, the boy is allowed to visit the girl on certain fixed days in her home, and an adult must be present there. This is not only the ideal pattern but the actual practice, as we were able to corroborate by direct observation. Most couples follow the rules most of the time. The courtship period is not a long one, usually a year or less.

The day of the wedding is agreed upon, and on the appointed date they go to Arecibo, where the judge will marry them.

After the marriage there is a reception at the girl's parents' house, where the kin of both sides, *compadres,* neighbors and guests join to celebrate. The couple change clothes and join the party. All receptions are held at night, and after the party is almost finished, the newlyweds leave in a car that takes them to a hotel in Arecibo, where they spend their honeymoon. In the meantime, the party goes on, but only then is there dancing.

The proceedings (wedding and reception) are simple compared with Catholic marriage, but the role of the different actors is basically the same.

Catholic Marriage

Catholic marriage is the most common form in Esperanza, and people refer to it as "marriage by the church." It must be remembered that in our survey 115 out of 133 unions were Catholic marriages. Courtship follows the same lines as described for civil marriage; but the wedding and the party which follows are more elaborate. Our observation of one wedding began in the house of the bride's father around seven-thirty in the evening. The girl was being dressed by the women of the house (her mother and sisters) and in front of the house there were six or seven cars that would carry the girl and many of the guests to the church. The church was outside the boundaries of Esperanza, as no weddings are celebrated regularly in Esperanza, where there is no resident priest. Only at mass can people be wed in Esperanza's church. At last the bride was ready and she entered one of the cars that was waiting for her. She was dressed in white with a veil over the head and face. The cars then headed towards the church in a procession in which the bride's car was the last. A small girl of around seven, dressed as a bridesmaid, was with the bride.

The bridegroom was absent, for it is only in church that they may meet before the ceremony. When the procession reached the church, we noticed that the majority of those present were women. Among those present were the bridegroom's parents, while the bride's parents were absent. The bridegroom was late, causing the girl to wait for him outside the church. The ceremony was conducted by a priest, and followed the regular pattern of the church. It lasted only a few minutes, and then the bridegroom and the bride entered their car, which, on the return trip, went first in the procession. All the cars sounded their horns and made as much noise as they could. They went straight to the house of the girl's parents, where they and some guests who had not gone to church were waiting. The house was ready for the party.

There was a moment of temporary confusion, as the newlyweds went into the house and the other people got out of the cars and followed them. A few minutes later the couple started giving away remembrance figures, a small ribbon with the names of the couple and small plastic figures; the bridegroom carried the box with the figures while the bride pinned them on the guests. At the same time the bride's parents started serving refreshments. The men were served alcoholic beverages, while the women and children got only nonalcoholic drinks and ice cream with sandwiches.

A few moments later the couple was called for the toast between those present and the couple, wishing them good luck. At the same time some photographs were taken, especially of certain groups which the couple wanted to remember. These included one in which both sets of parents and the couple appeared in front of the wedding cake.

After the pictures were taken, the cake was cut by the newlyweds and was distributed among the guests. The occasion had a feminine air about it, and the impression of the observer was that the women were enjoying the whole event more than the men, who were more restrained in their behavior. Kin on both sides were present, and also many *compadres* and neighbors of the girl's and boy's parents. This is a general observation, as we could not make a count. Among them we remember cousins, brothers and some uncles and aunts on both sides.

After the reception was finished, the guests moved to a nearby store where they danced until about four o'clock in the morning. This store had a small dance hall with a juke box which provided the music. All the guests, except some elderly people, went to the dance. Those that remained behind were served dinner. Among these were both the girl's and the boy's parents. The couple went to the dance (unlike civil marriage) where they remained for about three hours and then went to a hotel in Arecibo.

As can be inferred from this abbreviated picture of the proceedings, it takes some time and financial resources to celebrate a Catholic wedding in proper fashion. The costs of the party are borne by the bride's parents, the father especially, who always wants "to throw the house out of the window" (*tirar la casa por la ventana*). By this is meant that the wedding should be as expensive as they can afford. For the wedding and party described above, the father, a wage laborer with a relatively low income, spent around $200 in all, quite a large amount of money for him. This amount is probably about twice his monthly income.

Apart from the bridal couple, the most important personalities in the proceedings are the parents, both the girl's and the boy's. But the most hard pressed of them all is the girl's father. It is his duty to check on everything, and we could see that he was feeling the pressure even two or three days before the wedding. He is formally responsible for everything and is not expected to rest until his daughter has been married properly. Before the couple entered the church, there were a few minutes of tension when the boy did not arrive on time, and we could hear some of the girl's relatives remarking that they were afraid that he might have run away and the girl would be left empty handed. This situation is avoided at all costs by parents, as it brings great shame to the family of the girl. The father is supposed to see that everything ends well. From then on, responsibility for her care and support is transferred to the husband, even if he does not establish an independent household right away.

There seem to be two types of parties after the wedding. One type could be classified as modern and the other as traditional. We did not see both types, but informants repeated these differences constantly. We missed the traditional party. In both, the structural arrangements and the main roles are the same, but certain items have been altered. For the modern party there is no "live" music, while the traditional includes a group of musicians. In the modern type the dance is held after the party has finished, while in the traditional the dance and the party are together in the same place. The food and refreshments also differ. In the modern, there are sandwiches, ice cream, bottled drinks; in the traditional, roast pork (prepared at home) and illegal rum. The main difference is that for the modern party the food is bought in a store, while according to tradition the food is prepared at home. The modern party seems to be more frequent among families that live near the main road and where electricity is available, and the traditional appears to be more prevalent among the most isolated families, those who live miles from the road and do not have electricity in their homes.

Consensual Unions

This is the third type of union found in Esperanza, although it is not considered a true marriage. In our sample it is the least practiced of all, only eight persons living under this arrangement. As a regular pattern it does not involve either courtship or any ceremony; the persons involved only move to live under the same roof. The practice of elopement is closely related to this type of mating, and we will discuss the implications shortly.

Marriage and the Household Group

Legal marriage (civil and religious) in Esperanza as defined by custom and law clearly delimits the roles and the rights and duties between the parties in the internal structure of the household. As defined by the civil code in *Leyes de Puerto Rico Anotadas* (1955), the husband's role is one of provider (mainly) and in everything that concerns the family as a unit, he has authority. This corresponds very closely with the actual and ideal image prevalent and operating in Esperanza. Thus the role differentiation described in detail in the previous chapters and the legal framework correlate directly.

The religious factor is also relevant. Catholic marriage, the normal form in Esperanza, also sanctions this type of role structure. The man is the head of the house, and his wife (and children) should obey him. The wife should be a good wife and mother. This is the image of family structure that the church upholds, and it is very much the same as that which actually exists. What custom and law sanction and approve, the church also sanctions and approves.

Thus the relations between spouses are clearly defined. The man knows that he must support his wife and children, that he is their ultimate moral guardian. He can be sued in court if he fails. The wife knows that she must take care of all the internal issues of the household, that she is responsible to her husband, and that he has not only the ultimate authority in the household but also the duty to support her and the children.

This clear definition of the relations between the parties in marriage can be seen even in consensual unions. This type of union has all the characteristics of legal marriage, except legal and religious approval. It would be more correct to say that it is tolerated because the expectation is that they will marry as soon as they can, as most of the cases have done in the past, according to our informants. Consensual union involves coresidence and the rights and duties between "husband" and "wife" are recognized and practiced in everyday life. The children are registered and recognized by the father and carry his surname. Persons who start a consensual union in due time will marry "by the judge," that is, will have a civil marriage. In the meantime, the children are usually registered and recognized by the father, though there are some men who wait until they get married, and the "wife" will be known by the surname of the "husband" as in marriage. There is no open condemnation of these unions, only a mild disapproval. People emphasize that the husband and wife are good or bad in terms of what is generally understood by that, regardless of the type of marriage. If the parties perform their roles properly, public opinion is satisfied.

This does not in any way mean that consensual unions are thought to be on a par with marriage. A couple does not feel ashamed of living in a consensual union, and we did not observe signs of anxiety in people living under this arrangement. Women especially want to legalize the union, and they say they feel less secure than if married legally, but there is no urgency in what they say. The strong sense of paternity and the practice of coresidence appear to offer adequate security, and this is supported by the moral climate of the whole community, of which the husband is well aware. The general impression one gets is that the same norms that are binding in marriage are binding here, with less force, perhaps, but still effective.

Elopement is a frequent cause of consensual unions. The main reason given for it in Esperanza is conflict between the boy and the girl's father. The way to overcome the father's authority and force him to yield is to present him with the fact already accomplished. It is usual in cases like this for the father to display anger for a few days, after which he will think it over and, in most of the cases, concede victory to the couple and reconciliation will follow. The authority of the father continues in such cases. The couple will establish a household in Esperanza, and the father continues, by inspection, to insure that the couple live together. The expectation is that in due course they will be married, either by the judge or by the priest. The former is simpler, private and cheaper.

Marriage on the Barrio Level

Marriage is indeed a difficult factor to take as an index of social differentiation in Esperanza. The majority of people practice legal marriage, but through the church. Civil marriage is still practiced only by a minority, although perhaps in a given year more people will marry in that way due to generally adverse economic conditions.

But in general, the type of marriage in itself is not an index of social differentiation. Catholic marriage is not associated in Esperanza with the upper class, although the expectation is that people in the upper levels will always marry in church. The expectation among the lower classes (in terms of income, land and occupation) is that they, too, will marry in church although the pressure to abide by the rules is less. A rich person living in consensual union would feel more uncomfortable than a poor one in Esperanza.

In a very broad sense, consensual unions are associated with the lower class, but the fact is that the great majority of the lower class marries in church. The association is not really related to social class as such, but with the placing of different types of marriage and unions on a scale of values. Catholic marriage is the legitimate, and for many, the only true marriage (following Catholic principles). Some persons so married consider anyone married by the judge as not truly married, but they are a minority and have to recognize civil marriage in a *de facto* way. On the same scale, civil marriage tends to be recognized as a secondary form of marriage, with a lower rating than the Catholic one. Some people say: "At least they are married by the judge" when describing this type and comparing it with Catholic marriage, referring to the bottom of the scale, consensual union, which they consider only a quasi-marriage. This is brought out when one asks informants: "People who live in consensual union, are they married?" The regular answer is no. But if one pursues this question in more detail and inquires if this type of union is just a "come and go" affair they state that it is not the case, that these unions "are almost like marriages." In favor of this, they quote the stability and responsibility of the couple.

The three types thus presented on a scale are not then directly related to social class. To try to differentiate social groupings on this basis in Esperanza would be futile.

Choosing a Partner in Esperanza

In any society where people have some choice in the selection of their conjugal partners, there are certain factors that influence the decisions taken by the personalities involved. In Esperanza factors like social class, kinship and residence are significant.

There is relative freedom in the choice of the marriage partner, and nothing like family-arranged marriages is found. But there are certain factors that limit or influence the decision of the parties. Among these is social class. Social class in Esperanza, as defined by criteria such as income and property (mainly land) and prestige, influence one's choice of a partner. A member of one of the "best" families cannot marry below his class. Even if he tried, it would be very difficult indeed, and he would be courting trouble with his parents. This occurs in spite of the egalitarian tendencies present in the area of social intercourse, which tend to mislead the superficial observer.

The same tendency is found in the rest of Esperanza. Couples who marry generally come from families that "match" in income and other criteria. This unwritten rule is well known and it is followed most of the time. This narrows down the pool of available potential partners and is thus a limiting factor.

Kinship is another relevant factor. We refer here to the range of marriage prohibitions, which in Esperanza is very narrow if compared with other societies. Marriage between first cousins is prohibited; second cousins are eligible. We made some inquiries to try to find out how often marriage between kin occurs. Of the forty-nine couples questioned, only two of the nine having kinship connections are cases of first cousin marriage. The remaining seven married second cousins and distant relatives. This shows that cousin marriage from second cousin outwards is practiced with some frequency. Although formally people frown upon cousin marriage ("it may produce abnormal children," and so forth), in actuality they practice it. This practice widens the available pool of marriage partners and also shows in an indirect way how the independent household, the emphasis on close family relatives (father, mother, brother, sister, uncle, aunt and grandparents), and the prohibition of marriage up to the first cousin level form part of the same structure.

Residence is also among the conditions which affect the choice of the marriage partner. Physical proximity tends to associate people and to increase the chance of betrothals. This seems to be the rule in Esperanza as shown in Tables 11.1 and 11.2 Table 11.1 provides some data on the influence of residence. It suggests that anyone born in Esperanza has something like a fifty-fifty chance of marrying a person from Esperanza.

The significance of residence for the selection of marriage partners is even clearer in Table 11.2. The proportion of people reared in Esperanza and married to persons also reared there is greater than the proportion of people born there and married to persons born there.

People from Esperanza tend to marry within Esperanza, but within certain limits, some people marry outside the *barrio*. Esperanza is not a closed society, and the *barrio's* inhabitants interact with the town people and inhabitants of neighboring *barrios*. It is probable, however, that in the past the incidence of marriage within the *barrio* was greater due to the lack of roads and communication in general, which tended to restrict the physical mobility and consequently the amount of social

Table 11.1—Relation Between Place of Birth and
Marriage in Esperanza

Males

Husbands born in Esperanza	24
Husbands born outside Esperanza	25
Husbands born in Esperanza and married to wives born in Esperanza	14 out of 24 (same couples as above)

Females

Wives born in Esperanza	26
Wives born outside Esperanza	23
Wives born in Esperanza and married to husbands born in Esperanza	14 out of 26 (same couples as above)

Table 11.2—Relation Between Place Where Person was
Reared and Marriage Partner

Males

Husbands reared in Esperanza	34
Husbands reared outside Esperanza	15
Husbands reared in Esperanza and married to wives reared in Esperanza	26 out of 34 (same couples as above)

Females

Wives reared in Esperanza	32
Wives reared outside Esperanza	17
Wives reared in Esperanza and married to husbands reared in Esperanza	26 out of 32 (same couples as above)

intercourse outside the *barrio*. In a small sample of fifty (all classes), we found that 60 percent of the household heads under thirty-nine years old had married within Esperanza and 51 percent over thirty-nine had married within Esperanza. The sample is too small to allow for significant deductions but it does suggest a high degree of constancy of marriage within the *barrio*.

This pattern of marriage within the *barrio* is certainly affected by factors such as class. Informants tell us that the rich people now tend to look *outside* Esperanza for the selection of their marriage partners. What this means is that the percentage of marriage within the *barrio* is reduced by upper class marriage outside the *barrio* due to the limited choice available to them in Esperanza.

Partial view of the barrio cemetery.

CHAPTER 12

Religious Beliefs and Practices

Puerto Rico is by tradition a Catholic country and Esperanza is primarily a Catholic community. But its actual religious practices and beliefs include many elements that are at least partially condemned by the church as an island-wide institution as not being strictly Catholic. Esperanza's inhabitants, however, do not make any formal distinction in their lives between official Catholic practices and rituals and practices of an "extraofficial" character. For them, both are part of the same religion: Catholicism. They are interrelated with certain aspects of the social system, and also with family structure. For these practices do not operate in isolation: indeed, many of them take it for granted that the family is the main channel through which they do operate.

There are also certain basic themes that tend to be found in all these rituals and practices. They can be viewed as constituting the Catholic religion of Esperanza as interpreted and perceived by its inhabitants.

Vigils

Vigils perhaps form the main category of religious ritual and represent the most frequent way of expressing certain religious beliefs. They can be broadly divided into two groups: those of happiness (*de alegría*) and those of death (*de muerto*), that is, wakes. We shall discuss them in that order, beginning with a description of a vigil, a time of happiness, and the proceedings related to it, excerpted directly from our field notes:

"We were told by Pepín that Nico is planning a vigil, but that it was not yet definite. We went into Tristán's store, and he told us that was true because Nico had told him. Nico had also bought certain things in the store for the vigil, among them: beer, sweet drinks and candles. The vigil is in honor of the Virgin Mary, whose day it is tomorrow. We asked Tristán if Nico celebrated this vigil every year and he answered no, at least not to his knowledge. Nico is not at home, because he is at a funeral in town.

"In the afternoon, while we were again in Tristán's store, somebody mentioned that there were going to be many vigils during the night in addition to Nico's. Tano said that in David's house they were going to celebrate one (it is done every year, as in the house of Tribilín) that was 'better' (*quedaba mejor*) than the one celebrated by Nico. We were a little doubtful about which one to attend, but decided finally to attend the one arranged by David. Tano and Tiburcio said they also were going to David's vigil, and we set off for Tano's home in his car. While we were there, David came by in his small truck, in which we went on to his house. It seemed as though it was going to be a rainy night, but later the weather improved."

We reached David's house, but the vigil had not begun. There were about twenty people, who were talking among themselves, both inside and outside the house.

"The program of this 'devotion' is more or less standardized. There are two fundamental phases: the sacred and the secular. In the sacred, two couples of opposite sex sit down, one behind the other, in front of an altar which is adorned with flowers in an inverted U arrangement and with figures and drawings of the relevant saint, the Virgin in this case. The man in front leads the rosary, which is sung. Nobody else takes a direct part, except when they make the sign of the cross at the beginning and the end of the rosary. Three rosaries are sung during the whole night by different couples taking part each time.

"After the rosary is finished, the secular phase begins. People start chatting, and the household head or an adult serves alcoholic beverages to the men, while the women and children have soft drinks. In the early morning hours, coffee, cheese and crackers are served to everyone. If there are musicians available, they start playing and the festive mood continues for at least two hours.

"In David's house, an uncle of his was present. This uncle later took an active part in the rosary as one of the *rezadores* (those who pray). When this uncle came, David embraced him and asked for and received his blessing. The uncle then went inside where he was also welcomed by David's wife and other people.

"In the patio (front and backyard), not one woman was present, as all were inside the house, but it was full of men of all ages.

"The first rosary started around nine, with about thirty people present, and finished around 10:15 p.m. During the prayers no refreshments or drinks were served. There was no special attitude of solemnity and, although silence should be maintained during the prayers, some people went on talking in a low voice. Nobody asked them to be quiet, unless they made too much noise.

"The men in the patio talked constantly, the main themes being: dead persons, jokes, farm work.

"When the first rosary ended, some musicians appeared, among them Cipriano and Leandro who played the *cuatro* (a guitar-like instrument) and the guitar. They placed themselves at the front door and sang some *aguinaldos* (carols) to the Virgin. The singers were Cipriano, Tiburcio and someone else whose name we do not remember. After they had finished, David (the household head) invited them to enter the house, where they continued their playing. I remember a small fragment of one song which said: 'That is why I sing to you . . . with much happiness . . . O, Virgin.' Alcohol was served, controlled by David and Segismundo, who served everybody in the same glass, and then hid the bottle.

"We talked for a while with Menelao, who told me that in Esperanza they spend almost fifteen days in a row (during July, the month dedicated to the Virgin on the Catholic calendar of Puerto Rico) celebrating vigils in honor of the Virgin, and he himself is going to celebrate one next Friday.

"During this secular part, an old *cuatro* player called Santana turned up unexpectedly. He now lives in Arecibo but used to live in Esperanza. All the other musicians stopped playing and everybody's attention was focused on Santana, who started immediately to play a *cuatro* that Cipriano lent him. Santana is about seventy years old, and people regard him as a perfect "bohemian" (*bohemio,* a person who leads a very active life at vigils and parties, and can stay awake all night long). Segismundo stated that he had in the past been Santana's partner in a musical group and began talking about the good old days. Only the men took an active part in the musical proceedings, while the women remained 'inside the house': in the living room (a few), kitchen and sleeping rooms.

"The second rosary started at 12:05 a.m. Somebody told me that Santana has *compadres* in Esperanza, among them Perseo and Menelao.

"At about three in the morning, I returned home, when they were preparing to start the third and last rosary."

Vigils have the main purpose of "paying" a vow. This can be to Jesus, the Virgin or any saint, and points to the relationships between deities and persons in Esperanza. A person in some kind of trouble (illness, debts, accidents) may resort to an agreement with a saint. He promises that if he comes out well from the trouble, he will celebrate a vigil in his honor. The person makes the bargain and waits to see what happens. A "promise" can be made between an individual and the saint or between a group (family, couple) and the saint.

If all goes well, the preparations for the vigil are started, though sometimes the vigil is postponed until the persons concerned have the funds to hold it. Vigils are customarily celebrated a year or less after the trouble is solved. It is assumed that the deity helped in solving the problem, if it is solved; if it is not solved no vigil is celebrated, and it is said, "God did not wish it, we do not know why, only He knows."

Household preparations are started a day or two before the vigil is to be held. Women go to the store to bring supplies and children gather flowers. The vigil is always held at night, as it literally means keeping vigil (*en vela*) all night. People start arriving around nine o'clock, and by ten many of the guests are present. Most of them are kin, close neighbors and *compadres,* and sometimes guests from other places are present. The proceedings take place in the living room and certain arrangements are evident. A table is arranged with flowers surrounding the image of the deity or saint who conceded the favor. Other religious statues and images may also be placed on the table. Three candles are lighted in front of the images, and must be kept lit the whole night. In front of this table are four chairs, destined for the *rezadores,* the people who will say the prayers.

The head of the house announces that the vigil is going to start and pleads for silence. Everybody sits down, either inside the house or in the yard. The *rezadores,* four of them, two men and two women, sit on the chairs in front of the table with the religious images. They sit in mixed pairs, two in front and two behind. They do not have to be kin, and they are not professionals; they are people who know the prayers and are invited by the household head to come and *lead* the prayers in the vigil. They are going to recite (either singing or speaking) the rosary; this consists of a series of prayers to the Virgin Mary and to God. If the *rezadores* know how, it will be sung; if not, spoken. The leader is always a man who knows all the details of the rituals, and he starts either the chants or the spoken prayers. This part of the ceremony usually lasts from one to two hours. After it is finished, the first secular part begins. Refreshments are served and the music starts. There are no dances, and the audience just listens to the music. Some songs may be sung in honor of the deity or other religious figures, but most of the songs are based on secular themes.

This lasts a couple of hours and then the head of the house calls for the beginning of the second rosary. The second round is exactly like the first, as the whole vigil is a cycle of three religious and three secular parts. The ceremony lasts the whole night and usually finishes at dawn, when people are served coffee and, after a while, go home. It is then considered that the deity has been properly honored.

The whole character of the vigil is a festive one, and the mood is reflected in the happy behavior of the people. No special prayers are directed to the deity, and the rosary does not make any direct allusions to the events that brought the vigil about.

The important role of the household in the organization of vigils is reflected in the way they are announced, which emphasizes the house and household head involved. The household unit, under the leadership of its head, handles and is responsible for all the aspects (financial and otherwise) of the ceremony. During the ceremony the head and his wife act as the hosts, the wife attending to the women and children and the man to the male guests. The man also sees that no guests misbehave by getting drunk or fighting.

The male-female dichotomy so crucial in Esperanza's social structure can be seen in the physical segregation of the sexes during the celebration of the vigil. As has been pointed out, men stay outside the house or in the living room, and move constantly from one place to another. The women stay "inside the house," and most of them go into the kitchen or bedrooms and remain there. Inside the house, people of opposing sexes only mingle in the living room where everybody can see and watch them.

Apart from its manifest purpose, the vigil is one of the vehicles *par excellence* for cementing relations between households. Kin come into contact, discuss family problems, meet new members of the family and so on. *Compadres* and neighbors can discuss agricultural prospects and reinforce their ties by drinking and talking together. Children watch and run around and enjoy the excitement of the occasion. Adolescents of both sexes meet each other in a lawful way under the eyes of the adults. Indeed, many men told the investigator that they "fell in love during the vigils." The ceremony is not purely a religious occasion, but an event that provides the opportunity for social intercourse between members of different households. The emphasis is the recurrent one on happiness and harmony.

There are other "happy" reasons for celebrating vigils. It happens sometimes that a vigil is held every year because that was the agreement between a person and a saint on the original occasion, and it becomes a tradition, often sustained through generations. The original motive recedes into the background, and the force of tradition takes over. If questioned about the motive, the people will simply say that their parents used to celebrate it every year.

The result is that there are numerous vigils celebrated in Esperanza, and especially in the month of July, when we found that between twenty-five and thirty were celebrated in the whole area. Most of these were celebrated for different reasons; some traditional, others to fulfill a promise; there are some occasions when the real reason is very hard to pin down.

Death vigils or wakes have a totally different meaning and tone, although some vague structural similarities. The event is one of sorrow. There are two types of death wake, the vigil and the *novenas,* which together form a series. The vigil takes place during the period from the time of death until dawn of the day of burial. The body lies in state, prayers are said for the soul of the person who has departed, and people come to pay their respects to the kin. All night people come and go, while a group of people of both sexes say the rosary. The prayers end at dawn. Later in the day the body will be buried in the *barrio's* cemetery. The following is a short account of one of these vigils:

"On this day a woman died of cancer. Her husband had passed away about a year and a half previously.

"The news spread throughout Esperanza. Everybody was talking about it. Mayoral told us he was going to the house to pray for the dead. We also went to the house, where relatives, neighbors, and friends were already 'keeping watch' over the body.

"A group of men were sitting on chairs on the verandah. Another group, mostly men with a few wives, were in the living room. The blue coffin had been placed open in a bedroom. A large cross with a dark piece of cloth behind it was at the head of the coffin. Some lighted candles were placed nearby. Adults of both sexes surrounded the coffin.

"The kitchen was full of women and children; many men were in the yard, some smoking, others talking, a sizeable group praying. Some cars were parked nearby. Inside and outside the house people were saying the rosary, and between each prayer they asked Jesus Christ and the Virgin to intercede with God for the peace of the soul of the deceased. The rosary was led by a woman who was a close neighbor, and every so often there was an interval for rest and conversation.

"While we were there, Heriberto explained to us some of the customary practices. People 'keep watch' the whole night and say as many rosaries as they can. Coffee is served to the women and rum to the men at regular intervals. Men usually lead the rosaries because women are shy, although there is no explicit prohibition against women leading the prayers (see preceding paragraph). The body is interred the day after death, and one day later the novenas begin. After the last prayer of the novenas is completed, the cross is stored. Afterwards, an annual mass may be held for the dead for seven years.

"We made note of the following items: there was segregation by sex, although not clear-cut. People entered, stayed for an hour or so, then left. They seemed to have met their social obligations, had done their duty, or had expressed their condolences (*dado el pésame*). The general tone of the event was serious and formal.

"The next day the funeral was held (we were not present)."

The day after the funeral, the novenas (nine consecutive days of prayer) begin. They are always held where the person lived until his death. The ritual begins at about six-thirty or seven in the evening, earlier than in the case of the happier vigils. Usually some close kin of the deceased come to stay in the house and help in the preparations and celebration of the novenas. The rosary is said only once, and one person of either sex acts as leader. Some refreshment, such as cold drinks, or coffee and chocolate with crackers, is served, and people then return to their homes. In some homes a cross is laid over a black cloth, and candles are lighted. In the prayers the name of the deceased is mentioned, and then the words, "May he or she rest in peace, God." The prayers are said directly to God or through a saint who can intercede with God in favor of the dead person. The last day the cross is ceremonially removed and is placed out of sight by the wife, husband or closest kin present. This implies that the novenas have finished. A one-night wake, very similar in form to the one described here, is held on each anniversary of the death for the following seven years.

The impression one gets from the wakes is that the range of connections (kinship, neighbors, *compadres*) is more restricted than in happier vigils, and more close kin are present; fewer people, but more of them are kin, proportionately. The wake is an expression of solidarity, an attempt to demonstrate that the loss of the person is felt. There is a sense of duty toward the dead person and his surviving kin, and being absent from such an event can mean social ostracism by all the survivors, a thing avoided at all costs in Esperanza.

Another very powerful reason for attending is what we would call the principle of reciprocity. Every dead person must have his or her novenas if he or she is going to be saved in the Catholic sense. "If I always do my duty by everybody, and if I am on good terms with all, then there is more chance that my novenas will be kept. As the family group is the most vital in this duty, I feel more obligation to them." "Your turn today and mine tomorrow" is a common saying. The religious practices related to death increase the general sense of interdependence; but it is equally important that the sense of interdependence increases the efficiency of religious practices, and this is of the utmost importance to the people of Esperanza.

Funerals are closely related to this preoccupation with salvation, and everybody is anxious to have a proper one. Their concern is not only with the economic aspect, but also that the requisite rituals and prayers are properly executed at their funerals. When possible, relatives try to get a priest to visit a dying person, but because there are no priests resident in Esperanza, it is difficult to do this.

Arrangements for the funeral are made by undertakers from the town of Arecibo. The body is taken into the cemetery in a hearse, although often the hearse drives in front loaded with flowers while people on foot carry the coffin. In the latter case men take turns in carrying the coffin. Generally no priest accompanies the funeral, nor does one officiate in the cemetery. By the time the cortège enters the *barrio* cemetery, the grave is already prepared. The bearers lower the coffin and start covering it up. All this is done by the men: neighbors, *compadres,* kin and regular gravediggers. The attitudes of both men and women during the proceedings reveal in a very clear way their respective roles. Men are expected to "know" how to deal with these situations, and they are expected not to weep. Women, by contrast, do not "know" how to deal with the situation and they *are* expected to weep. It is considered a normal part of the behavior of women.

While the coffin is being covered with earth, the closest kin stand on one side of the grave while somebody takes charge of the situation and begins a rosary. All then kneel on the ground while the rosary is said. The prayers are full of intercessions made by the *rezador* before God in favor of the deceased, and as he (the *rezador* is usually a man) prays aloud, the rest of those present, repeat the prayer aloud. Meanwhile the grave has been covered with earth, and flowers are placed over it. At this juncture the closest male kinsman usually serves some refreshments to those present, but especially to those who helped in the funeral and in digging the grave. This is done in the cemetery and is the way in which the family of the deceased thank them for their help. (In many cases even these few formalities are waived and only a rosary is said.) With this, the family feels that the funeral has been a proper one. What remains is the *novenas*. The pattern is identical for all social classes in Esperanza with minor exceptions. For example, the only differences in funerals of the well-to-do consists of higher-priced coffins, more expensive hearses, and so forth.

By watching carefully at a funeral, one can infer the degree of affection and esteem people in Esperanza had for the deceased. We attended six or seven funerals, and we can state that a person with a reputation of being respected and well liked will have many more kin, *compadres* and neighbors present at his funeral (and the novenas) than one who is not respected or not liked. The funeral of Doña Remigia, a popular old lady of good standing, was attended by more than 100 persons. Sinforoso, a relatively isolated resident, was not well liked by the *barrio* and only a handful of people were present at his funeral, mostly neighbors who were acting out of charity as Sinforoso and his son were said to be very ungrateful and hostile characters. Remigia's funeral lasted several hours while Sinforoso's was finished in less than an hour.

Other Ritual Beliefs and Practices

Although Catholicism dominates the religion of Esperanza, there are other beliefs of a religious nature that play an important part in the lives of the people.

EVIL EYE

The belief in "evil eye" (*mal de ojo*) is widely held in the *barrio*. This is a belief that a person can "destroy" some things just by looking at them. This ability to "destroy" things might be involuntary, and the person might not be conscious of it. A beautiful baby or a healthy animal can be affected by the evil eye. The baby might become sick, and the animal might die. If an adult is affected with illness or misfortune, tries to fight it but fails, then he or she says, "I think somebody is casting the evil eye on me."

This implies that there is a voluntary aspect too, in the sense that one person may consciously try to injure another one. This means in effect that people in Esperanza are thought to resort to the evil eye to cause damage to those they dislike. In Arecibo there is a marketplace where "magical" prayers and all sorts of incantations are sold, and many go there to try to find these remedies or formulas. (There are also other kinds of prayers. For example, there are prayers that can be said to certain saints so that a desired person will fall in love with one.) If they do not find what they want there, they can resort to an interview with a medium or a *curandero,* literally "healer," for help.

It is difficult to discover who exactly is casting the evil eye, and the impression we have is that the guilty person is seldom recognized and pinpointed. Instead, those affected apply the countermeasures and try to ward it off. The attitude of the people, when questioned about the existence of the evil eye, is to deny that it is practiced in modern times. In informal life situations, however, we were able to see it in operation.

It seems that belief in the power of the evil eye is related to the inability to find a cause for evil or misfortune that has taken place, and that, in spite of all efforts, still persists. A man may have a sick daughter, and the cause of the sickness (according to informants, it can be *any* sickness that persists for some time) may not have been diagnosed in spite of many visits to doctors. After this, he may take the child to a spiritualist medium who states that somebody is casting the evil eye on the child and prescribes a "medicine." Or the father by his own reasoning might conclude that it is the evil eye. In a sense this provides the person with a supernatural cause where apparently there was no real one.

SAINTS' MIRACLES

The plea for the intervention of saints is a natural recourse, since they inhabit the world of the supernatural and might thus succeed in solving the problem. The peasant always has a number of religious images at home, but there is a special form of relationship between a type of religious art and what are called *promesas* (promises). There are wooden figures of saints and deities called *santos de palo* (wooden saints) made by local artisans that, in many cases, have been handed down through three, four and five generations. These figures are considered to have the power to cure certain ills. For example, Saint Blaise is supposed to be able to handle well any kind of trouble related to the throat, and any such trouble is laid before him. Not all the houses have a wooden saint, but many of them do. People know which house owns a particular figure, and when a special trouble appears, the "specialist" is visited. Those afflicted pray to the saint and promise for instance that if the illness is cured, they will hold a vigil, or the person may promise to say the rosary every week. In any case a contract of some sort is supposed to be made between the saint and the supplicant. If everything goes well, the latter is expected to fulfill his part of the contract. If the trouble is not cured, then it is said that "it was the will of God and who are we to doubt His wisdom."

If a cure is successful it is called a "miracle," and this deserves some consideration. The miracle is symbolized by a small piece of metal called a votive offering (*milagro*) hung from the figure. This represents the miracle in a graphic form. For example, a small metal leg would symbolize a sickness of the leg that was cured. In this way one can almost tell what the specialty is of a particular figure by looking at the votive offerings hanging from it. Everybody whose trouble has been cured must produce a votive offering. These can be bought in Arecibo's marketplace.

Many of the miracles are associated with human health and accidents; but there are also numerous animal figures symbolizing animals that have been "cured" by these wooden saints. Indeed, the relationship between the daily life of the peasants (as exemplified by the health problems and accidents), and this cult of saints is striking. It is as if there was always some saint at hand who could be expected to solve or help solve one's daily problems. The figures are consequently kept in a prominent place in the living room, and excellent care is taken of them. Saints with a speciality are very much in demand, incidentally providing yet another mechanism for vitalizing interhousehold relationships.

HEALERS

There are still some healers, *curanderos* or *santigueros* as they are called in Esperanza. However, many people, especially among the very old, assert that they have been disappearing with the advent of modern medical practices and facilities. We made the acquaintance of two *curanderos,* but only one was "practicing." Both of them were men, although informants told us that this is not an occupation limited to males. Menelao, the only practicing healer, was a specialist in bones and muscles. He would manipulate and massage an arm or leg until the patient was cured. We were not able to inquire into details, but Menelao told us that he said certain prayers while "curing," and spoke about a direct relation between certain prayers and certain parts of the body. Menelao could only teach his "profession" to three people, because if he taught more than that number, the cures would not be effective. In this case, we have a mixture of folk medicine (Menelao claims his physical manipulations place things in their natural locations) and an appeal by prayer to supernatural agencies (God, Jesus and saints) to help the healing process. Thus even normal physical ailments not caused by the evil eye, are cured with the aid of inhabitants of the spiritual world of Catholicism.

GHOSTS, SOULS AND APPARITIONS

There are many stories about ghosts and apparitions. Certain places are related to particular ghosts, apparitions or wandering souls. Here we shall mention only a few samples.

There is the legend of the three dogs, which has strong moral overtones. There are three large dogs which appear at night only to certain people. They appear only to married persons who quarrel frequently, and it seems that they only appear to the guilty one. These dogs represent the devil, and people describe them as the "three evil dogs." We met one person who told us that they appeared to his father. Perhaps we have here a symbolic representation of a guilty conscience in a specific context (marriage) and some kind of mechanism of moral control. But the information available is scanty.

There is also the story of the rich man who hid his money in a hole underground but forgot the location. He died and now searches restlessly for the money. People say that a light circulates the place at night, and that it is the owner searching for his money.

Here we have moral condemnation of rich people who are not generous with their money. As they were "tied" to their money, they cannot enter heaven. As they have died, they do not belong to the world of the living. They are in-between and have not reached heavenly peace.

The same happens with other types of wandering souls. When a person "sees" a ghost, it is a sign that something went wrong with the death of that person. He or she died "an unnatural death" and is trying to tell the living to intercede for him or her with God. The people of Esperanza are really afraid of these apparitions and those who are known to have had an "unnatural death" are especially feared. They are described as "souls in torment." The reference to an unnatural death means that the person died in a state of sin according to the ten commandments. Most of the inhabitants of the area avoid passing certain locations at night, afraid of an apparition or ghost related to that place. Places connected with murder or suicide are particularly feared.

A case like this happened in Esperanza while we were there. A man murdered a woman and later committed suicide before the police could arrest him. All the *barrio* was shocked by this happening, and the climate at night was one of fear because these two people had died a violent and unnatural death. Nobody dared pass the place where the crime took place for fear of seeing either ghost, let alone both of them. The first thing that people did was to place a wooden cross to indicate the place and perhaps to placate their own consciences before God. "This has been a terrible thing for Esperanza," the people said constantly. A religious procession was organized a few days later by the households who lived nearest to the place of the crime with the declared purpose of "driving the evil away" (*alejar lo malo*). They carried religious images and the rosary was said many times. The belief is that by praying to God directly or through intermediaries, such tormented souls will be admitted to heaven in due course and the ghosts will cease to appear. Then the souls will "rest in peace" (*descansan en paz*).

Religious Processions

This is a more formal device used by church authorities. Processions are held several times during the year. Most of them commemorate a religious occasion like Good Friday.

They are mainly attended by women and children, especially girls, as men try to avoid attending formal ritual activities, even though the local church leaders are men. The few men who attend behave rather awkwardly, while women participate more freely. These processions take place around the church, religious images are carried, and prayers are said aloud. As these are official church activities, they are performed under the direction of a priest, who visits for the occasion.

This does not exhaust the range of religious beliefs and practices, which is indeed rich and varied, but for us the limits are narrower and the interest is not in the matter *per se,* but in its sociological implications.

Catholicism in Esperanza

We said at the beginning of the chapter that Catholicism permeates religious life in Esperanza. But Catholicism is more than just a religion for its people. It is a way of life, a philosophy in the strict meaning of the term. It is also a moral system, a whole set of norms that guide the behavior of Esperanza's inhabitants. In this aspect, religion provides for the definition of proper and improper (or good and bad) behavior. The formal principles of this religion have been assimilated and modified by these people, so that in a sense it could be said that Esperanza has its own peculiar brand of Catholicism.

Catholicism, then, forms a set of principles and these can be inferred from Esperanza's religious beliefs and practices. Common themes run through all of them, and this is what gives unity to the principles. We shall try now to summarize and discuss those principles.

There is a preoccupation with salvation in Esperanza's Catholicism. Salvation means that eternal happiness, as defined by religion, is attained in heaven. All the practices are a means to this end. But salvation does not come by itself, there are certain things that must be done to achieve it. The wakes, vigils and novenas are specially vital in this respect. Death is the last chance that you have to be saved, and that is why the wakes or vigil and *novenas* are so important.

As death is so important, provision is made to insure that everybody has "his prayer said" (*se le digan las oraciones*) as they put it in Esperanza. The principle of reciprocity and all the emphasis on cooperation and harmony is part of this: "I help you and you help me" is applied in this crucial situation.

The notion of contract is another characteristic of this system. There is a constant flow of petitions directed to God and the saints. They are asked for help and promised prayers and special acts if they provide the help. The *promesa* is the clearer expression of this, and also the cult of saints, where the person makes a contract with the saint or deity and both parties are put under mutual obligation. This constant mutual relationship is the crucial feature of the system.

In a very broad sense, we find also a concept of fate. Human beings can try to alter each other's lives and deeds, but in the last resort everything is determined by God, and to try to alter His will would be a heresy. They describe this acceptance of God's will as *resignación* (resignation) but this framework provides some freedom of the human will. There must be some indication of God's will manifested in His acts. But when do you know that He has acted? This doubt leaves room for human intervention, and you can still appeal to God through the various intermediaries to see if He can act in your favor. It is here that the relationship of the peasant to the saints is significant. It explains why the peasants reject the importance of the clergy in their relations with God. The priest is a human being, a man like us. He is in the same position as us, why then do we have to appeal to him, when we can do it through prayers and the saints, which is all he does?

The emphasis on the role of the family in religious expression is another important theme. The rosary, an essential element in almost every religious act, explicitly requires that the family be assembled under its head, who is supposed to lead the prayers. This is not always achieved, but in the rituals where the rosary is said, it is the man (as leader of the *rezadores*) who starts it and directs it, while the women follow with the rest. Religious beliefs and the principles of family structure reinforce each other.

In the organization of the church in Esperanza, it is the man who has the most important positions, while the women compose the bulk of the congregation who attend church most frequently. The male-female dichotomy has been projected into religious life. Men are in charge of the structure (as in the family) but it is the woman who does the everyday work (as in the family).

The moral influence of Catholicism is another way in which this system of values has come to form part and parcel of the lives of the people in Esperanza. The emphasis on respect and harmony is indeed closely related to Catholicism, which emphasizes these aspects of social intercourse. The image of the good father, of the good mother, of the good son or daughter held by the people in Esperanza does not diverge from the one held by Catholicism. Indeed, if one were forced to use a single word to characterize the moral system of Esperanza, it would inevitably be "Catholic." But the term is misleading, and only careful and systematic research on the grand scale would be able to solve the problem completely in a satisfactory manner. The main passage rituals, baptism, marriage and funerals, are conducted according to Catholic principles. The structure of the family and the ideal image of its members is sanctioned by the church. The relations between individuals (at least in certain aspects) show the influence of the church. The religious beliefs and practices clearly show their Catholic imprint.

CHAPTER 13

Social Patterns of Conflict at the Local Level

The local social system in Esperanza is not always able to control the behavior of the people. There are occasions when direct physical violence breaks out and people resort to fights (*peleas*). Esperanza is a well-integrated community, involving all *esperanzeños* in a wide diversity of everyday relations. Instrumental and affective ties develop, but out of just such close integration, discord can arise, and this provides the raw material that can result in an open fight. The nature of the fights almost always involves a definition of the situation in terms of ultimate, basic values, as seen from the perspective of the participants. This does not mean that it is a rational, calculated process, simply that there is invariably a claim by the people involved that "something basic" was at stake. It can be either the fear of losing masculinity (*miedo a dejar de ser un macho*) or the sense that the normal situation in which everyone knows how to operate is being disturbed.

The first instance is closely related to the *relajo* pattern that develops in the cafes and public places. This mode of social interaction implies a type of aggressive conduct toward the other person; you assault him verbally and wait for his reply, he replies, somebody makes a joke and so on. It is here that a man proves his maleness; the other is the constant enemy; he is also forced to prove and assert his manhood. Bourdieu (1966) has called this type of interaction "the dialectic of challenge and riposte." Speaking about some aspects of this way of behaving he says:

For a challenge to be made, the challenger must consider whoever he challenges to be worthy of it-to-be, that is to say, in a position to riposte. This means that he must recognize him as his peer in honor. To issue a challenge to someone is to acknowledge his manliness, an acknowledgement which is the prerequisite of any dialogue as well as the prelude to the dialogue; it is to acknowledge in him also the dignity of a man of honor, since challenge, as such, requires a riposte and consequently is addressed to a man thought capable of playing the game of honor and of playing it well (1966:197).

Bourdieu's comments could be applied almost entirely to a similar process in Esperanza. The only minor modification, not mentioned in the fragment quoted, is that this assumed equality must be proved; that is, the status of equal is not an ascribed one but achieved. It is assumed that you are his equal, but in your reply (riposte) you must demonstrate it. Otherwise, there is a tendency to consider you a social inferior, and sarcastic comments emerge, with cynical implications. In Esperanza, if you cannot prove your equality and worthiness you are considered a coward, or in other terms, a *pendejo*. The *pendejo* is the man who is at the mercy of others, who has lost his equality as a male. People joke and make derogatory comments about him. In a community where everyone knows everyone else, moral pressure builds up, and you must face it or assume by implication the role of *pendejo*. This is considered a very inferior role, negating all the ideal and positive aspects of manhood. The role of man, as perceived by the women, can be seen in O. Lewis's work about Puerto Rico (1969). This work is full of negative remarks by women about their men. The term *pendejo* appears frequently; women seem to be dissatisfied with the incapacity of their men to fulfill their expected roles. Women have a clear knowledge of what a *macho* and a *pendejo* are; they want a *macho* and disdain and avoid *pendejos*. The *pendejo* thus summarizes almost all the negative qualities of the male.

When a fight erupts, the limits of the situation have been reached; the man sees his equality with others threatened, so he resorts to violence. This is frequently marked by throwing a few punches at the other without giving warning; those attacked are caught unprepared. In some cases any object close at hand may be used as a weapon, or knives may be drawn. What follows shows some variation and no definite pattern. People may allow the antagonists to fight or friends might intervene. It depends on many factors. In some cases, people do not want to get involved; in others, it can be sheer indifference (very rare indeed), or the spectators may actually want them to fight. In this last situation the fight is seen as a solution. It is worth mentioning here that the force of law is distant from this community. There is no local rural police force. Police operate regularly from Arecibo, but there are none stationed in the *barrio*. The town is about twenty minutes by car from Esperanza, or a distance of approximately 6 miles of narrow road.

This first type of fight usually involves the presence of both parties and of other men, as when they are in a cafe. The second type does not necessarily need both parties to be present at the outset. An act of one person against an absent one can start and result in a direct struggle. The absent one hears about the act or the comments of someone in the *barrio* and interprets it as an affront. He sees the fulfillment of his normal roles threatened; the normal aspect of his social personality is being upset. The reaction is to move towards the aggressor and demand an explanation or issue a challenge. The challenge is an invitation to engage in physical combat. In many cases the challenge is accepted and a lonely spot is chosen. Both contestants meet there and the fight starts. When the first drop of blood is drawn, the fight usually stops, but this is not always the case. In extreme cases, one of the contestants can be killed.

As stated previously, this can be interpreted as an attempt to restore a normal situation which was perceived as being disturbed. For example, the following incident took place in Esperanza. Roberto and Felipe are both married adult males in their early forties. Both of them have lived in Esperanza for a long time, and have plenty of kinship and other connections in the community. Roberto's daughter and Felipe's son, both of whom study at the *barrio*'s elementary school, got involved in a fight. The first of the fathers to know about it was Felipe. He scolded Roberto's daughter for fighting. Later he had an angry exchange of words with Roberto, with the result that they agreed to meet in the *barrio*'s cemetery to fight. Both men came, Roberto armed with a *machete* and Felipe with a gun. Roberto started to advance towards Felipe in a menacing way; Felipe opened fire and wounded Roberto. Felipe stopped shooting, left the place and surrendered himself to the police. A few weeks afterwards, he was brought to court and put on probation. Both men continue to live in the *barrio*.

Although other explanations are possible, and other factors are involved, the case can still be interpreted as the attempt to restore a normal situation. The normality under discussion here, we hold, is the concept of the father. Felipe took for himself rights that belonged to Roberto; he scolded Roberto's daughter. He trespassed on the latter's paternal rights and duties, violating sacred territory. The fight can then be interpreted as an attempt to restore Roberto's prerogatives. In the light of Bourdieu's (1966) comments about the "dialectic of challenge and riposte," Felipe accepted Roberto as an equal by participating in the fight with him, restoring the normal situation in this way. We can venture to speculate, with a certain amount of caution, that the fact that it was Felipe who shed the first drop of blood allowed him to "save face." He "won" the duel. This is intimately related to the fact that the fight stopped immediately and nobody was killed. It was a form of "limited" violence within the framework of a normative conflict.

For students of Mediterranean societies, the pattern sounds familiar in the way violence is handled at the communal level. Campbell (1964) and Peristiany (1966) and others have described similar processes. This tends to show, as we hold in another work (Buitrago Ortiz 1970) that patterns of behavior in the traditional Puerto Rican rural society are not merely of Spanish origin, but of Mediterranean (and North African) origin. Further research is needed on this point, but the similarities of values and institutions are too striking to be ignored.

A brief comment on another aspect of the *peleas* is in order. Fights are not always merely between individuals. The kinship system and other types of systems can be activated and its members become involved in a group fight. We witnessed this when we were present at a wake and went into the kitchen to have a cup of rum. A group of men were present in the kitchen (something unusual; later they went to the patio), busily conversing among themselves in an orderly way. But we noticed that a middle-aged man and a young man of about twenty-five were exchanging words in a somewhat aggressive manner. The language was not entirely offensive, nor was the challenge direct. From what we could hear, the middle-aged male asked the youngster, "Where do you have it?", referring to the knife that ideally males should always carry. The youngster replied, pointing to his trouser pocket: "I have it here . . . we can do it (fight) anytime you want." It seems the youngster was either a relative or a close friend of a person that had been attacked on a previous occasion by the brother of the middle-aged man. The youngster had a low opinion of these two brothers and had said something about their being drunkards and people who were always looking for a fight. The incident, though apparently slight, points to the kind of solidarity that emerges between persons related by ties of kinship, friendship or both. Both of these men had taken a stand in a conflict they had not created, involving themselves to the point of *peleas*. A conflict between individuals was transforming itself into one between groups.

Other aspects of *peleas* also illustrate the principles operating in the social structure of the community. For instance, open conflict reveals the operation of the class system. People who get involved in an open fight are usually from the same social level. Persons of a lower level do not engage themselves in fights with people of a higher one. In case of conflict, they avoid an open confrontation and engage instead in gossip "behind their backs" (*a sus espaldas*). As we commented previously, this is done mainly by women. An individual of the higher class can

initiate a fight with one of the lower levels, but the latter will not recip-
rocate. In addition, there are considerations of age and sex. People who
fight are more or less of the same age and usually the same sex. To
violate these criteria, one has to go against the values of what is proper
as defined by the community. If a man attacks a woman he is considered *un abusador* (one who abuses) and a negative reaction sets in
against him. A youngster who attacks an elder can, in some cases, be
considered an *abusador,* especially if the elder is not able to defend himself. A young or middle-aged man who attacks a child is placed in the
same category. Regardless of the justification for the hostility, such an
attack will lose the *abusador* much support and sympathy.

There is a final point worth mentioning. One can find in Esperanza
some men who are considered the drunkards and vagrants of the *barrio*.
When these vagrants are present in a cafe, some of the others present
activate the *relajo* pattern. If two vagrants are present, and they are
drunk, they are stimulated to fight each other. They are pushed physically and stimulated verbally until they engage in a real fight. All this
is done with a sense of humor. Men say that such a fight is just a kind
of game and that nobody is really injured, the contestants being so
drunk they do not have the strength to damage their adversary. Some
liken it to a dance. The whole thing is not considered serious by the
community. What this implies from a theoretical viewpoint is that these
drunkards are not men from a sociological perspective. They are the
opposite of what men should be. That is the essence of the humor, an
inversion of the normal values of maleness; that is why they are ridiculed and why the fight has no further implications. The vagrants are outside the normal definition of men and are kept outside; they are not taken
seriously. By the very contrast they offer, they reflect the aspects of the
social system and culture which define the social personality of maleness.

At the local level, then, Esperanza still maintains the traditional ways
and patterns of fighting. In this aspect it is close to a community like
the one described by Pitt Rivers (1961) in the south of Spain. Social
change has not yet modified the manner in which the inhabitants of
Esperanza fight among themselves, and we adhere here to a thesis of
relative continuity and permanence of some modes of behavior. We
would even expand our thesis to include La Esmeralda, the urban slum
described by O. Lewis (1969). In spite of the assertion that men are
less aggressive, which may hold in comparison with a community like
Esperanza, there are still men who conform to the patterns we have
been discussing. Women may have invaded some areas of masculine
behavior, but this appears to be a new element in the situation, which
has more stability (although with increasing tensions) than many stu-

dents of Puerto Rican society are willing to grant. There may also be a class element in the situation. The communities we have been speaking of are basically lower middle and lower class. In spite of there being a common general (or national) culture there is some kind of segregation in the Puerto Rican society between these lower levels of society and the middle higher levels.[1]

If this point is valid, then we see that the continuity we have been speaking of is limited to only one sector of the Puerto Rican society. This type of social phenomena modifies Lewis's concept of the "culture of poverty," which tends to assume an almost 100 percent isolation. We hold that these are continuities within both the rural and urban sectors in the lower classes, while Lewis implies discontinuities (Buitrago Ortiz 1967). All that we have said above does not deny the stresses and strains inherent in the process of proletarianization. What is more, the stresses and strains felt by the males highlight the intensity of the values and orientations internalized by the men. They are proletarianized at the economic level but the psychological level is harder to change. The women in La Esmeralda tend to be more aggressive and outspoken, but they constantly complain about the incapacity of the males to fulfill aspects of their expected roles. If they are expected roles, they have not lost their moral legitimacy, in the Weberian sense. We think this aspect has been neglected by students of social change in their anxiety to demonstrate that everything is change.

Territoriality and kinship are powerful factors in the operation and resolution of conflicts at the local level in Esperanza. This does not mean that there exists anything approaching corporate groups in the African manner, acting as a unit in religious, economic and political levels. But households of certain sectors of the *barrio* tend to form clusters in terms of consanguineal, affinal, ritual, kinship and friendship ties. They do not see themselves as a completely discrete unit, but a process of differentiation and contrast with other clusters gives some degree of identity and solidarity.

We remember very clearly the ways in which they expressed their differences. During our fieldwork we made comments to others about people who were not immediate neighbors, trying to obtain some information. The only information given, and given with reluctance, was that, "All those people are always fighting." They were portrayed in a nega-

---

[1]The problem of a national versus regional and/or class cultures in Puerto Rico is discussed by Mintz (1966:339–434), by authors in *Revista de Ciencias Sociales,* 2:235–39, and in Steward (1956).

tive way. Alongside this negative portrayal, it was observed that there was a minimum of social interaction between them.

Usually, we could see people of one cluster moving from house to house within the cluster. People from outside that cluster and who "belonged" to another would behave in a similar fashion within their own cluster. Only in special events would the isolation be broken, as in wakes (*velorios*). But everyday interaction seems limited to each one's cluster. A member of one cluster can pass by a neighbor's house and salute, but he will continue on his way if he does not "belong" to this cluster. The cluster, then, creates a sense of solidarity and provides for some daily collaboration among related households. This tends to lessen the conflict among these people. The constant claims to solidarity among themselves was a feature when we visited them, and it was also constantly reiterated at social events. "In this area we are all good people" (*Aquí todo el mundo es bueno*). The fact of living nearby and of being enmeshed in all kinds of ties created this sense of "belonging." Loyalties were created that were expected to transcend conflicts at the level of the cluster.

Certain surnames stand out in these clusters, such as Ayala, Rivera, Correa, Seín, Ramírez and González. The Ayala cluster included about five households, the Correa four, the Rivera six, the Seín three, the Ramírez five, and the González three. Taking as an average a number of five persons per household, we have here a total of 110 persons. This is just an estimate, as there are other clusters in the *barrio*. The households are mainly headed by a married male, with his wife and children. This is the basis for the relationship between households in the cluster. Men may collaborate among themselves in agricultural or other tasks, although our impression is that this is not a highly formalized and ritualized process. Migration affects these relations, as men move out of the *barrio,* either temporarily or permanently. Women may also collaborate in some jobs, such has harvesting tobacco.

The cluster is then more than a mere collection of houses located in the same area; it has moral, economic and kinship functions, though it is not a corporate group in any sense. In opposition to descent groups, it is not a political group. Every household head manages the affairs of his own household. The individual household is a *relatively* autonomous unit within the cluster, and the links we have mentioned are tenuous. We are of the opinion, on a highly speculative level, that in the past the households as a group approached more closely the model of a political unit and acted more as a corporate entity. The older informants commented along these lines and even today, in many clusters, one finds an old man who is the father of a group of sons (and daughters), many of them married and living on his farm, though in their own households. The land is controlled and managed by this old man. He makes the decisions, and only he can dispose, sell or rent the land. Many of these sons and daughters appear to be "waiting" for the old man to die to be able to receive their share of the inheritance.

But the process is not so simple. These farms are not big. A division on the death of the father may leave many sons and daughters with three, five, or less than ten, acres. The values of urbanization and of an industrial society seem to have changed (increased) the level of aspiration of the sons and daughters. They appear to prefer the values of city living to those of a rural setting. In Esperanza, as farmers, they would have to operate a relatively small farm, with a relatively low return. This expectation results in a pattern where some of the sons and daughters (and potential members of the cluster) migrate, move to Esperanza, to Arecibo, some other town, or to the United States. This diminishes the number of persons living in the clusters. It is probable, then, that there were more people in the clusters in the past, as migration was less. The demographic situation was more stable and there was less mobility.[2] Thirty or forty years ago, migration to the United States was microscopic. The intensity of cooperation within the cluster, in a general sense, has been modified by social and economic processes. Today it appears to be less structured, more open, less stable, and in some cases in a process of dying out. But the cluster is still a social unit that has the function of creating solidarity, insulating conflict, and providing a web of relations for the individual in Esperanza.

---

[2]For a discussion of a process of change due to different causes and in a *Bantu* setting see Fallers (1967).

CHAPTER 14

Social Stratification in Esperanza

To the newcomer, Esperanza appears to be a fully egalitarian society. The way people behave towards each other in regular daily intercourse very easily leads one to assume this. People behave in a friendly way, making jokes and assuming an apparent equality. But even the newcomer after some time starts noticing that all the behavior is not the same, and that behind the apparent homogeneity, there is great diversity.

Several factors enter into the formation of social strata or classes in Esperanza among which land, income, occupation, education and prestige are the most relevant. They do not operate in an isolated way, but are closely interrelated one with the other. In the analysis that follows, we shall try to assess their relative importance, but we shall also try to keep these interrelations in sight.

Land

Land is a very scarce commodity in Esperanza. The topography of the area, the great degree of erosion, and population pressure have all had and have their effect in making usable land available only at a relatively high price. Geographically, there is plenty of land in the area, but when the factors just mentioned are taken into consideration, the usable amount is very much less. This makes Esperanza a land hungry community. In an agricultural community like Esperanza, land is the main economic factor, and men will resort to many different arrangements to acquire a suitable plot to farm and on which to build a house.

People may buy outright, rent, buy on installments, or just get land free. The important thing is to have it. Men who emigrate for many years often do so with the idea of being able to acquire a plot in due time. This being the situation, peasants look with a mixture of admiration and envy upon the people who control and own the best land. They are the people who have a true farm (*una finca verdadera*) in the full meaning of the term. And if the farm has a water supply within its boundaries, this increases its value as not all farms have wells or other local sources of water.

Farms are classified according to size, location, topography and the quality of the soil. A farm near a road, on level land, with "black soil" commands the highest price on the market. Less fortunate farmers regard men who own the best land as superior to themselves and speak of them with respect. In Esperanza, a person with around 40 to 70 acres of land is a "big farmer" and is treated as such. He is addressed as *usted* and may address others by the term *tú* (implying in this context inequality). He is placed higher not only by virtue of having a big farm but also by the fact that he owns the farm. Ownership of a big farm, with no mortgages or other claims upon it, rates a higher prestige than renting a farm of similar size. People usually explain this rating by remarking that the land owner must have worked hard and honestly in the past and that his success is evidence of that.

The scale is then from those who own large good farms to those who do not own or control any land, although other factors are taken into consideration at the same time. Inquiries in 205 households revealed the following details: 140 households owned no land at all, 49 owned plots ranging from ¼ acre to 20 acres, 12 owned plots ranging from 21 acres to 50, and 4 owned plots of 51 acres or more. The tendency is for the biggest plots to have the best quality in type of soil and topography.

Income

Closely related to this land factor is income, which in Esperanza is mainly derived from the land. Peasants produce for a market, and the biggest and best farms are almost fully dedicated to cash crops. This means in a very general way that the bigger and better the farm the higher the income of the owner or operator: land and income vary in direct proportion.

The relatively wealthy farmers also tend to be the ones who employ wage labor on their farms in the production of cash crops (such as sugarcane), so the wage workers tend to be dependent on them for getting at least some of their cash incomes. Many of these wage workers are squatters who do not own land and have just a small piece for growing subsistence crops, and others are small farmers who work as wage laborers to increase their incomes.

Peasants are well aware of income differences. One has only to mention any individual in the area, and they can classify him (or her) very quickly into rich or poor. They speak mainly about *ricos y pobres* (rich and poor) or about *los que tienen y los que no tienen* (the ones that have and the ones that do not have). They infer the income of a person by the amount of land, the size of the house, the amenities (car, television, and the like) and similar visible items, but they do not judge by the clothes a person wears. They say, "A poor man can dress in fine clothes and look like a rich one," or "A rich man can dress like the poor when working, and you cannot distinguish between them." We were once told that some of the rich folk of Esperanza dressed like the poor, in a very humble fashion, but that some poor people dressed like the rich without being able to afford it and with the declared aim of imitating them. The latter were disapproved of on the grounds that, "Each one should stick to his own level."

Occupation and Education

These are two factors that always go hand in hand in the mind of the peasant when making social distinctions. They associate education with work of the mind (*trabajo de la mente*) and divide occupations into two categories: those of manual character (*con las manos*) and those of the mind (*de la mente*). Those of manual character are ranked lower than those of the mind. Those of the mind are made for intelligent persons, and those of manual character are made for the less gifted (*para los brutos*). Most of the wage workers consider themselves not very bright because they never could learn anything at school and could never pass beyond their primary school level, and so they are doing manual work. It must be noted that this is not a rejection of manual work, but clearly places it low on the scale. Farmers do not protest at manual work as such but at the values it carries. They place it low on the scale, but see it as a necessary part of life and attempt to justify it with their image of the hard worker.

Occupations of the mind require more education that those of manual character. But there are also levels within both types of occupation. The headmaster of the local school is placed higher than the teachers of the school because he has more education. The foreman of a farm is placed higher than his assistant, although both of them do manual work (or more specifically, semimanual work). A storekeeper (owner of the store) is placed higher than the assistant or the supervisor, because he is more literate (*sabe más de letras*).

Prestige

Prestige is one of the most difficult things to define in Esperanza. Many factors enter into the situation, but the main ones are those discussed in the preceding paragraphs: land, income, occupation and education. Prestige depends on these factors, but they must be augmented by what persons in Esperanza call by different terms: *consideración* (consideration), *disciplina* (discipline), *caridad* (charity). But before entering into this issue, let us place it in context.

There are some families in Esperanza that are considered the "good families" (*buenas familias*). Most members of these families own some big farms, have a relatively high income and have had above average education, that is to say, beyond the primary school level. These people are farmers who employ wage labor and grow cash crops. Most of them and their parents and grandparents have lived in the area for at least forty or fifty years, or in some cases up to 150 years, and they are considered the old, established families of Esperanza. In a very real sense they are considered members of the upper class of the *barrio*. They comprise about thirty to thirty-five persons in four or five households.

But it is not just the total sum of land, income, education and occupation that places these families at the top. There is the element we have labelled "prestige," for lack of a better term, that complements the situation. These families, to be classed as good families, have to behave in a certain way toward the rest of the community. If somebody needs some money and comes to them for help and gets nothing, all the community will label them as *esmayaos* (misers) and would place them low in the prestige scale of the community. If somebody who is in difficulty with the law comes to ask them to intercede with the town's authorities on their behalf and they refuse, the same lowering of prestige occurs. One informant, a wage laborer, put it this way during an interview: "We call a person high in class when he has some land, money and has consideration in his relations with the people of the *barrio,* a person who serves the community. When that person has all these qualities, he is called an upper-class person. But there are some persons who have land and money and who are ungracious and do not help people, and they are lower than poorer ones."

Social Strata

The people of Esperanza tend to cluster certain families in the same reference group when speaking about them. They do this on the basis of the criteria discussed in the previous section. It must be remembered that these are not clear-cut criteria and, as such, the picture is not a sharply defined one. But there is enough grouping of the units to justify speaking about social strata in Esperanza.

The upper class is a very limited group indeed, composed of something like four or five families. These families are the most respected in the *barrio,* and they own a lot of land. Most of this land is used for cash crops, and they employ a large amount of wage labor, although they have tended to restrict the use of labor in recent years in favor of mechanization. One or two also own some of the stores in Esperanza. The combination of land and commercial enterprises give them great power in the area, both economic and moral. In general, the prestige of these families is very high, and people refer to them as considerate and good-hearted.

The families in this group have quite a high income probably more than $5,000 per family per year. Their houses are the biggest and most comfortable in the *barrio.* They are classified as farmers, even though the work of their farms is done by wage laborers whom they supervise. Only one of them engages in manual work, and he has only recently begun to do so.

These families are well integrated within the *barrio,* and do not anticipate moving to the city, as is the case with other upper-class families in Puerto Rico. They feel that Esperanza is their home and do not wish to leave it. Their ancestors lived in Esperanza for many generations, and they would not like to abandon the place where they were born and reared. The rest of the population shares this feeling, and the general opinion is that these are the "real" families of Esperanza.

It is significant that the children of these families also remain in the *barrio,* and when they get married they continue to live there, not far from their parents. This is particularly the case with the men, who often continue to work as assistants to their fathers. Their parents occupy the dominant positions in the economic system, and they have no motive for moving out of the *barrio* or emigrating abroad, so most of them stay.

There is a group of families in Esperanza that we have defined as lower upper class in relation to the "real" upper class. The main differences between them are that this lower upper class includes newcomers and that the disparities in income and land are such as to justify their inclusion in a different stratum. The people of the *barrio* also make these distinctions when they say, "X is rich, but not so rich as Z."

There are some members of this stratum who are related to people in the upper class by close kinship ties (brothers for example) and there is some degree of intermarriage with the upper class. Their inclusion in a different group is explained basically on economic grounds; they do not have the income or land that their brothers (if this is the relationship) have and so are not considered real upper class. People generally justify this by saying that one worked harder than the other.

The newcomers are people who may have been born in the *barrio* or who have lived there for many years, and who gradually have accumulated some money and land. They have moved up in terms of income and land, and one of them owns a general store in the *barrio*. Some of them proudly state that in time past they were wage laborers and had to work hard, adding that now that they have some money, they behave in a "charitable" way and that they do not put on airs on account of their rise.

The majority are farmers, and they also engage in cash crop cultivation, but on a lesser scale than the upper class. They employ much less wage labor than the larger farmers, and unlike the latter, do not have any form of mechanization on their farms. All of these people own the land they operate, and they never work for others as wage laborers.

Most of the families are well integrated in the *barrio*. Many of them have deep roots in Esperanza, and consider themselves bound to live there for the rest of their lives. A few, however, have some doubts about the wisdom of staying in Esperanza, as they think they do not have much to leave their children after they die. They say that they do not have the resources the upper class has to allow them to send their children to school and even to the university in the capital.

It is very hard to calculate an average income for this class, but perhaps a figure between $2,500 and $3,000 would not be far from the truth. People in the upper class have at least 50 or more acres of first-rate land, while those of the lower upper class would own something like 30 to 40 acres at the most, and in some cases a large part of the land is of poor quality. Most of the land of the upper class has been inherited from their ancestors, but in the lower upper class the method of land acquisition is in many cases by purchase.

Families on this level rank high in prestige, although lower than the upper class. People resort to them as they do to the upper class, but with less frequency. They have less power than the class above them, and people in Esperanza know this. This class includes from fifteen to twenty families.

The middle class is a very broad stratum and includes many more individuals than the two preceding strata combined. It includes around eighty to ninety families in all of Esperanza. This is the class of the small farmer, who owns or controls a small piece of land that can range from a minimum of 5 acres to a maximum of 15. This includes those who rent, share (sharecroppers) or otherwise control land. We are justified in calling it a middle class within Esperanza, because there are considerable differences between it and the two upper classes on the one hand and the lower class on the other.

This stratum includes a small group of people who do clerical work for the government, either in Esperanza or outside. These are persons who approximate the income average of the middle-class peasant, which we estimate at more than $500 but less than $2,000 a year. We also include some small storekeepers and the drivers of the *públicos* that provide public transportation between Esperanza and Arecibo. All these nonfarmers would add up to about fifteen families; thus the bulk of this class is of agricultural origin.

The farmers in this stratum also produce cash crops, but they employ little or no wage labor, as they cannot afford to pay for it. This is the class that makes most use of the *compadrazgo* and other connections when trying to establish themselves as cash crop farmers. Even if they are successful in producing for this market, they are likely to supplement their income by working as wage laborers in the big farms.

Many of these farmers belong to families which have lived for generations in the *barrio,* and many of them can remember when they did not own or control any land and were *agregados* (squatters). They recollect the time when they or their forebears worked and lived on the land of the big families of Esperanza. Others have come to Esperanza from nearby regions and gradually became established there. As a group they consider themselves as belonging to Esperanza and look forward to residing there permanently.

These families have limited resources and are seldom in a position to give help to others. They are more likely to seek help, especially in emergencies, from people in the wealthier classes. They do not emigrate much, if we compare them with the lower class, and they make a conscious effort to avoid emigrating.

The majority of families, numbering almost 200, belong to the lower class. Most of them do not own land, and they live as squatters on the big farms. The land they live on is the most unsuited for cultivation and is not used by its owners, as it is usually hilly and inferior in quality.

These people are not strictly farmers, and they do not show much interest in cultivating the soil for themselves. They are wage laborers who work on the farm where they live, or when work is finished there, on adjacent farms. It is only in time of need that they plant anything, and this only on a small scale. If times get really bad, they occasionally plant some cash crops which they sell in the market in Arecibo.

These people are perhaps the most class conscious of all the strata in Esperanza. They constantly refer to themselves as *los pobres, los arrimados, el obrero mal sufrido* (the poor, the squatters, the poor and suffering laborers), and state that others in Esperanza have at least a piece of land of their own. They emphasize their condition by stating that they can be evicted at any time from the plot they occupy, though this, incidentally, is not allowed by the law.

In terms of income, they are also at the bottom, and most of them probably make less than $500 a year. They can only alleviate their position by subsistence farming or other activities which bring return in kind rather than in cash. Many of them also emigrate and work in the United States.

Many of them were born and reared in Esperanza, although some have come from nearby regions. But they are not a mobile class, as most of them have lived on the same plot for at least a decade, and some for twenty or thirty years.

All in all, the squatters know that they are at the bottom of the scale, and as such orient their behavior when dealing with others, especially with the rich, on whom they depend so much. The squatter may call the big farmer *usted,* and the big farmer reciprocates by calling him *tú.*

ROLE OF DIFFERENT STRATA IN GOVERNMENT

It is hard indeed to pinpoint the role of social class in relation to local government, as this term (local government) does not make any sense in the area. Esperanza is administered from the town of Arecibo, and the people who are in charge are members of a bureaucracy. They are essentially professionals and technicians. When the people want to deal with government matters, they have to go into town and into the offices.

They have to deal with two levels of government: the so-called *insular* (island-wide) government and the *gobierno municipal* (municipal government). The latter is similar to local government bodies in England. At the municipal level the most important position is that of mayor, which is an elective position. So in a very real sense, the mayor depends on the people to get reelected. The position of the mayor has created the following situation: when people from Esperanza (and from other places too, naturally) have a problem (e.g., need medicines and do not have the money to buy them), they ask for an interview and often the problem is solved through the mayor's efforts. This process has become institutionalized, and the mayor has regular hours to deal with these requests.

In a situation like this, a recommendation from the members of the families of Esperanza can be valuable. It ensures that the mayor will try to do his best in the case, as many of these families have kinship connections with other families in town who have some power and influence in the city hall and in the political party in power, of which the mayor is a member.

This is practically the only channel through which the upper class can exert some influence in governmental matters. The centralizing tendencies in the Puerto Rican governmental structure, in which the central government in the capital gets more and more power, has greatly reduced the powers of the municipal government. This, in turn, has reduced the power of the mayor and the influence of this upper stratum. For example, many specialized medical services (e.g., psychiatry) are controlled by the insular government, and it is harder for the upper class of Esperanza to exert influence in the complex bureaucratic structure of the health service to obtain such specialized help. A lower-class person with a *recomendación* will probably have to abide by the rules in the same way as those without one.

The role of other classes in government is much more passive. It is almost limited to the exercise of the vote every four years or the voicing of a complaint to the mayor when he visits Esperanza, a very infrequent event indeed.

ROLE OF DIFFERENT STRATA IN CHURCH AFFAIRS

The role of the upper classes in church affairs is minimal or practically nonexistent. Their only participation is by attendance at regular but not invariable intervals at church events like anybody else in Esperanza. The church in Esperanza is in a very similar position to that of the government, being heavily centralized and directed from the outside. There is no resident priest and during the week (Monday to Friday) the church is closed. It is only on Sunday and on special occasions that the priest comes over from a nearby area. On these occasions he is helped by two or three persons of the middle or lower class who are considered by the rest of the people to be very religious. Most people limit their participation to being part of the congregation.

Other Aspects

There is no institutionalized charity in Esperanza. The emergence of government welfare services, with offices in Arecibo, has altered the situation in which the upper classes could have played a role in the past. In time of need, (poverty, illness, death of a member of the family, and so forth) an individual goes either to the welfare services or to the mayor, perhaps with a recommendation. It is true that in an emergency the neighbors, *compadres* or kin might help, but that is considered a temporary measure, and the final aim is to obtain assistance from an official source. Private charity, such as it is, now supplements government services.

Visiting can perhaps be taken as an index of social differentiation. Two different types of visiting need to be distinguished. There is the visit called *dar la vuelta a ver cómo están* (to drop in for a short visit to inquire about family health, for example). This type appears to follow both class and kinship lines and is a good indication of how the different strata are arranged. This visit would only be made by a member of one class to another member of the same class. The other type of visit is called *molestar un momentito* (to bother you just for a minute). This would be made by a member of a lower class to a member of a higher class, perhaps to request a recommendation or to obtain his wages.

Special Groups

There are some people who do not live in Esperanza, but who come there frequently on account of their jobs or professions. Among them are the school teachers, who arrive in the *barrio* every morning but leave it in the afternoon. Once in a while people from other branches of government also come to the *barrio*. All these persons are more or less classified as "literate people" by the inhabitants of Esperanza and are treated as such. They are addressed by the term *usted,* implying in this case the great respect felt for people who work for the government. But even within these groups they make another differentiation. There is the *empleadito* (the small employee), and there is the *profesional* (professional). By the first they mean that the person is not important (in terms of authority and income) and is just another employee performing a job under the direction of somebody more important than he. The *profesional* is a person (like the school teachers) who has more authority and self-reliance, and probably earns more money. He also *sabe más* (knows more) and must be respected on that account.

All other persons are measured in the same way, and in case of doubt the peasant calls the person *usted* until he can find out more about him.

Examples of Social Differentiation

The following short examples illustrate some of these general principles of social differentiation.

UPPER CLASS

Armando is a member of one of the old families and is considered by many to be the richest person in Esperanza. He has a $10,000 home, about 80 acres of land of excellent quality, and something like 30 head of cattle. There are rumors that he has something like $100,000 in the bank in Arecibo, and once he told us that this was true.

Armando is married and has two children, both of whom are studying, one in the United States and the other at the university in San Juan. He and his family hold high prestige in Esperanza, and everybody considers that he is from a good family. Armando has good connections with the mayor and the party in power, and many times in the past he has written recommendations for persons, which have produced the desired results. Apart from this, Armando states that he does not care about politics, and our observations confirm this, at least for the time we were there. Informants state that he has not been in politics for many years.

Armando does not consider himself a religious man, and neither he nor his family goes to church. He says that he does not care about church matters.

He and his wife are always very busy, but from time to time they pay short visits to kin, brothers, and cousins and others, who live in Esperanza. He is well respected by all in Esperanza and is addressed by the term *don* (implying respect), especially by the members of the lower classes. By contrast we have heard Armando call other people by the term *tú,* also implying social differentiation.

Armando used to cultivate sugarcane on a large scale in the past, but now he has a dairy and is engaged in milk production. He runs the dairy with the occasional help of his wife and son and sometimes wage workers. In the past he used to employ a lot of wage labor. Now he has partially mechanized his dairy, and the cows are milked by machines.

LOWER UPPER CLASS

Heráclito is a man in his sixties, who lives alone on his farm with his wife. All their children are married and have gone away. People in Esperanza say that Heráclito has plenty of money, but not so much as Armando and other members of the upper class.

Heráclito has a farm of some 42 acres and a small herd of ten cows, which are looked after by two full-time laborers.

Heráclito stated that his income (cash) is around $3,500 a year, and there are many products that are produced in the farm and do not have to be bought outside, such as milk, meat and eggs.

He and his wife are well liked and respected by the people of Esperanza, who say that in the past, when he had more money and power, Heráclito used to have a lot of influence at city hall. Heráclito is a sick man now and lives a very quiet and sedentary life. He never goes to church, nor does his wife, who says her prayers at home. The couple never go out visiting and, instead, receive fairly frequent visits from their kin.

MIDDLE CLASS

Clemente has a small farm of about ten acres, which he bought with the help of his father, a retired farmer. He operates the farm himself, and sometimes hires one or two laborers. Clemente sometimes works as a laborer to supplement his income and to help *compadres* when laborers are not plentiful.

He is married and has two children, both of whom attend the local school. Clemente's income is difficult to calculate, but he estimates that it is something like $1,500 a year. He considers himself a "poor man" but states that there are others who do not have any land and are poorer than he. He says that his income and land allow him to lead a decent life and that the future could bring better things as he plans to buy more land if he can get the money. Clemente never goes to church, although he considers himself a religious man.

He is quite an accomplished musician, plays the *cuatro* well, and is always in demand to play at vigils, especially in the homes of his kin and *compadres*.

LOWER CLASS

Macario is a squatter who lives on a plot of land that belongs to a big absentee landowner who owns more than 600 acres of land planted with sugarcane. During the sugarcane harvest, Macario works as a cane cutter. The rest of the year, during the dead season, when the work in the cane has finished, he works in any way he can find (*chiripeando*).

He is married and has two daughters. Macario stated that his income was $500 to $600 a year, adding that sometimes he does not have any work, and they have to tighten their belts. He was able to get permission from a landowner to plant some plantains in a small lot near his house, so that they could have some food for the dead season. Macario used to be a Catholic but was converted to the Pentecostal Church, along with many of his fellow laborers. He says that he has many *compadres* in the area, but that all are poor like himself. He is

Chart 1—General Analysis of Social Stratification in Esperanza

Upper Class

4–5 households
own 51 or more acres of good land
employ plenty of wage labor
some also own stores
high prestige, "old families"
$5,000 or more yearly income
well integrated in *barrio*

Lower Upper Class

15–20 households
own about 30–40 acres
employ some wage labor
some own stores
less prestige, some are related to "old families," some are "newcomers"
$2,500–3,000 yearly income
relatively well integrated in *barrio,* some marginal

Middle Class

80–90 households
own 5–20 acres
employ little wage labor, work partly as wage laborers
some are clerks (some who are not farmers)
more than $500 but less than $2,000 yearly income
many have lived for generations in *barrio*
seek help from upper class and lower upper classes
some migrate

Lower Class

200–250 squatters (households)
do not own land
wage labor, not farmers
low prestige
income of less than $500 yearly
class conscious
emigrate
sense of dependence on upper and lower upper classes

gloomy about the future and states, "If the government does not help us and give land to us, we are going to die of hunger."

The factors we have discussed tend to divide the people of Esperanza into different social groupings (Chart 1). In general, it can be said that social intercourse in all its aspects tends to be carried on more among members of the same class. But there is also plenty of social intercourse among members of different classes. Ties of kinship, *compadrazgo*, neighborhood, often cut across social class, though in a limited way. Thus, although there are social strata, four as we see it, there are many cross-cutting divisions. The system is not a closed one, but neither is it fully open. There is, however, one factor that tends to unit all the people of Esperanza into a single community. This is the sense of belonging to the *barrio*, reflected very clearly when they say, "I am from Esperanza." This conveys a real sense of identity, of belonging to the same social entity. It is not just an amorphous feeling, but a very precise and clear sentiment. If you belong to Esperanza and see a fight between two men in Arecibo, and then discover that one is from Esperanza, you automatically intervene on his behalf without waiting to see who is right or wrong. This sense of identity outweighs all class distinctions and is one of the prime sources of Esperanza's very real unity.

CHAPTER 15

Relations With the Government:
Community *vs.* State

Despite its apparent isolation, Esperanza is related in multiple ways to the outside world. This contact with the exterior is mediated by a series of institutions that operate at different levels and in different patterns. One such institution is the police. The police force in Puerto Rico is an island-wide organization with headquarters in San Juan, about 80 miles from Esperanza. As mentioned earlier, there are no local policemen in Esperanza. The nearest local police force operates from the town of Arecibo. The police are then not a permanent factor in Esperanza; they appear only occasionally, and they usually operate within very specific circumstances. For example, many persons in Esperanza engage in the manufacture of illegal rum. This is distilled in secret. When police come into the *barrio* it is usually to arrest somebody who operates an illegal distillery. They regularly find them through the use of undercover agents, who pose as civilians and who visit the area. The casual comment, "X was arrested for making *cañita*" (local name for illegal rum), is heard around Esperanza with some frequency.

There are also some special community activities where the assistance of the police is requested. For instance, when a *velada* (school party) is celebrated, at least one policeman is assigned to watch and maintain order among the many who attend. On other occasions two or three policemen dressed as civilians can be seen in the *barrio,* indicating that somebody (in many cases the school authorities) filed a complaint with the police in Arecibo. They may be making sure that the cafe near the school does not play the juke box during school hours and that small children do not play billiards instead of attending classes.

Sometimes uniformed police come in groups, perhaps looking for someone from the community who was in jail and has escaped. We remember one case of a young man who escaped from the jail in Arecibo. According to rumors, he had escaped in order to kill his wife, who, it was said, was having an affair with another man while he was in prison. We saw a group of five policemen driving about in a jeep. They came during the day and returned to Arecibo at night.

These are the few kinds of situations in which Esperanza and the police come into contact. At this level of conflict, the situation is structured and defined from the outside; Esperanza is not a politically independent community, but is part of a bigger society. The referent here is Puerto Rico, and in some cases the United States. The rules of the game are drawn by the state. They are defined as laws, and it is the job of the police to apply the law. *Esperanzeños* meet the law through the police and in doing so they meet the state. This is really the political level, where communal behavior is being judged by the state. We have then two sectors: the community and the state.

The situation, or relation, is a very tense one. People do not trust the state. In general, they see it as a kind of enemy, but in some instances, they see it as a patron, with whom they must interact in a ritualized and formalized manner. An individual must humble himself, but as a way of maximizing his profits. The relationship, then, is one of opposition in terms of values and institutionalized referents. People do not have a friendly and close relationship with the state or its representatives. They speak of *el gobierno* (the government) in opposition to their communal and personal levels of interaction.

This attitude of rural societies can be found in many places (for example, see Wolf 1966:1–35). In some instances it assumes the form of a rural versus urban opposition. Government officials are seen as urban types with urban interests, and when they come into contact with rural society, it is with the intention of exploiting it. The city is seen as the embodiment of centralization, bureaucracy, impersonality. In many cases the rural society is subordinated to the political and legal power and authority of the state. This can force the emergence of some professions and occupations which act as mediators between the state and the people. Similar patterns, with some local variations, have been described by many students of rural societies. In the study of Mediterranean societies, the clearest discussion of patron-client relationships can be found in Campbell's (1964:195–281) study of the Sarakatsani. In that pastoral society, patronage is the link between the rural local community and the city and the government.

Some of the elements Campbell finds in these relations can be found in Esperanza when the people interact with the police. Local people distrust the police, and relations with them are ambivalent. They appear to respect them but they also fear them. We have the impression that there is also an element of hate. What is completely absent is a sense of identification with the policeman as the representative of the state. When police intervene and begin asking questions, people do not talk; they try to avoid any involvement. The attitude is one of "let them do their own jobs," and is even more clearly manifest when they are asked to testify before the government attorney. The documents available in the court of Arecibo contain many pages of declarations given by witnesses from Esperanza during the last twenty or twenty-five years. We examined all of them and the pattern was always the same. Their answers were stereotyped and as brief as possible. It was plain from the records that the attorney was having trouble eliciting information from his "informants," who were trying deliberately to evade giving any kind of information.

Two additional examples can give more force to our argument. We mentioned the *veladas* (school parties) as one occasion when policemen are sent to the *barrio* to maintain order. The relationship with the police officer in attendance is always a tense one. He keeps shouting as he moves around and makes abusive comments. His attitude is one of trying to impose his will over the local people, who react by playing around, often angering him. Youngsters particularly pretend not to hear his orders. The relationship tends to be antagonistic, something like the one found between males in the *relajo* pattern in the cafes. The other case is a more specific example. On one occasion in the middle of the day, the body of a murdered woman was discovered in Esperanza. We rushed, with many other *esperanzeños,* to the place where the body had been found. We had a camera and began taking pictures before the police arrived. Many of those present jumped out of range immediately, as they did not want to appear in the photographs. Some commented that they did not want any trouble. No one had touched the body, as everyone was waiting for the district attorney to initiate the investigation. But being photographed with the body would, in their minds, have somehow connected them too concretely with what they perceived as being a problem pertaining to government offices. It would also have made it impossible to deny having seen the body if called on to be a witness.

The people in Esperanza have not internalized the moral legitimacy of the state's law. They see the law of the state as power, as the capacity to force them to conform to certain patterns of behavior. The law is seen as something imposed from the outside. They avoid and hate the whole legal process, including the police and the courts. The rational and profound moral understanding of the law as the basic norms of social interaction is clearly lacking. The two basic concepts that are fundamental for analyzing this process are the concept of community and that of the state. The community is affected by the law, but persists in using its own criteria to deal with conflict. The result is tension between the two levels as the different systems of values come into contact. The maker of illegal rum, when caught by the police and fined by the courts, does not feel any guilt in a moral sense; he merely resents being caught and fined. *Esperanzeños* who hear of the incident do not condemn the person at a moral level. For them the fact that he was caught was merely an unfortunate mistake. They evaluate the person in his conflict with the law in individual terms; it is the man against the law. If somebody from the *barrio* helps the law he is called *un alcahuete, soplón* (a pimp, informer), a very negative evaluation indeed. Such a person who works for the police will not be trusted by his fellow *esperanzeños*.

This opposition between these two levels transcends the mere example of Esperanza. In many communities studied by anthropologists in the Mediterranean, the distinction between some kind of concept of community and the state is found. The point to emphasize is that the relation between the community and the state is not one of integration. The fundamental characteristic is opposition, some kind of distrust and tension.

Even in a community where there is a formal local political organization, the tendency is to transcend the formal process of law and engage instead in informal arrangements. The fundamental thing is that the communal-moral level puts pressure on the state-legal one, and the final decision is given in some cases in terms of the former. It can be argued that this is a characteristic of every social system where there is a state in the modern sense. We do not pretend to portray this process as peculiar to Mediterranean or Caribbean societies, but it is, however, a profitable area for comparison.

Pitt Rivers comments in relation to the Andalusian town he studied: "A strong distaste for formal justice, a distrust of it and a preference for an equitable arrangement are to be found in the sentiments of the whole *pueblo* including those of the legal authorities" (1961:129).

Another variation on the same theme relating Puerto Rican and Mediterranean patterns is implied by Wilson when he concludes:

In Puerto Rico observers have pointed out the prevalent indulgence in illegal activities such as the lottery and numbers (*bolita*), drinking illegally-distilled rum ("bushy" in most Caribbean societies), living in consensual unions, fighting and so on (Mintz 1956:364). In studies of European peasantry (e.g. Pitt Rivers 1961) similar activities and proclivities are noted and those who are most proficient become folk heroes enjoying great "reputations"—bandits and smugglers, for example. A similar, though not necessarily identical feature, seems to be characteristic of Caribbean societies. It is surely not accidental that the very activities most central to the achievement and maintenance of manhood and reputation are those proclaimed illegal by the total society (gambling, smuggling, fighting or readiness to fight, banditry, embezzlement and bribery, for example) (1969:70).

The two examples correspond in general to the pattern we have examined in some detail for Esperanza. The communal and the state level appear in a relationship of opposition, of contrast.

Another complex of state institutions that becomes relevant at the external-internal level of conflict is the educational system. It is represented in Esperanza by the local school and its fifteen teachers. The school is public and education is compulsory. It provides a nine-year course for students of both sexes. As described elsewhere, none of the teachers or the principal are residents of the *barrio*. Normally, the school is accepted by the *barrio* inhabitants as a useful and legitimate institution. *Esperanzeños* see the school as a means of providing a diploma (*darles un diploma*) for their children, although a limited one. If they can afford it, and the government backs them up, they send their children to study at Arecibo's high school.[1]

The conflict between the educational system, as represented by the school, and the people of Esperanza operates at different levels and in a variety of situations. Among the older generation there is some sense of dissatisfaction with the school. They criticize certain aspects of the educational system. For example, they state that education was better when they went to school and that a person with an old "eight-year diploma" (eighth grade) knows more than one with a modern twelve-year diploma (high school). The implication is that today's education is lower in quality than yesterday's. This is a latent conflict that most of the time is only verbalized, but it indicates how the older generation perceives the aims and the system. There is no direct confrontation in this respect with the teachers and other school officers.

There is another level of conflict that can emerge into the open, though in many cases without a direct confrontation between teachers and parents. This involves the requirements of agricultural activity versus school attendance. As stated previously, school attendance is compulsory; parents are obliged to send their children to school. If they do not comply with this law, school officers can coerce the parents through the police. The police have a special organization for dealing with these problems. They usually visit the parents and conduct an

---

[1]The relationship between education and mobility in Puerto Rican society has been examined with some limitations by Tumin (with Feldman 1961).

investigation. This situation can occur when a farmer does not have enough people to harvest his crops. The parents resort to using their own children temporarily, and the children will not be able to attend school.

We remember a case in point which dramatizes the issue. One day we met Nèstor, a peasant who owns a farm of some 60 acres. He was angry and made derogatory comments about the teachers. He had needed some of his younger sons to do some work on the family farm, and they had been absent from school. Some of the teachers had commented that they would request the assistance of the police if the sons continued to be absent. Nèstor was angry because he thought it was his prerogative as a father to order and have authority over his sons. He said that they were his sons and he was their father and that the teachers and the police did not have any authority over sons.

The basis of the conflict is very clearly the exercise of paternal rights versus the state's rights to demand compulsory education of its younger citizens. The domestic realm of the family, which operates at a household level within the *barrio*'s limits, was being opposed by the requirements of the state through the educational system. The tensions of the two levels manifest themselves in a kind of subtle fight, where the use of the police by the teachers (both as a potential and actual resource) serves as a mediating and connecting link between the contestants. In this way a direct confrontation is avoided. If the children are needed by their parents and start being absent, the teachers warn the children about the possible use of the police. The children will tell their parents, and they will react accordingly. The result is that an indirect process of interaction sets in, and the mechanisms of conflict-solution operate. This is what happened to Nèstor. The police may be substituted by the social worker, who will visit the family and inquire as to the cause of the children's absences. On such occasions, the parents often seem to adopt a humble and apparently submissive pose in front of the government officer. There is no overt aggression, either verbal or physical, towards the visitor. The questions and interrogation are met with smiles. The attitude taken by the parents tries to communicate the idea that they were helpless, that they were forced to use their children during school hours. The pose is basically a defense mechanism, an attempt to avoid *some* guilt or shame (*vergüenza*).

It is reminiscent of similar ways of behavior observed in other sectors of Puerto Rican society. Seda Bonilla (1969b) has commented that this type of conduct is related to antidemocratic practices. For him it reflects a servile attitude, an accommodation to a highly centralized and autocratic government and society. This leads to patronage and to the manipulation of the governmental structure in extragovernmental terms.

Campbell's (1964) interpretation is somewhat different in the sense that the element of servilism is not so clear-cut. The Sarakatsan shepherd appears servile and submissive, but he knows that he is manipulating the system and expects something in return. He has entered into the relationship because he needs something and in so doing he tries to circumvent bureaucracy and formal authority. In this sense the situation of the parents in the context of Esperanza is different from the Greek shepherds; they are forced into a situation, but the shepherd has entered in a relatively voluntary fashion. We are not stating that the Puerto Rican parents do not know that they are manipulating the situation; they know it fully. But the type and content of the relationship is different. Similar levels (communal-familiar and state) are involved. The general structural pattern is similar; the specific level is different.

There is an additional level of conflict which illustrates the relationships among the local community, the state, and the spoils system at the municipal and *barrio* level. The *barrio* had a bus that transported the local school children to and from their homes. The bus driver was a resident of the *barrio* who belonged to the party in power in Puerto Rico, and who presumably got the position due to political patronage. When the elections took place again, the party in power lost and a new party came to power. The driver lost his position, and the bus was moved to another *barrio*. The position of bus driver formed part of the spoils system: Esperanza lost its bus as the result, not of an educational decision, but as the result of a purely political one. This behavior brought protests from many of the *barrio*'s inhabitants. Political forces operating inside and outside the *barrio* had created a conflict within the *barrio,* between two *barrios,* and between the *barrio* and the political party that had won the elections. This last factor controlled the town of Arecibo where all the political and administrative decisions are made at town hall by the mayor (for an understanding of the political process in Puerto Rico, see Anderson 1965).

In relations with the townsman, there is a kind of tension, a defensive mood. We perceived it immediately in our own relations with the peasants and other inhabitants of Esperanza. And even after almost two years of living and interacting with the people, there was always something in the conversation, in their way of reacting, that gave us a sense of social distance. This tone could assume many forms. Sometimes it was the comment that we made a lot of money (*usted gana mucho dinero*). This was stated in a mixture of implied irony, envy and cynicism. On other occasions it assumed a more direct form. For instance, if we left early from a vigil or any social festivity, the host would comment that "you do not like to be with the poor" (*no quiere estar con nosotros los pobres).* At other times they would say, "You know much about books" (*usted sabe mucho de letras*). We used to ride horseback around the *barrio,* but to begin with we had little control over the horse. Once a peasant commented: "You may be a school-master (*maestro de escuela*) but you are not a master of horses (*maestro de caballos*)"—something that to *esperanzeños* is much more important than books.

The situation reflects what Caro Baroja (1963) has described as the "two elements of the dichotomy." He argues in favor of a historical structural and functional approach when studying the relations between town and countryside:

In summary, I believe it would be worthwhile to study the people of the Mediterranean in terms of the structural and functional relations between the two elements of the dichotomy, paying more attention to the historical reality than to the abstractions of the moralists and their disciples, the sociologists. The general problems of the culture and society of the country-side and of the city are not easily discussed without taking into account the dimensions and constituents of the polis or its equivalent. Following Socrates, I believe that one must examine the essential ties which relate those who may be considered the characteristic representatives of *"rus-ticistas"* with those who typify *"urbanitas."* Their cultural universe is con-ditioned at each point in time by the strength of the traditions which link them to their past (1963:40).

The several instances mentioned previously in this chapter can be studied using the dichotomy rural (community) versus urban (state) in terms of a relational model characterized by contacts of contrasted relationships. The interrelations are basically those of opposition, of antagonism. The examples discussed constitute some of the "essential ties" which relate the inhabitants of Esperanza to the state.

CHAPTER 16

Conclusions

The traditional picture of Esperanza is one of a peasant community with patrifocal family patterns and where males control all the systems outside the domestic one. Land has traditionally been held in three ways, by relatively big local landowners, by a middle and small sector of peasants, and by one or two big landowners who do not reside in the *barrio*. To this general picture we can add the heavy migration to the United States that has taken place in the last twenty years. This is the configuration we confronted. But changes initiated from the outside are taking place, and they are going to have quite an impact in the structural patterns this community presents. One of the forces with which we will have to reckon is the dependence on the American economy that brought about the migration process. This influence is likely to continue in the next years, as the *barrio* has suffered changes. As is typical of a dependent area, most of the transformations have come from the outside. Tobacco, heavily dependent on American buyers, is on the decline. The peasants depend on this product to maintain themselves as proprietors and as controllers of the means of production, although on a small scale. As indicated, this is closely related to the patrifocal character of family patterns. Any change in this important economic factor of ownership would have a great impact on family patterns. If they lose their land (something like this is beginning to take place), their position would be very similar to the *agregados* (squatters), where patterns appear to be less patrifocal.

In terms of some of the directions that change may take, some structural changes can be expected. In the first place, family patterns are likely to be transformed in the direction of more formal and *de facto* equality for women, who are beginning to abandon the traditional role that limited them to the domestic sphere. The channels being used to transcend the domestic role are several: education, migration or employment in industrial concerns outside Esperanza. This will probably affect the distribution of authority within the traditional household. Thus patrilocality will begin to change in the direction of a more "democratic" family structure. The economic basis of the whole family is expected to be different with the emergence of a more proletarianized family (although imitating urban middle-class patterns) less economically dependent on the land. It will depend more on salaries derived from manufacture or from agricultural work (especially for males) done in large agricultural and capitalistic concerns in the United States or in manufacturing work in Puerto Rico. Thus the mobility of the labor force, its inclusion of women, and the different basis of economic activity (proletarian instead of peasant ownership) will undoubtedly bring about change in family patterns. This would be especially accelerated among the quasi-peasants whom we labeled *agregados*. Naturally, all these trends and their impact will depend on the continuation of the present direction.

There is another area that seems ready for change. We expect that interaction models based on kinship and *personalismo* will be transformed and that relationships will be of a more individualized and contractual type. *Compadrazgo* and kinship connections are thus likely to be replaced. This is fully consistent with the changes expected in the sphere of family roles. The family is becoming more democratic and is breaking away from the system of traditional (*personalismo* and *compadrazgo*) relationships. Relationships outside the family system follow other channels. This trend will show even in the area of religion. In the past, and in the period when we were doing our field research, Esperanza has been more or less a Catholic *barrio*. But this unity is being broken, and religions are competing for clients. This fits nicely with the individualized and contractual level of relationships. Thus the traditional integration of several structures (patrilocal family structure, economy based on the use of property or land, *compadrazgo* and *personalismo* systems of relations, a relatively monolithic Roman Catholicism) into a coherent whole at the *barrio* level is being broken and substituted by a more mobile and less localized one.

These trends are likely to continue and will in the long run transform the *barrio*'s whole fabric of social relations. It is unlikely that Puerto Rico will be able in the near future to divorce itself from the United States and from the heavy economic and political influence that it exerts on the island. The colonial status of the island, the conservative trends in local politics (and in the metropolis) still hold firm since the formal structures of power are reinforcing instead of lessening these influences. The dynamics of the migration process are also solidifying the ties between Puerto Rico and the United States. As we see it, there is no way of reversing these trends, short of trying a military and political revolution, which would be suicide from the strategic point of view. As part and parcel of Puerto Rico, Esperanza will have its share of these processes now at work.

Anthropology and Fieldwork: A Critique

So-called research, as practiced today in many places and especially in Puerto Rico, consists of what we characterize as the "dictatorship of the questionnaire." The investigator, usually called the chief investigator, is a respected member of the academic community. He is regularly a well-connected person who can command sufficient resources from private or public institutions. In this manner he can group around him a whole staff of research assistants with plenty of clerical help, office space and all the material resources available. With all this accomplished, the process starts. The chief or his deputy gathers all his people. Something must be said about the deputy, as this role often reflects the colonialism rampant in the social sciences. In Puerto Rico, the deputy is frequently a "native," that is, a Puerto Rican. He is the one who does the dirty work. The chief investigator is regularly a foreigner, usually a North American. He is considered the "expert," the "mind" behind the project.

The mechanics of research operate in the following manner. The chief investigator decides on the subject to be studied, or is invited by a research center, government agency, or some other institution. Two main tasks must be achieved; the construction of the questionnaire and the training of the interviewers. These two are sacrosanct, and any deviation from this main pattern is implicitly forbidden. The questionnaire is usually a very rigid document.

It is structured under the premise that it will be the basic (and many times the *only*) tool and means of gathering data. The questions are made up in such a way that the subtleties of the culture and society are ignored; a dualistic manner of perceiving and living is assumed. You are either in one place or in the other, you cannot be in-between. The complexities, shades, gradations, changes so characteristic of social life, remain ungathered, are totally ignored. The dogmatism of the questionnaire emerges. There are several reasons for this way of doing research. The questionnaire is available for quantification, as the questions and answers have been prepared with this in mind. Numbers, then, due to their symmetry, provide the illusion of being able to grasp social reality. They can be controlled easily. The intention is to offer a closed image of reality. This is clearly revealed in the process of gathering the data and also in the training of the research assistants. The training is merely the manner of learning the questionnaire, in many cases by memory, in such a way as to be able to gather the data by the most efficient method. This last concept is interpreted in quantitative terms: time and money. The process of becoming a research assistant should not go beyond, does not transcend, the technical level. No theoretical training is needed.

When we were confronted with the problem of doing research in our own country, the reaction was one of alienation. We were working towards the doctorate at Cambridge and had been thinking on a series of themes for the dissertation. All of them were exotic and seemed far away in our minds, like the anthropological study we intended to do on the work of the French novelist of the last century, Henri Beyle (Stendhal), or a similar one about Dostoevski. We were being bookish and intellectual; we wanted to work on a "respectable" theme. When we arrived at Cambridge and started suggesting those themes, the authorities felt that they were not within the competence of the Faculty of Archaeology and Anthropology, and implied that perhaps we should move or get transferred to another faculty within the university, like classics. Our initial reaction was one of hostility and later of confusion. During some months of rethinking, we gradually came to realize the positive aspects and the limitations of the faculty, as we were able to perceive them. They worked under a heavily positivistic and empiricist tradition, with an emphasis on fieldwork, and within the province of certain restricted themes, such as kinship, political systems and the like. There existed a kind of distrust of broad theoretical schemes, and some aversion for themes like social change.

We became interested in the subject of family structure and its relation to certain aspects of the economic system, more specifically, with the occupational system. All this within a dynamic perspective, assuming there was such a thing as a family cycle. We were still heavily influenced by the limited approach (in some respects) of the Cambridge School. But there was something in this "limited" approach that developed an incipient reaction in our perspective of the social sciences and in particular towards social research. The work we were going to do in

Puerto Rico was very specialized, but the preparations (readings, drawing up questions, specific subthemes to be developed, models to be used) were developing within a very flexible and individualistic framework. We had also come to realize a very simple thing indeed; we were going to do research about our own country—in spite of our attempts to work with an "intellectual theme." The fieldwork tradition at Cambridge had pushed us towards our own country, where the custom was to work on "serious themes about Western Society," and where it was left to foreigners (Americans) to do research and to become the standard authorities on Puerto Rico. The "natives" would adopt an elitist view, study the classics, Spanish society. But to engage in serious and systematic social research about Puerto Rico was unthinkable. Consequently, there exists a large bibliography of works done by Americans in our island, but the standards, by any kind of measure, are mediocre, to say the least. Only one or two rise above this level.

During the period we spent preparing for the fieldwork tour, the reaction was to get away from the dogmatism of the questionnaire. In this respect we were working in a kind of environment that would make things easier, as social anthropology has a more open approach to research. It can be criticized on other grounds, for example, in its exaggerated empiricism, or in trying to avoid the problem of social change; but for us, in this particular situation, with this kind of background and experience, it was facilitating things and opening paths by which we could transcend dogmatism. It should be stated very emphatically that we were not (nor are we now, at the moment of writing this) rejecting the questionnaire as *one* of our resources, but as the *only* one. All this process was, at the moment, a purely intellectual and theoretical one, as we had never done fieldwork previously. We were wary of the unidimensionality of social research and were trying to grasp a multidimensional and flexible approach to fieldwork.

We arrived at Esperanza armed with an intellectual arsenal and with a plurality of preconceptions. We had decided to be open and multidimensional, but this was a mental attitude. The first two months confirmed our experience with the "imported experts." At first all we got from the study of the community were disconnected facts. Later we began to see connections, and later still, the subtleties began to emerge. We might add here that this last stage was the most difficult and prolonged. No questionnaire can grasp (we even hate the term) the subtle shades of different colors and tonalities of life, of humanity.

We have talked at length of situations and fieldwork and have attacked the unidimensionality and technical approach of social research in Puerto Rico. If we learned anything about fieldwork during our tour in Esperanza, it is that there is no substitute for hard work, flexibility and for what we would call sensitivity to human beings and human situations. Oscar Lewis, in a discussion we had some years ago, said that "the British (anthropologists) lose their people." He was attacking the structural-functional approach so characteristic of this tradition, and which in its worst aspects resorts to an institutional-normative approach and neglects the unique and individual aspects of humans. In a reply reminiscent of Durkheim's attempt to give sociology its own "area of study," we made a defense of social anthropology as a theoretical science and evaded (unconsciously?) the fundamental challenge that Lewis had made (for another critique, see Banaji 1970). The reader can notice that this work reflects the limitations of the institutional-normative approach criticized by Lewis. This is a challenge that has not been answered on our part, and one that we think is still valid. Lewis focused his attention on a dimension that was being neglected by anthropologists; his interest in the microscopic and minute parts of the social system and culture, and in the ways people perceived their life and others' lives, is similar to what has been happening in some sectors of sociology in the United States, and in other sectors of the social sciences. The so-called (and we use a very stereotyped label) "institutional" approach has been supplemented by a kind of psychological one where the individual is taken into account, and where the institution (as defined in a normative and sometimes idealistic manner) is only one of the factors under consideration. The works of Goffman (1959) and Laing (1959) are a good example of this trend. In the case of Lewis's work, this was his merit. His limitations are found on the other side of the fence; in his lack of a general and comparative model from which to arrive at the theoretical level.

There is an aspect of the institutional approach that has been overlooked by its critics and which links Lewis's approach and intentions with this mode of operating. It may sound odd, but here it is. Both approaches start directly from the people, although they may arrive at different points. Both form part of a tradition of fieldwork in anthropology, and in spite of Lewis's remark that "the British lose their people," and our remark that Lewis does not have a theoretical framework, both started from direct contact with human beings. We emphasize this aspect, because there is a way of operating today which neglects these common aspects. Anthropology is in a state of crisis today, but we reject the unidimensional perspective which sees only differences and breakdowns, and which tries to reduce the discipline to the label that it is a "colonial area of knowledge or activity." The matter is more subtle and complex.

We think that we have offered the reader a more or less competent monograph of a Puerto Rican rural community and the connections or relationships among its different parts. The approach is an institutional one, quite traditional in other regions of the world where anthropologists have worked (Africa, for instance), but absent in studies done in Puerto Rico. In Puerto Rico, research in the social sciences has oscillated between two points. The first one has already been mentioned when we referred to the "dictatorship of the questionnaire"; the second one will be called "descriptive." Information is given to the reader, but there is no theoretical framework, nor any sense of the relatedness of social life. This book goes somewhat beyond these two trends. It evades the unidimensionality of the questionnaire and demonstrates the relevant relationships between different segments of social life. This was learned through experience and hard work, and under the influence of different schools of thought.

There is another aspect in which this work can serve as a starting point for much needed research. We have called Esperanza a traditional society, and we cannot ignore the fact that a brutal process of social change is taking place, although we have not treated it in depth. This process is destroying whatever is left of traditional society in Puerto Rico, and the average islander contemplates the spectacle of the countryside's being converted into a city—urbanized. In Puerto Rico, the traditional community is doomed. All values and decisions operate in favor of a modernized and urbanized society. *Esperanzeños* are being subjected to this process, and traditional Esperanza is giving place to a new Esperanza. The book, then, can serve as a base from which to study change and its implications. What will happen to the peasant, to the *agregado*? What will happen to traditional religion? What new types of economic activities will take place, and what changes in the social structure can be expected? To be able to project, one must know what exists.

There is a more specific aspect of this process in which we became interested later, and which we have just started to explore with our students. In a seminar on peasant societies, the question of what has been the role of the countryside in the formation of modern capitalist society was brought up. Moore's (1966) classic work, *The Social Origins of Dictatorship and Democracy,* was used as a means of exploring this theme in modern national states. After much discussion, we turned our attention to Puerto Rico and discovered that we did not even have any basic general information on how this process took place in our own society. As a suggestion for further research, this is a challenge that both social historians and anthropologists must answer. Investigators must explore questions like the following in a manner similar to the way Moore and others have done it in modern industrial states. How was the social and economic organization of the countryside in Puerto Rico structured? What were the main characteristics of the productive process in the countryside? Was there any surplus, and if so, to where was it channeled? What were the relationships between the internal agricultural economy and the outside world? To this should be added research on the economic role of the upper classes, the peasants and the agricultural workers. There is also the extra work involved in tracing how the idea of private property developed and was implemented in such measures as the enclosures, and the gradual alienation of the land from the small peasant through indebtedness, and in some cases, actual expropriation. All this enormous task is right there, waiting for rigorous investigation.

Certain problems closely integrated into an anthropologist's life and vocation emerge when one is dealing with a book like this, which involves relating, in a direct manner, to human beings. In the first place, there is the problem of "objectivity." Up to this day, we do not have a clear picture (must one?) on this theme. When one is doing research among poor people, how should one behave? Is there not a sense of hypocrisy in asking them about their incomes and asking for and getting other information from them, and professing to practice a profession with a humanist background? Can this be properly called humanism? We give ourselves different, and many times contradictory, replies. We can answer that we are intellectuals, that we are interested in theory, and that if we want intellectual development in the discipline, theory must be separated from praxis. On other occasions we jump to the opposite side, and nihilism takes hold: to hell with anthropology, there is no sense in what we are doing, only praxis counts; one must go into politics, or whatever type of "real" activity, and do something. But we perceive our inability to do anything about it, and we see ourselves as academics in the worst meaning of the term. The only answer of any real significance that we have given is to continue nurturing our paradox and to be conscious of it. We noticed the poor in Esperanza, we did our research and expressed our sympathies for their problems. Sometimes, not very many, we were able to give a little help. A book was written, but the poor are still living in poverty in Esperanza.

There is another part to this "guilty conscience" complex. Deloria (1969) has written a very perceptive and cynical (in the positive sense) book about the Indians and the white man. In a chapter entitled "Anthropologists and Other Friends," he draws a picture of the anthropologist and his manipulation of his "subjects." Reading this, we became aware that we too, had manipulated ours. We became friendly with our subjects because we needed them, and we needed them because we were working for a degree to be able to operate in the market, in Academia. For the researcher, this poses a problem. He is using human beings as means. The relation, then, becomes a purely instrumental one. One uses a rhetoric of consideration, of kindness, mixed many times with the classical anthropological paternalism, which we seem to have inherited from the founding fathers and their tours of colonial possessions. In our relationship with the people of Esperanza they are fading away in our memory and in the frequency and intensity of contacts. The brutal question we repeat to ourselves constantly then is: what is anthropology? Is it only a way of living, of earning a salary, of doing some work and getting paid for it? What values should we have, or should we be indifferent to all this? What is the human value of having done research in Esperanza? Are we a better sort of human being after this experience, or are we just a "living curriculum vitae" with a college degree, a profession, but without humanity?

An additional dimension makes our situation and that of other fellow anthropologists more inconvenient and tragic and paradoxical. In these days, we hear a lot about liberation and about the crisis in anthropology, especially at its academic level. Many investigators go to the poor, the marginal people, and throw away all that has to do with "traditional anthropology." But the result in many cases represents a return to what they were trying to reject. The most repugnant and representative example is the so-called study of the "culture of poverty," where the final result is that the poor stay poor and the investigator becomes a professional (and rich) and lives off this "racket." Anthropology is then transformed into an immoral discipline or endeavor. In Puerto Rico, we have this type of scholar, who lives on a diet of seminars, research projects and coordinated activities. Much money flows, people travel, have cocktails, dramatize the poor poor (*los pobres pobres*) but continue their alienated and immoral activity. And to add to the crisis in the discipline, what comes out, in terms of quality of their studies, is mediocrity itself in the form of reports.

A final comment on the dialectics between fieldwork and theory. Today it is the fashion to speak in almost exclusively favorable tones of fieldwork: experience, contact with the "real" thing is what counts. In our opinion (and our own work reflects this handicap), this posture leads only to a sterile empiricism, and there is no transcendence of the particular, which always should be one of the basic features of anthropology. Anthropology should be a theoretical discipline and should look for universals. Fieldwork, then, is the "dialectical husband" of theory, the flow which nurtures generality. Within the confused and critical anthropological environment that we live in today, this outlook is a constant for us. Anthropology, if it is to survive (and this is the issue that faces us today as a discipline) must search in this direction.

Bibliography

Part I: Puerto Rico

Anderson, R. W.
1965 *Party politics in Puerto Rico.* Stanford: Stanford University Press.

Batchelder, R. B.
1951 The subhumid plain of northwestern Puerto Rico: a study on rural land utilization. Unpublished Ph.D. dissertation, Northwestern University.

Blanco, T.
1948 *El prejuicio racial en Puerto Rico.* 2d. ed. San Juan: Editorial de Biblioteca de Autores Puertorriqueños.

Buitrago Ortiz, C.
1967 *La vida* de Oscar Lewis. *Revista de Ciencias Sociales* 2(2):235–39.

Hernández Alvarez, J.
1967 *Return migration to Puerto Rico.* Berkeley: University of California Press.

Jones, C. and R. Picó
1955 *Symposium on the geography of Puerto Rico.* Rio Piedras: University of Puerto Rico Press.

Landy, D.
1959 *Tropical childhood.* Chapel Hill: University of North Carolina Press.

Lauria, A.
Respeto, relajo and interpersonal relations in Puerto Rico. *Anthropological Quarterly* (37):53–67.

Lewis, O.
1967 (*as subject*) Discusión en torno al libro *La vida* de Oscar Lewis. *Revista de Ciencia Sociales* 2(2).
1969 *La vida.* (Spanish) Mexico City: Editorial Joaquín Mortiz.

Manners, R. A.
1956 Tabara: subcultures of a tobacco and mixed crops municipality. In J. Steward (ed.), *The people of Puerto Rico.* Urbana: University of Illinois Press.

Mintz, S.
1956 Cañamelar: the subculture of a rural sugar plantation proletariat. In J. Steward (ed.), *The people of Puerto Rico.* Urbana: University of Illinois Press.
1960 *Worker in the cane: a Puerto Rican life history.* New Haven: Yale University Press.
1966 Puerto Rico: an essay in the definition of a national culture. In *Status of Puerto Rico, selected background studies.* United States Puerto Rico Commission. Washington: U.S. Government Printing Office.

Padilla, E.
1956 Nocorá: the subculture of workers on a government-owned sugar plantation. In J. Steward (ed.), *The people of Puerto Rico.* Urbana: University of Illinois Press.
1958 *Up from Puerto Rico.* New York: Columbia University Press.

Puerto Rico, Government of
1953 *Informe estadístico del uso de la tierra en el municipio de Arecibo para el año 1950.* San Juan.
1955 *Leyes de Puerto Rico anotadas.* Stony Brook, L.I.: Equity Publishing.
1970 Junta de planificación. *Informe economico al gobernador.* San Juan.

Rosario, J. C.
1935 *The development of the Puerto Rican jíbaro and his present attitude towards society.* Rio Piedras: University of Puerto Rico Press.

Seda Bonilla, E.
1969a *Interacción social y personalidad.* 2d. ed. San Juan: Ediciones Juan Ponce de León.
1969b La socialización de la personalidad en el contexto de la cultura y del poder. Paper read at the annual meeting of the Society for Applied Anthropology, Mexico City.

Steward, J. (ed.)
1956 *The people of Puerto Rico.* Urbana: University of Illinois Press.

Stycos, J. M.
1958 *Family and fertility in Puerto Rico.* Mexico City: Fondo de Cultura Económica.

Tumin, M. (with A. Feldman)
1961 *Social class and social change in Puerto Rico.* Princeton: Princeton University Press.

Wolf, E.
1956 San Jose: subcultures of a "traditional" coffee municipality. In J. Steward (ed.), *The people of Puerto Rico.* Urbana: University of Illinois Press.

Part II: General

Arensberg, C. M.
1937 *The Irish countryman.* London: Macmillan.

Arensberg, C. M. and Kimball, S. T.
1940   *The family and community in Ireland.* Cambridge: Harvard University Press.

Banaji, Jairus
1970   The crisis of British anthropology. *New Left Review* no. 64:71–85.

Bourdieu, Pierre
1966   The sentiment of honour in Kabyle society. In J. Peristiany (ed.), *Honour and shame.* Chicago: University of Chicago Press.

Buitrago Ortiz, C.
1970   *Estructura social y orientaciones valorativas en Esperanza, Puerto Rico y el Mediterráneo.* San Juan: Editorial Edil.

Campbell, J. K.
1964   *Honour, family and patronage.* Oxford: Clarendon Press.

Caro Baroja, J.
1963   The city and the country: reflections on some common ancient commonplaces. In J. Pitt Rivers (ed.), *Mediterranean countrymen.* Paris and La Haye: Mouton.

Deloria, Vine
1969   *Custer died for your sins.* New York: Macmillan.

Fallers, L.
1967   *Bantu bureaucracy.* Chicago: University of Chicago Press.

Fortes, M.
1957   *The web of kinship among the tallensi.* London: Oxford University Press.

Fortes, M., J. Goody, and E. Leach
1958   *The developmental cycle in domestic groups.* Cambridge, Eng.: Cambridge University Press.

Foster, G.
1948   *Empire's children: the people of Tzintzuntzan.* Mexico City: Imprenta Nuevo Mundo.
1961   The dyadic contract: a model for the social structure of a Mexican peasant village. *American Anthropologist* 63(6):1173–92.

Frankenberg, R.
1957   *Village on the border.* London: Cohen & West.

Freeman, J. D.
1953   Family and kin among the Iban of Sarawak. Unpublished Ph.D. dissertation, Cambridge University, Cambridge, England.

Gluckman, M. (ed.)
1962   *Essays on the ritual of social relations.* Manchester: Manchester University Press.

Goffman, E.
1959   *The presentation of self in everyday life.* New York: Anchor.

Hunter, G.
1969   *Modernizing peasant societies.* London: Oxford University Press.

Laing, R. D.
1959   *The divided self.* London: Tavistock.

Lewis, G.
  1970   Romans, natives and helots. *Caribbean Review,* Spring 1970, pp. 3–5.

Lewis, O.
  1951   *Life in a Mexican village: Tepoztlán restudied.* Urbana: University of Illinois Press.
  1960   *Tepoztlán: village in Mexico.* New York: Holt, Rinehart and Winston.
  1964   *The children of Sánchez.* London: Penguin Modern Classics.

Lopreato, J.
  1967   *Peasants no more.* San Francisco: Chandler.

Mintz, S., and E. Wolf
  1950   An analysis of ritual coparenthood (*compadrazgo*). *Southwestern Journal of Anthropology* 6(4):341–68.

Moore, B.
  1966   *The social origins of dictatorship and democracy.* Boston: Beacon Press.

Murra, J.
  1957   Discussion. In V. Rubin (ed.), *Caribbean studies: a symposium.* Institute of Social and Economic Research, University College of the West Indies, Jamaica.

Padilla, E.
  1957   Contemporary social-rural types in the Caribbean region. In V. Rubin (ed.), *Caribbean studies: a symposium.* Institute of Social and Economic Research, University College of the West Indies, Jamaica.

Parsons, T., and R. Bales
  1955   *Family socialization and interaction process.* Glencoe, Ill.: The Free Press.

Peristiany, J. (ed.)
  1966   *Honour and shame.* Chicago: University of Chicago Press.

Philpott, S. B.
  1968   Remittance obligations, social networks and choice among Montserratian migrants in Britain. *Man* 3(3):465–66.

Pierson, D.
  1951   *Cruz de las Almas: a Brazilian village.* Smithsonian Institution, Institute of Social Anthropology, Publication no. 12. Washington, D.C.

Pitt Rivers, J.
  1958   Ritual kinship in Spain. *Transactions of the New York Academy of Sciences,* Ser. 2. 20(5):78–79, 206–7, 254–58, 424–31.
  1961   *The people of the sierra.* Chicago: University of Chicago Press.
  1963   *Mediterranean countrymen* (ed.). Paris and La Haye: Mouton.

Redfield, R.
  1956   *Peasant society and culture.* Chicago: University of Chicago Press.

Smith, M. G.
  1962a *Kinship and community in Carriacou.* New Haven and London: Yale University Press.
  1962b *West Indian family structure.* Seattle: University of Washington Press.

Smith, R. T.
1956   *The Negro family in British Guiana.* London: Routledge and Kegan Paul.
1957   The family in the Caribbean. In V. Rubin (ed.), *Caribbean studies: a symposium.* Institute of Social and Economic Research, University College of the West Indies, Jamaica.
1963   Culture and social structure in the Caribbean: some recent work on family and kinship studies. *Comparative studies in society and history* 6(1):24–45.

Warner, W. L.
1949   *Social class in America.* Chicago: Science Research Associates.

Willems, E.
1962   On Portuguese family structure. *International Journal of Comparative Sociology* 3(1):64–79.
1966   *Capitalism and slavery.* New York: Capricorn Books.

Wilson, P.
1969   Reputation and respectability: a suggestion for Caribbean ethnology. *Man* 4(1):70–84.

Wolf, E.
1962   Types of Latin American peasantry. *A Preliminary American Anthropologist* 57(2):123–130.
1966   Kinship, friendship and patron-client relations in complex societies. In M. Banton (ed.), *The social anthropology of complex societies.* New York: Frederick Praeger.

Index